Airimagination

Unprecedented social changes, accelerated by facilitating technologies and the COVID-19 pandemic, are calling for airlines to think deeply and non-conventionally on what will be important to existing and new travelers, as they change their lifestyles. New thinking requires airlines to extend the boundaries of their businesses to go beyond their traditional domains. This need goes beyond the renovation and iteration of conventional products to the transformation of products requiring new ideas and ways to scale them. Examples include the development of cost-effective urban air mobility, intermodal passenger transportation, door-to-door travel that is sustainable, and personalized offers.

Airimagination: Extending the Airline Business Boundaries raises some thought-provoking questions and provides a direction for practical solutions. For example, what if airlines developed products and services that finally meet end-to-end needs of customers seamlessly by collaborating in the value-adding open ecosystems, using platforms that facilitate effective engagement with both "digital and nondigital" customers and employees in real time and at each touch point? Ironically, the current time is an advantage for some airlines as they already have had to deal with a deep and wide disruption caused by the pandemic, leading operations to start from ground zero.

This book, the latest in a long and well-regarded series by Nawal K. Taneja, explores innovative best practices within the airline business world, complemented by numerous insightful perspectives contained in multiple forewords and thought leadership pieces. This book is aimed primarily at high-level practitioners within the airline industry and related businesses.

Nawal K. Taneja, whose experience in the aviation industry spans five decades (starting with TWA at its headquarters in New York City), has worked for and advised major airlines and related aviation businesses worldwide. Currently, he is an executive-in-residence at the Fisher College of Business at the Ohio State University.

Airimagination
Extending the Airline Business Boundaries

Nawal K. Taneja

LONDON AND NEW YORK

Cover image: Getty Images

First published 2023
by Routledge
4 Park Square, Milton Park, Abingdon, Oxon OX14 4RN

and by Routledge
605 Third Avenue, New York, NY 10158

Routledge is an imprint of the Taylor & Francis Group, an informa business

© 2023 Nawal K. Taneja

The right of Nawal K. Taneja to be identified as author of this work has been asserted in accordance with sections 77 and 78 of the Copyright, Designs and Patents Act 1988.

All rights reserved. No part of this book may be reprinted or reproduced or utilised in any form or by any electronic, mechanical, or other means, now known or hereafter invented, including photocopying and recording, or in any information storage or retrieval system, without permission in writing from the publishers.

Trademark notice: Product or corporate names may be trademarks or registered trademarks, and are used only for identification and explanation without intent to infringe.

British Library Cataloguing-in-Publication Data
A catalogue record for this book is available from the British Library

Library of Congress Cataloging-in-Publication Data
A catalog record has been requested for this book

ISBN: 978-1-032-32746-4 (hbk)
ISBN: 978-1-003-33282-4 (ebk)

DOI: 10.4324/9781003332824

Typeset in Times New Roman
by SPi Technologies India Pvt Ltd (Straive)

Dedicated to Angela, Matthew, Sophia, and Ravi

Contents

List of figures xi
List of tables xiii
Forewords xv
DOREEN BURSE xv
STEPHEN FITZPATRICK xvii
CHRISTOPH KLINGENBERG xix
BOET E.J. KREIKEN xxi
LE HONG HA xxiv
CHANG-HYEON SONG xxv
DECIUS VALMORBIDA xxvi
DEE K. WADDELL xxviii

Acknowledgments xxx

1 What if airlines adapted to consumer lifestyle changes? 1

Implications for airlines 3
Outline of chapters 9

2 What if airline products were reengineered? 13

Short-term improvements in the core product 16
 Clean-sheet scheduling 21
 Scheduling for profitability and reliability 23
 Producing operations-friendly schedules 24
 Improving forecast accuracy 25
 Dynamic scheduling 26
Medium-term improvements in the core product 28
 Door-to-door travel 29
 Small electric aircraft 30
 Air taxis 31
Long-term improvements in the core product 33
 Supersonic aircraft 33
 Hyperloop vehicles 34

viii Contents

      Hydrogen-powered aircraft 34
      Highlights 35

3 What if airlines rethought their revenue approach?   36

    Traditional revenue approach 36
    Offer management 39
    New pricing/revenue management techniques 42
      Seat buy-back 42
      Ancillary pricing optimization/revenue management 44
      Customer choice model 44
      Dynamic pricing 46
      Offer revenue management 49
      Network planning/revenue management integration 49
      Real-time revenue management 51
      AI (algorithms) 52
      Strategic pricing 53
      Next-generation revenue management 54
    Selling differently 55
      Selling more products on airline.com as a natural retail
        channel 55
      New pricing schemes 55
      Better shopping displays 56
      In-flight shopping 57
      NDC and distribution 57
    Highlights 58

4 What if airlines reimagined and redefined customer experience?   59

    Customer service versus customer experience 59
    Two insightful examples 62
      Amazon 62
      DBS Bank 63
    Personalization 64
      Challenges 65
      Opportunities 65
    Digital experience 71
    AI and machine learning 72
    Highlights 75

5 What if the aviation industry contributed no carbon emissions?   78

    Developments relating to climate change 79
    Sustainable Aviation Fuels (SAFs) 81

The net-zero-by-2050 scenario 83
Implications for airlines 84
Making sustainability the core of an airline's business strategy 88
Highlights 90

6   What if airlines could do more with less?   93

Collaborating by design 94
Building digital resiliency capabilities 99
Strategizing for positional superiority 101
Highlights 105

7   What if airlines could truly differentiate themselves?   108

Applying the principles in practice 108
  JetBlue Airways 108
  Alaska Airlines 109
Characteristics of Agility Airlines 109
  Network and schedule planning 110
  Revenue and offer management 113
  Designing customer experience through a holistic approach 115
  Sustainability as a competitive advantage 116
  Doing more with less 117

8   Thought leadership pieces   120

The unifying nature of customer choice 121
JIM BARLOW

Turning air into magic 127
EVERT DE BOER

The operation's support for a new airline customer proposition 136
CHRISTOPHER GIBBS

Everything will remain different—a different view on change 141
PETER GLADE

Stop playing copycat 145
GLENN HOLLISTER

Contents

Enhancing revenue management analyst effectiveness with human-machine symbiosis: learning to work with machines 150
JASON KELLY

Whatever you do, start with the customer 158
JORDIE KNOPPERS

Creating unexpected compelling experiences to increase bookings and ancillary revenues 166
KERSTIN LOMB

What if airports changed into mobility hubs? 172
MICHAELA SCHULTHEIβ-MÜNCH AND DR. JENNIFER BERZ

A new dynamic approach to network planning 185
PHILIPPE PUECH

Making clean-sheet scheduling real 191
RENZO VACCARI

About the author	200
Index	202

Figures

2.1	The Vertical Aerospace VX4	32
2.2	DJI M600 drone, operated by 42air	33
3.1	Pricing/revenue management capabilities ladders	43
3.2	Pricing strategy considerations	54
5.1	Airbus ZEROe concept planes	82
6.1	Value propositions of an airline	102
6.2	A simple conceptual map of airlines	103
7.1	Major hubs and focus cities of JetBlue and Alaska Airlines	111
7.2	Potential transatlantic and transpacific opportunities for Agility Airlines	112
8.1	Process of choosing preferred flights	122
8.2	Customer preferences for schedule, price, and airline	123
8.3	Customer choice at the center	125
8.4	Loyalty program strategies	134
8.5	Competitive scope versus competitive advantage	146
8.6	The undifferentiated middle	147
8.7	Ticket revenue versus disposable income	148
8.8	Air travel spend as percent of firm revenue	148
8.9	Case study: extra legroom seating in the US market	149
8.10	The RM analyst bears the burden of translating the airline business problem into the language of the RM system	151
8.11	The evolution of communications	152
8.12	An early visualization of Kambr's architecture from 2019	156
8.13	2019 XMI customer ratings	166
8.14	Impact of trend categories on the airport business model	176
8.15	Positioning Fraport as an intermodal mobility hub with increased connectivity	177
8.16	Important aspects when booking a trip through a mobility hub	178
8.17	Important factors for digital connectivity of means of transport at a mobility hub	178
8.18	Satisfaction levels concerning intermodality at Frankfurt Airport	179

xii *Figures*

8.19	Coverage offered by American Airlines' Dallas and Charlotte hubs in July 2021	186
8.20	Part A and B Spatial and temporal components for O&D viability	187
8.21	DFW 30-minute rolling departure count pre-pandemic and during summer 2020	188
8.22	Key airline scheduling processes	193
8.23	Clean-sheet scheduling in two steps	194

Tables

2.1 Recent calibration of airline customer preferences 15
3.1 Preferences from a customer choice model with a price variable 45

Forewords

Doreen Burse
Senior Vice President Worldwide Sales, United Airlines

Change is a funny thing. It can be sudden or tectonic. It can be a starburst or the briefest flicker of flame. Without a doubt, it's constant, and for businesses, it has long been a matter of how (or if) we're prepared to respond to it. The premise of this book makes the case that the pandemic has forced a period of accelerated change and I have found this to be true for airlines. Change wasn't just on the horizon for the travel industry as a whole—it was already in motion. And what followed has been extraordinary. The industry responded in such a way that we're able to *be* the change, not just respond to the change. At the beginning of the pandemic, we spoke often about the idea of "the new normal"; little did we know that "normal" was about to become a concept of the past.

Throughout his writing, Mr. Taneja inquires, "What if ...?" and over the past two years, many businesses have shifted that simple question out of the theoretical and into their business plans. For airlines, that has been true in this industry where many long-held paradigms (an airline as a catalyst for innovative ecological change?) have been challenged. But like consumer lifestyle trends that have been slowly evolving and now accelerated by the pandemic, airlines are addressing bigger picture concepts that have always been there but have shifted to the forefront of the conversation today. What if, to borrow Mr. Taneja's question, an industry historically known as a contributor to climate change suddenly became the one leading the charge to solve it? Additionally, what if airlines and transportation companies could collaborate to rally around the reality that climate change is coming, thus we must work together to address it?

I'm proud about what United has done around sustainability and the tough but impactful goal we have set to be 100% green by 2050. To quote United CEO Scott Kirby, "*When I became United Airlines' new CEO at the beginning of the pandemic, I did so with a grand vision for our company: to make sustainability the new standard in flight. I realize it's an ambitious vision for someone in an industry that depends on burning fossil fuels to operate. As the leader of one of the world's largest airlines, I recognize our responsibility in contributing to climate change as well as our responsibility to solve it. It's no longer enough for us to connect the world without making sure it has a future."* As an organization, it's a point of pride; I firmly believe that people do business with companies (really people) that share their same values. Today I'm speaking about sustainability, but the same holds true for efforts in equally important spaces like diversity, equity, and inclusion.

The technology that exists in the sustainability space is revolutionary—we are literally capturing carbon dioxide from the air and storing it safely underground for future use. We're also investing in aircraft that will redefine what it means to travel within the next decade. United holds conditional orders for electric aircraft that will leverage battery power to connect smaller U.S. cities to our hubs. We're bringing supersonic travel back to the skies with our investment in Boom Overture. Traveling at twice the speed of today's passenger jets, these aircraft are projected to connect London and New York in just over three hours—all while net-zero carbon and flying on 100% sustainable aviation fuel. And our efforts don't end there. This is just the beginning of our journey.

The airline business is incredibly competitive, so the idea of industry-wide cooperation may seem antithetical. But on important topics like diversity and sustainability, we don't want to be in this space alone. Airlines working together and collaborating with other industries will accelerate real solutions and lasting change. This of course raises a whole host of new questions: What will it cost? Won't this raise our operating expenses? The answer is yes, it likely will—but we are resolute that the short-term pain is worth the long-term gain. The path to decarbonization is one that will be built through collaboration. We're willing to walk the walk, and we're confident that this shared sentiment will result in a linking of arms down that path.

Without question, the pandemic has been difficult for everyone, and the travel industry was no exception. But the pandemic also created a rare moment of pause, a period of reflection to question all we hold to be true and to reassess our actions and our business purpose. We imagined "what if" and in short order were asking "what now" as we took on a generational level of change a short 24 months ago. We emerged tired but spirited and ready to do more. Is it accurate to say this has been good for us and our customers? I believe so. Hindsight is always 20/20. I am confident it's just the beginning of a new chapter that will cast the airline industry in a new light that is equal parts accountable and celebrated for the economies we drive, in an environmentally conscious, inclusive, and authentic way that was previously thought unachievable.

Chicago, Illinois, USA

Stephen Fitzpatrick
CEO, Vertical Aerospace

On a bright November morning in São Paulo, I was in a car heading for the 2015 Brazilian Grand Prix. After a 15-hour trip from Europe I was eager to get to the track as the first day of practice sessions began. My team, Manor Racing, was struggling in the face of stiff (and heavily financed) competition—but that wasn't my immediate problem. The issue occupying my mind, as I looked out of the window, was that for the last hour we had barely moved.

Sao Paulo has the largest urban rail system in Latin America, but that morning it felt as though the city's 12.33 million inhabitants had opted for the car instead. The distance from the airport to the race is about 45 kilometres; that day the journey took four hours. Things didn't improve when I arrived at the Autódromo José Carlos Pace. Overhead, I could see that most of the competition had avoided the traffic—most other owners (as well as drivers) had hopped over it in helicopters.

This episode was the start of a new journey. It demonstrated to me the real potential of urban air mobility (UAM) in cities. Using available technology—I reasoned—someone might create a solution that would fundamentally alter the way we travel in cities and beyond.

It was around this time that my team and I were looking at further commercial opportunities in the technology we had at our disposal. The obvious application of F1 design and engineering is to put it toward making a car. But after some research, we discovered that all our advances in carbon fibre, lightweight composites, aerodynamics, computer simulation, and hybrid powertrains, what we really had were all the tools and capabilities we need to build electric aircraft—not cars.

Meanwhile, the problems connected to urbanisation aren't going away. The World Bank estimates that over 50% of the global population live in urban areas today, and by 2045, the number of people living in them will increase by 1.5 times—to 6 billion. As megacities boom, enabling people to travel to, from, and within them will become a greater challenge than ever before. As Nawal Taneja explores in this book, *AIRMAGINATION: Extending the Airline Business Boundaries*, UAM represents the best commercial and practical opportunity we have in meeting this challenge. Evidence also shows that the public is ready for the aerospace industry to come forward with solutions that make travelling in cities less painful. According to the European Union Aviation Safety Agency's (EASA) 2021 report, 83% of people it surveyed have a "positive initial attitude towards UAM, with 71% ready to try out UAM services."

It is advantageous that citizens are in favour of UAM solutions taking flight in their communities, because there is a huge risk if we do not innovate. Urban centres are the driving force of modern economies. In the UK, cities account for more than 80% of the national economic output. They are where leaders govern, where companies conduct business, and where cultural institutions flourish. When cities don't work properly, economies lurch, and quality of life recedes. According to research by McKinsey, urban congestion can cost as much as 2–4% of a country's gross domestic product (GDP) due to lost time, fuel burnt in idling engines and the increased cost of doing business.

Meanwhile, fast movers in the UAM space will find themselves presiding over a new growth industry. In the UK, this fledgling sector is thought to be worth 1–2% of the country's GDP in the coming years. Specifically, the air taxi market is forecast to become a multi-billion-pound industry, with the UK government predicting it will lift GDP by 1.8% by 2030.

This new era of UAM will usher in an unprecedented level of convenience. While the car is poorly suited to the modern cityscape, vertical take-off and landing vehicles (eVTOL) will mean passengers or products will be able to travel to locations that have, until now, been inaccessible by air. Cities themselves will become more liveable. Moving traffic from the street to the sky will free up space in dense urban areas. Roads will no longer have to double as storage space for cars. Multistorey car parks will vanish and in their place will sprout dedicated take-off and landing ports for eVTOLs. According to our calculations, the operating cost of such an aircraft will be $1 per passenger mile. That's for a short route. For longer routes, this figure would decrease.

While cities form centres of productivity and economic activity, they are also major contributors to climate change. Research from the UN indicates that cities consume 78% of the world's energy and produce 60% of greenhouse gas emissions. They account only for 2% of the Earth's surface. Poor air quality is becoming the biggest environmental crisis impacting residents of cities. The World Health Organization (WHO) estimates that pollution in cities and rural areas caused 4.2 million premature deaths globally in 2016. The technologies that built cities in the 20th century are now choking them in the 21st. The most urgent problem that must be solved by new UAM solutions is to dramatically reduce transport emissions.

The key to reducing transport sector emissions is transitioning from internal combustion engines to electric motors. Fossil fuel–powered modes of transport have marginal year-over-year improvements in efficiency and thus a reduction in emissions. Commercial VX4 services will have a carbon footprint on par with an electric car being used for commuting or business travel over the same distance using grid power. eVTOLs and other UAM vehicles will become the unrivalled option for decarbonising transport.

Bristol/London, UK

Christoph Klingenberg
Head of Operational Excellence at Deutsche Bahn

You are looking for a high dose of independent thinking on aviation? This book is for you. The author bypasses the standard "in every crisis there is opportunity" and dives right into the main question: "What does customer centricity mean in the post-COVID world?" He gives a bright analysis of how consumer behavior changes and how this affects aviation. The emergence of platforms and of lifestyle brands challenge traditional airline thinking. The author calls for a massive expansion of the airline business model to provide full-scale mobility solutions instead of simple airport-to-airport services.

Airlines are now—somewhat ironically—in a perfect position to master this change. The COVID measures have turned even the most traditionally run businesses into agile machines. Rapidly changing travel restrictions and an ever-increasing pent-up demand for air travel forced the airlines to adapt their destination portfolio, their schedules, and their active fleet on a weekly and sometimes even daily basis cutting the usual multiyear planning process down to just a fraction. The most noticeable effect of this "forced agility" is the fleet restructuring. In particular, the legacy carriers are emerging from this crisis with a (much more) uniform fleet of highly efficient aircraft: customer-friendly, cost-effective, and with a small ecological footprint. The fuel consumption per passenger mile is half of that in public ground transport (German data)—something to be proud of.

Besides fleet restructuring and schedule flexibility, there are some important changes "behind the curtain" that eliminate competitive disadvantages of legacy airlines. Just one example from my experience as Head of Direct Services at Lufthansa managing all non-hub flights: the area of highest internal regulation and complexity is crew planning and rostering. At Lufthansa, the fleet rotation plan was fixed more than 10 weeks before the flight (when less than 10% of short-haul seats were booked) to start the cumbersome rostering process with crews being able to request certain flights. This led to tremendous planning inefficiency of cockpit and cabin personnel—and perhaps did not even increase their work satisfaction because the whole process was opaque. Agile crew planning allows for real-time adaption of capacity and schedules to the customer demands increasing customer satisfaction and airline profitability. Maybe we will see—for the first time in 50 years—the legacy airlines emerge as the stronger segment gaining an upper hand over the low-cost carriers.

One of the many highlights of this book is Chapter 5 outlining the path to net-zero carbon emissions for the airline industry. Reduce short-haul air travel by shifting to ground travel and use sustainable aviation fuel for long haul. For the substitution to work airports must integrate railway systems and airlines have to become mobility solution providers. This redefines the hub and spoke structure: a hub is no longer 60% feeder flights feeding 40% of long-haul flights, but changes into an intermodal hub with most flights going long haul with carbon-friendly technology.

All mobility sectors should work together towards a sustainable traffic system. And there is much that other sectors can learn from aviation: First, running at an 80% load factor, the global airline system is the most efficient mass transport system compared to other systems like railways and public urban transport (in Europe) running below 50%. Second, another lesson is in capacity allocation: the transparent assignment of slots at the twice-yearly IATA slot conferences with more than 1,000 delegates distributing the slots at 180 airports in a fair and transparent manner. If the number of slots matches the airport's capacity, no major airport congestion can occur. This is in sharp contrast to the overcrowding of some railway corridors operating sometimes far beyond their capacity.

The grand synthesis of the book is contained in the description of the business model of an airline that the author calls Agility Airlines. He uses this clean-sheet approach to paint a vivid picture of how a post-COVID airline looks and feels and how it generates customer enthusiasm.

So, enjoy this high dose of original thinking, but feed it carefully to those still caught in the thinking that "everything will be the way it used to be."

Frankfurt, Germany

Boet E.J. Kreiken
Executive Vice President, KLM Customer Experience, and former CEO of KLM Cityhopper

The core of the airline business will remain to deliver, also in the future, a safe, efficient, and comfortable "time-compression" system between two geographically distant points. Even though current electronic "Teams" and "Zoom" solutions will become even more sophisticated as alternative communication substitutes for actual travel the conscious traveler, who wants more solid relations and connections between people, organizations, businesses, nations, and cultures, will continue to choose for airline mobility. Advanced materials, sophisticated propulsion technology and new aircraft/wing designs have always played a pivotal role to shape the future of aviation. With the urgent need to tackle the global energy transition, to limit the use of fossil-based fuels and the negative CO_2 impact that flying has, the quest for sustainable aviation is bigger than ever. This point is made quite well in Chapter 5 in this book. In fact, it has become our purpose, as a company, to make it happen for now and future generations. We have invited already in 2019 with our "Fly Responsibly" campaign, all our staff in KLM, all our customers, partners, and competitors to join us in this challenge and share all our common knowledge in this field without any hesitance. New initiatives abound, including the role of science-based targets, sustainable aviation fuel (SAF) as a good alternative and many collaborations between airlines, top universities and key suppliers. Examples include KLM's initiative with the University of Delft concerning the "Flying-V" aircraft, Delta Airlines' recent initiative to team up with Airbus on developing a hydrogen-based aircraft fuel, and Pratt & Whitney having their Gear Turbo Fan engine certified for 100% SAF fuels. And there are many other examples. Engineers with the proper support of entrepreneurial spirits in airlines and scientific and governmental institutions will solve many of the challenges ahead. Next are some interesting initiatives for short-haul electric flying (or initial flight training purposes for new pilots). The race is on to use lighter materials and constructions (seats, galleys, carpets, monitors, containers and nets, trolleys, food and by preordering meals we can avoid full inventory in the air and unnecessary waste, unbundling in fares for weight and luggage). The pressure must also continue for better air traffic control and more efficient, quicker and faster flight paths. This involves so many partners and coordination between airlines and suppliers as well as between intergovernmental parties. New design-and-decision rules are needed to deliver double-digit impacts.

From a passenger point of view the "time-compression" of both the flight and of the total required journey of all touchpoints to deliver the products and services, as demanded, will become even more important. Customers want, next to safe and punctual operations, two other things related to the use of their valuable time:

(1) The avoidance of time wasted (reliability, full choice, and control if things do go wrong, smooth /effortless/walk through airports, easy luggage drop off, security, customs and boarding/deboarding processes, luggage pickup)
(2) Rest of the time in the overall journey should be well spent from customers' perspective (personalization, relax, work, sleep, entertain, seat comfort, digitally connected, and/or get the right food and drinks and personal service as they require and/or are willing to pay extra for)

Apart from having your key processes under control, every day, every flight, and for every kind of customer, we see seven other major trends:

(1) A revolution in the home/curb to gate processes in the next 5–7 years. Biometrics, digitization, better international cooperation in customs, health attestation, security, and all kinds of preclearance, far earlier in the customer journey than only at the airports, will create more physical space at airports and ease the stress related to travel for the passengers involved. Check-in as such will be minimalized and basically disappear.
(2) Given the new availability and performance of combined 5G, LEO and GEO satellite, the commercialization of space, the long-haul aircraft cabin will be fully digitized for new uses by passengers, between the airline and its passengers, for operational purposes and or other services related to choice and control. We call it "The Cabin Digitization".
(3) Functional and continuous customer communication will reach new levels, the need to inform on events and the use of the preferred customer communication channels of choice will become a key differentiator. The PNR will slowly disappear and the customer as the "one-ordering driver" will become the main input data for sales, service, and maybe also operations.
(4) Customer case management will get the same importance. Being a service product in time with so many hundreds of touch points, things might not work out or may be perceived differently by passengers. It is important that the airline care systems and service staff detect and solve problems as fast as possible and solve them quickly and before the customer journey ends.
(5) Genuine mobility needs of passengers stretch beyond airport-to-airport, of course, so multimodality solutions with mainly fast train and express bus partners at hubs and final destination network points will arise.
(6) The human aspect of customer culture centricity will become even more important as an airline experience differentiator. People want to be

  recognized as human beings as well. There is no substitute for helpful and professional service and cabin staff.
(7) The attractiveness of an airline's brand and the reputation of the airline (even beyond an airline's prime services and products) remains key for current and future customers, but also to attract the right creative talents, (software) engineers, service staff, and the right suppliers and partners to build your 'ecosystems' for continuous innovation and improvements.

Marketing's main purpose used to be "turning needs into profitability". Today and tomorrow, we must create a net-positive company, in conjunction with all our partners, and new ecosystems and deliver other positive outcomes also for society, our employees worldwide, our suppliers, public institutions, and co-innovators and engage our millions of conscious customers as well in the process toward sustainable aviation. The author makes a clear point throughout this book for collaboration within the ecosystem. This is precisely the KLM Royal Dutch Airlines' flight path for the future. We know the challenges ahead and we need all the aviation enthusiasts, experience, skills, and knowledge available to cooperate with us in order also to create it.

Amsterdam, The Netherlands

Le Hong Ha
President and CEO, Vietnam Airlines

The COVID pandemic reset the game for airlines when most of the established airlines restarted at ground zero and many new airlines entered the marketplace, increasing competition in the industry. At the same time, the pandemic also accelerated the already rapidly changing demands and behaviors of airline customers, as well as employees.

Airlines' competitors now are not only other airlines, but also other businesses that can offer customers better solutions, or a more seamless journey. With the support of digital systems, processes, and data, a start-up can now become a serious competitor in a short period.

In the context of the massive digital revolution affecting people's lives, incremental innovation will not enable an airline to survive, let alone thrive. On the other hand, while the dramatically changing marketplace is calling for a fundamental transformation of airline business models, there are major questions relating to transformational strategies and their execution—the need for change in corporate culture, financial resources required, talent needed, and the continuation of constraining legacy systems and infrastructure, just to name a few challenges.

The book will inspire your imagination (in a very practical way) on how to engage with customers and employees, and how to collaborate within the internal and external ecosystems to develop new products and services to offer customers, in both the short- and long-term future. And keep in mind that customers are looking for not just value-adding products but also an experience that is consistent and seamless throughout the journey. This book gives a precious blueprint to think about the business model that an airline can pursue. However, you should also be prepared for this book to make you think of totally changing the business philosophy of your airline.

Hanoi, Vietnam

Chang-Hyeon Song
President, Hyundai Motor Group, and Founder and CEO, 42dot

The theme of this book is that, going forward, companies need to extend the boundaries of their businesses to meet the changing needs of consumers whose lifestyles have begun to change in dramatic ways. And, according to the author, one way to undertake this task is to collaborate within the ecosystem and deploy smart platforms. The automotive sector is already way ahead in these areas. Think about the auto manufacturers that are enhancing, for example, their core competitiveness by focusing on software rather than hardware. In the case of the Hyundai Motor Group, it has established a TaaS division to provide transportation solutions to the mobility and logistics market. Furthermore, it is transitioning from an automaker to a services and solutions company that excels in software and AI.

The TaaS Division is building strategies and all aspects of global mobility services including planning, development, and operations. The division also streamlines the group's existing mobility services, then introduce new service models, based on user data to enhance the competitiveness of its global mobility business. The division also plans to create a mobility ecosystem that will promote collaboration among diverse players within the industry. Hyundai Motor Group's new automotive software department will speed up the establishment of the software-defined vehicle development system to enhance the automotive group's electronics and infotainment capabilities.

Think also of a comprehensive mobility and logistics platform, called Urban Mobility Operating System (UMOS), developed by 42dot. UMOS integrates all forms of ground and air transportation services such as e-hailing, fleet management, demand-responsive transport, smart logistics, autonomous driving, and more.

42dot has been recognized for its excellence in the Pohang Smart City Challenge project, hosted by the Ministry of Land, Infrastructure and Transport, and has overseen the demand responsive transport operation. Demand Responsive Transport is a new concept public transportation method that flexibly operates the operation section, frequency, and time within a set route. 42dot is also developing autonomous driving technology that moves by itself and a mobility platform that provides optimal mobility at the same time, connecting technology directly to services and businesses. The 42air division of 42dot will pioneer the future drone delivery services for not only the maritime and last-mile but also middle-mile deliveries. The platform includes many layers of functionality built with robust technology that enables scale. The object is to create an ecosystem that transforms the way people and goods travel, using autonomous and frictionless services.

This book clearly underscores the inevitable changes and challenges in the airline industry, which is very similar to those of the automotive industry and suggests what to embrace and how to prepare to win the market.

Seoul, South Korea

Decius Valmorbida
President of Travel Unit, Amadeus IT Group

In this new book, Nawal Taneja asks big, foundational questions of the aviation industry. What if airlines could rethink their core product? What if they could change their business model and generate more revenue? What if they could inspire more loyalty? For there is power in reimagining the future of the industry that many of us serve.

Of course, there are many books on airline transformation and the word itself is overused. Yet, given the recent disruptions in our industry—for example, the COVID-19 pandemic, higher fuel prices, route closures, and so on—it is clear that some kind of transformation is exactly what is needed for our industry to reliably deliver sustainable profits. And let us not forget the importance of our industry to the world. There are many communities for which air service is not just a matter of profits but also of survival. Our industry is a vital part of the global economy and any book, like this one, that can provoke thinking to make our industry better is a true contribution to the literature.

We at Amadeus are a proud member of the airline ecosystem. We are honored and humbled by the trust our airline and airport customers place in us to manage their distribution, their reservations/check-in and other important functions. We are committed to innovation in the airline ecosystem to meet the changing needs of our customers. We appreciate that the kind of transformation that Nawal speaks of requires airlines, airports, travel suppliers and other partners working together to realize the vision of a more sustainable industry. We are dedicated to this important collaboration.

One of the features of Nawal's book that I especially enjoyed was that he ensured new kinds of thinking by asking provocative questions and went on to show how these questions could be answered in practical and real ways. At Amadeus, our experience with our own transformation journey is that it is important to first establish a compelling vision of the future but ground that vision with real-life experiences. Achieving a vision and executing upon a strategy requires building a realistic plan and carefully monitoring progress of that plan. I believe Nawal balanced this tension between possibility and reality quite well.

Of all the chapters, I found two of them particularly important. The first one is about sustainability (Chapter 5). The climate change crisis is an existential one for our planet and clearly, we in the aviation industry must play a role to address this crisis. He mentions that there are long-term solutions, such as sustainable aviation fuel and electric aircraft, but that there are still short-term actions that we, as an industry, can take now to contribute alleviate this crisis while the long-term technologies are developed. What was especially interesting to me was hearing that these long-term technologies may not, in fact, be that far off, which is very encouraging. I believe such initiatives deserve more attention and I look forward to the additional attention Nawal's book will create.

Another important chapter asks the question how airlines can do more with less. From Nawal, this deliberately thought-provoking question generates many interesting ideas. Through this question, Nawal points out the many changes in society and customer behavior and suggests that airlines find ways to adapt to them. This type of approach—treating each major change as an opportunity—generates a true sense of innovation thinking rather than the kind of incremental thinking a lot of us have seen in the industry.

In summary, I highly recommend this book. If you want to move away from "business as usual" and toward a more inspiring and achievable vision for the future, then you have come to the right place.

Madrid, Spain

Dee K. Waddell
Managing Partner, Global Industry Leader, Travel & Transportation Industries, IBM Corporation

Nawal Taneja, now in his sixth decade of sharing his deep passion, knowledge, and expertise in our global aviation industry, does it again with *Airimagination: Extending the Airline Business Boundaries*—his 14th book. Nawal's real-world approach for the everyday leader and practitioner in aviation is a testament to his ability to articulate the challenges and opportunities in our industry but, more important, provide provocative questions and discussions about the most impactful ideas, innovation, and potential solutions for our post-COVID-19 pandemic world.

It's no secret the travel industry, and particularly aviation, continues to be the wistful example of discontinuity with such ravaging effects from global disruptions and crisis. However, even amid such devasting impact and grim ongoing prospects, our industry has always adapted and found a way to roar back and overcome.

Perhaps a reflection of innate human resiliency and progress, Nawal's key topics and questions in this book connect my mind to the human desire to overcome and be resilient in finding ways to elevate empathy, diversity, human connection, and social good. Travel and flying across the world extend our own boundaries as we realize that people are people no matter their nationality, religious ideals, skin color, or other identities and preferences. We rediscover the childlike goodness in ourselves and begin to respect, appreciate, and even love people and cultures who are unlike our own.

In aviation leadership, as we empathize with our customers, partners, employees, and other stakeholders, may each of us be reminded of our ultimate goal—to extend and elevate the humanity of all people. Whether it be transforming shopping of flights with artificial intelligence (AI), enhancing inflight entertainment and overall operations with 5G and edge computing, employing cross-border self-sovereign identity on blockchain, flying optimized networks and schedules leveraging quantum computing, employing non-bias AI for hiring diverse and competent staff, or empowering all individuals with mobile capabilities for collaborative teaming, may each of our next-generation innovations be well-grounded in elevating each human experience.

Additionally, for airlines to extend the boundaries of their own businesses, they will benefit from the discussions Nawal provides around digital transformation, including end-to-end process and operations transformation, especially as it relates to the customer and employee experience. Many airlines have already accelerated their shift to a digital-first environment and will find additional benefit in executing their transformational journey and always ensuring new technology, innovations, and capabilities can be leveraged for true competitive advantage.

As we consider this broader mindset and the implications of Nawal's book, perhaps we can truly help our airline industry overcome the pitfalls of continual discontinuities and even move beyond our traditional boundaries. To see a more noble opportunity in travel and airlines of helping the world elevate peace and prosperity for all.

Silicone Slopes, Utah, USA

Acknowledgments

I would like to express my appreciation for all those who contributed in different ways, especially Angela Taneja (my business research analyst), Peeter Kivestu (formerly with Teradata and now a principal with Oplytix), Dietmar Kirchner (formerly an SVP at Lufthansa and now Senior Aviation Advisor and co-Chairman of the International Airline Symposium Planning Committee), Zhihang Chi (Vice President and General Manager of North America for Air China), and Eric Leopold (formerly with IATA and now with Threedot.io) for discussions on challenges and opportunities facing the global airline industry and related businesses.

The second group of individuals that I would like to recognize include at

Aeromexico—Nicolas Rhoads;
Airbus—Robert Lange;
Amadeus—Jim Barlow, Adam Hill, and Matthieu Quehen;
American Airlines—Philippe Puech;
Apple—Sean To;
Fraport AG—Michaela Schultheiß-Münch;
IATA—Dany Lima De Oliveira;
IBM—Kerstin Lomb;
KLM—Jordie Knoppers and Liesbeth Oudkerk;
Salesforce—Scott Barghaan, Jacqueline Nunley, and Mark Reusser;
SunExpress—Peter Glade;
Tampa Bay Realty Development—Louis Buccino;
United Airlines—Marcel Fuchs, Glenn Hollister, and John Slater;
Vietnam Airlines—Le Minh Tuan; and
42air—Chul Lee.

Third, there are several other people who provided significant help: at Routledge of the Taylor & Francis Group (Guy Loft—Senior Editor, Routledge Professional, Law, Transport, Health & Safety; Amelia Bashford-Editorial Assistant, Routledge Professional, Law, Transport, Health & Safety); and Suba Ramya Durairaj, Project Manager, Straive; Wendy Jo Dymond: copy editor.

Finally, I would also like to thank my family for their support and patience.

1 What if airlines adapted to consumer lifestyle changes?

Societies worldwide are undergoing major transformations that are impacting buyers, sellers, workforces, government policymakers, suppliers, contractors, and providers of infrastructure. The resulting alterations of societies in the digital era call for the significant transformation of corporate visions and core products of most businesses. Think about just a few trends that are bringing about social changes:

- the fundamental change in cultures (people's interactions and relationships);
- the way people interact through social networks;
- the changes in the flow of information, from credible centralized media to decentralized (social media), with multiple major impacts;
- the continuing economic gap (measured in income or wealth between the richer and poorer segments);
- the shift in the balance of power between employees and employers;
- the continuation of racial discrimination, for example, in the US and other countries;
- the changing trends in the migration, again; for instance, in the US in which some workers are leaving major urban cities (such as San Francisco, California) and moving to smaller cities (such as Austin, Texas);
- the mobile technology revolution, and the advent of platforms (Uber, Netflix, Airbnb, Spotify, Tinder, Amazon, and so forth), setting a new standard in terms of customer-centricity; and
- the availability of incredible amounts of data.

And, within a broader context, what if China, in addition to its *Belt and Road Initiative*, also succeeds in its *Digital Silk Road* initiative that would connect and control future networks? "It could reshape global flows of data, finance, and communications to reflect its (China's) interests."[1] And let us not overlook a salient trend reported by Fareed Zakaria in his recent opinion in the *Washington Post*: Whereas, for decades, economics trumped politics worldwide, now, politics is trumping economics, also worldwide.[2] Then there is the US Congressman Ro Khanna thinking about "how to expand technology-driven opportunities to the people and places who have been left out of

DOI: 10.4324/9781003332824-1

the first wave of the digital revolution."[3] Some of these trends, which have been underway for many years, have simply gained significant momentum from the current and the ongoing pandemic.

Just think about how the education landscape is changing fundamentally with technology, enabling students and educators to identify new opportunities for learning and teaching with a focus on what is important to students. Think about the financial sector. Some non-banking businesses, that have a high frequency of engagement with their customers and have achieved a high level of loyalty, are considering providing some banking services to their customers. If these businesses are extending the boundaries of their businesses, should banks develop partnerships with them? Think about the changing healthcare landscape facilitated by breakthrough innovations in the medical field and in digital technologies. The intersection of innovation in just these two areas will lead to early detections and self-diagnostics. Think about the speed with which some pharmaceutical companies created vaccines for the COVID-19 pandemic by collaborating in their ecosystems. On a broader level, think about the impact of these social changes on

- how and when people interact with each other;
- how they want not just a good experience but a good "digital" experience (think about how consumers have become accustomed to smartphones, smart TVs, and smart appliances from the value provided, especially smartphones);
- how personal priorities, relating to work, for example, are changing; how employees want to work and the emergence of the hybrid working model;
- how governments and consumers are putting climate change and global warming front and center;
- how the alarm for data privacy (General Data Protection Regulation; GDPR) and protection (cybersecurity) has begun to ring more loudly; and
- how people are concerned about the growing impact of the strategies being followed by high-powered social media companies, as well as data-hungry and algorithm-focused companies.

Based on the emerging social changes, some business sectors, and individual companies within sectors, have already started their transformation processes by extending the boundaries of their businesses to go beyond their traditional domains. The airline industry has shown great resiliency and will return but with changes in business models. A fundamental change in the transformation of businesses is how they are starting to compete, moving from competing with traditional products in their well-defined business sectors to working within their wider ecosystems. Some automakers, for example, are expanding into the area of mobility; some banks are moving into the fintech area (mobile payments, for instance); and some journalism organizations are becoming technology businesses to adapt to social changes by capitalizing on emerging technologies. Some railroads not only are rebranding themselves, but one, EURAIL, is going for a "Digital-First Rebrand." The company is rebranding itself based on the values of "curiosity, flexibility and openness."[4] In the case of the automotive sector, it is being transformed radically by such forces as electrification, self-driving vehicles, and the proliferation of in-vehicle software. To adapt to the influence of these forces, Volkswagen, for example, is positioning itself to become a brand that provides sustainable mobility. In the journalism sector, the *Washington Post* has transformed itself to become a "technology, software, and media" company.[5] In the car-rental sector, Hertz is positioning itself to capitalize on a greener future by forming an alliance with Tesla and Uber. In late 2021, Hertz announced a decision to buy 100,000 Tesla Model 3 sedans by the end of 2022 and to rent Tesla cars to Uber drivers for about $300 a week. What if some customers were willing to pay premium rates for car rentals for an environmentally-based experience?

Implications for airlines

The unprecedented social changes, coupled with facilitating technologies, could substantially impact the airline industry, calling for deep thinking on what is now important to existing and new travelers as they change their lifestyles, including health safety, for example. As such, some airlines are beginning to focus not only on strategies but also on the skills needed to acquire new customers and meet their new expectations. This book raises some thought-provoking questions. For example, what if some leading airlines do manage to innovate by thinking unconventionally to create value for customers, employees, and a broad spectrum of other stakeholders? What if they manage to

- overcome their fear of change,
- figure out how to change,
- find ways to obtain the necessary information to adapt to the change,
- become much more proactive as opposed to remaining reactive,
- decide how to function within a bimodal framework—how much new conventional thinking and how much new thinking (90%–10%, or 70%–30%, or 50%–50%), and
- introduce intrapreneurship within their large legacy systems by partnering much more effectively with start-up groups?[6]

Ironically, the current time would be an advantage for some. Airlines have already dealt with a deep and wide disruption caused by the COVID-19 pandemic. In some ways, airlines have already ended up starting their operations from ground zero. Think about Cathay Pacific Airways, which has reduced its passenger capacity in January 2022 to just 2% of the pre-pandemic level[7] and can now take its strategy of developing into a lifestyle airline to the next level. Think about when Delta lost 95% of its revenues in 30 days after COVID-19 struck and how it managed to post adjusted third-quarter profits of $1.2

billion in 2021, without any help from the government.[8] Consequently, a starting point for some airlines could now be to realign their organizational structure, leadership style, and their basic products, for example, by

- recognizing that the pandemic has accelerated the change in "people's attitudes towards institutions in general, and towards employers in particular";[9]
- diving not only deeply into the multigenerational challenge relating to customer expectations of different segments, at least for the US and parts of Western Europe,[10] but also into each generational segment to redesign products and strategies to reflect the changing behavior within each segment;
- understanding that the "most significant change influencing customers over the past decade, has been the massive increase in the role 'digital' plays in their lives";[11]
- focusing on how technology is empowering travelers, at an accelerating rate, to demand products and services on their own terms (time, channel, screen, etc.);
- recognizing that there are now differences not only in what people buy but also in how they buy and how they pay for what they buy (e.g., not just with the use of the "digital wallet") and for products the use of the "buy now and pay later" framework;
- keeping in mind that consumers now have at their fingertips access to competing products and services, meaning that airlines must focus not just on wallet share but also mind share;
- developing a broader ecosystem of partners to deliver service and value to the customer during the end-to-end traveler journey;
- also keeping in mind that the Google environment enables leading sellers to anticipate what consumers want;
- enabling travelers, through painless processes, to (1) find suitable flights and fares (with the combinations based on value) without using multiple websites and search engines (a large and complex issue) and (2) easily make and pay for reservations;
- thinking about the possibility of customers "posting" their "request for travel" and then airlines and others coming up with solution proposals;
- getting travelers on time from their points of origin to their points of destination, not just from airports to airports;
- introducing more point-to-point services, even in thinner markets, using a new generation of single-aisle aircraft;
- minimizing airport processing times, from arrival at one airport to arrival at the other airport, including the processing of connections through airports, easy access to ground transportation services and new ways of handling baggage (e.g., could the baggage be picked up at the exact point of origin, say, a home, and be delivered to an exact point at a destination, say, a hotel?);
- removing friction in the end-to-end travel process;

- developing new loyalty programs, given customers' desires for efficient mobility systems that may call for, for example, travel on one airline on the outbound leg and a different airline, or another mode of transportation, for the inbound leg;
- developing new ways to stimulate air travel shoppers to book, for example, using a metaverse for shoppers to "visualize" their seat selection process and experience at destinations; and
- making sustainability a high priority, given the rise of eco-friendly travelers who may be searching for itineraries that generate less CO_2, for example, with new aircraft, offer nonstop flights, and fly to and from less congested airports.

What if some airlines figured out the process for redesigning products that calls for steps well beyond renovation and iterations to lead to the total transformation of products that, in turn, calls for the generation of new ideas, particularly with insights coming through extensive engagement with employees? While there is no shortage of ideas, the challenge is twofold. The first part of the challenge is to identify those ideas that are worth pursuing in the fundamentally changing environment. The second part of the challenge is to find ways to "scale" the ideas. As one business researcher, John List, explains, "But scale isn't just about accumulating more uses or capturing more market share. It's about whether an idea that takes hold in a small group can do the same in a much larger one."[12] The new thinking would need to consider the changing needs of customers, the changing needs of employees, and the changing needs of airlines. Customers want seamless and frictionless travel experiences, even more so with an increase in the causes of disruptions. In the case of employees, frontline, for example, the need is for the development and empowerment of employees to provide real-time solutions to customers' problems. In the case of changing needs of airlines, think about this example: What if London Heathrow Airport kept increasing its prices, especially if it moves forward with the development of the third runway? What should IAG do or not do to realign its hub-and-spoke structure? Flexibility is needed in the decision-making process. For example, given the importance of Heathrow Airport to the UK economy, wouldn't political leaders intervene to ensure the staying power of the airport, eliminating the need for IAG to realign its hub-and-spoke structure?

To generate new viable ideas, readers are referred to the work of Bouquet et al, who have coined the term *A.L.I.E.N Thinking*.[13] In the authors' terminology, A.L.I.E.N stands for "Attention, Levitation, Imagination, Experimentation, and Navigation." According to these three business researchers, attention relates to seeing the world with fresh eyes, levitation relates to executives elevating their thinking, imagination calls for thinking out-of-the-world ideas, experimentation relates to the ability to test smarter to learn faster, and navigation relates to the capability to "maneuver to soar … and to avoid being shot down."[14]

Based on the author's experience, while there is no shortage of ideas in the airline industry, the challenge is to identify which hypotheses to test to determine their viability and how. Take, for example, the need for empathy to develop a deeper understanding of travelers' needs. While the idea is not new for airlines, what if they found the operative tactics for determining effective ways to understand empathy and to find new ways to solve travelers' problems? Empathy is a complex topic, and employees need special skills to understand travelers' needs in unique situations. "Empathy is accepting and seeking to understand their (customers') perspective."[15] And listening to and understanding a customer's problem in real time, and at an *emotional* level, requires frontline employees to have relevant skills, data, and time. Empowerment of frontline employees with the necessary skills and data, as well as making the necessary time available, would provide an airline with a real competitive advantage. Think about the current situation in which an airline needs to explain delays. There does not seem to be any empathy for passengers. How many executives have walked in the shoes of ordinary in-frequent travelers?

What if airlines developed products and services that finally meet end-to-end needs seamlessly by collaborating in the value-adding and open ecosystem (airlines, airports, surface transportation providers, and so forth)? What if they used platforms that facilitated the engagements with customers and employees in real time and at each touch point? Just as individual businesses within the automotive sector (e.g., Volkswagen), and individual businesses within the banking sector (e.g., the Royal Bank of Canada) are expanding their product lines by collaborating within their respective ecosystems, leading airlines could also begin to take a fresh look at new ways to compete for their existing and new customers. As the business researcher Ron Adner explains, the focus should now be on "winning the right game" as "winning the wrong game means losing." There are key insights that airlines could get from the two examples that Ron Adner provides, based on the strategies of Wayfair (an American online home furnishing retailer, formerly known as CNS Stores) to compete with Amazon and Spotify (a Swedish music streaming service provider, founded in 2006) to compete with Apple.[16] What is the right game for airlines? Could it be to focus more on nonbusiness travel? Could it be door-to-door travel?

Wayfair, now a multibillion-dollar business, was started around 2002 as an online store that enabled shoppers to see images of different products offered by different sellers (accompanied by information about the products), took orders, and then planned for delivery. The concept worked fine to connect small sellers with buyers. However, to compete effectively with larger organizations, Wayfair began to transform its business model by first helping its partners, small manufacturers of products and small shippers, to become more efficient. Second, Wayfair innovated its online search channel to help customers improve their experience in their selection process by "inspiring content to help guide their purchase decisions." In fact, innovation in this area stepped up when Wayfair introduced technology that helped customers select complementary products based on their "lifestyles."[17] Transformations along these lines helped Wayfair to compete effectively with Amazon.

Similarly, Spotify faced significant competition from Apple but managed to survive and thrive by continuously transforming its business model. The first competitive advantage was customers' access to remarkably comprehensive content using two types of offers—a free ad-based offer, or an ad-free subscription. Second, Spotify made high-quality algorithm-based recommendations using the data derived from listening choices made by consumers. The key point of this strategy was to provide a compelling product that engaged with customers. Third, Spotify developed a relationship with Facebook that posted users' playlists on its network, enabling the further matchmaking of listeners' playlists, based on the type of music. Fourth, Spotify persuaded some large record labels to allow consumers to upload songs without buying them, but instead providing revenue based on a royalty basis. Fifth, Spotify provided a linkage between artists (enabling the bypass of record labels) and listeners—a win–win situation for both artists and listeners. This linkage was also developed based on different aspects of the data derived from users. Spotify's ability to compete effectively with Apple resulted from the strategic use of data, meaningful engagements with consumers, and strategic collaboration with the ecosystem.[18] If Spotify was able to compete effectively with Apple, could a small airline learn how to compete with a giant airline or a giant distributor?

Imagine if a global airline were to transform itself in similar ways to Wayfair and Spotify by making personalized offers through much more effective collaboration within the ecosystem and the use of integrated data. Imagine also if an airline decided to "work backward" to design a radically new product. As described in Chapter 4, two former employees of Amazon, Colin Bryar and Bill Carr, explain in detail how teams at Amazon worked backward to design incredible products and services and the accompanying customer experience.[19] The role of design thinking, discussed in a previous book, cannot be underestimated.[20]

Think about the application of such design thinking within the "work backward" framework for several very different airlines and their situations. Cathay Pacific has been almost totally grounded (except for its cargo operations) as of the beginning of 2022 and would be starting its operations from ground zero. Allegiant Air, an ultra-low-cost airline, ordered 50 Boeing 737 Max jets to expand beyond its capacity during the pre-pandemic level. What about the new competition coming from the proposed merger of Frontier Airlines and Spirit Airlines, two other ultra-low-cost airlines? Wizz Air reportedly grew its capacity by 20% during the pandemic and placed an order of more than 100 Airbus 321s.[21] The expansion is based, presumably, (1) on the development of a subsidiary, based in Abu Dhabi; (2) plans to compete more effectively with Ryanair; (3) new services in the Norwegian market; and (4) the airline's application to fly to the US. China Airlines posted record profits from its cargo operations, developing a "cargo-centric business model."[22] What would be the new business model? And, Hainan Airlines, which had financial problems linked with its parent group, The HNA Group, which had problems even prior to the pandemic, has now just completed its restructuring plan. How would the products be designed for the new environment?

Some airlines have begun to think about and understand the future of travel in the emerging landscape. JetBlue, for example, is trying to evolve from being an airline to being a travel company, using its JetBlue Technologies Ventures. One example of moving toward becoming a travel company was for JetBlue to invest in Joby Aviation, a group involved in the electric vertical takeoff and landing (eVTOL) sector that could help JetBlue start transforming its services in the ultra-short-haul segments.[23] JetBlue also reported that it wants to become a lifestyle brand by diversifying its revenue base and by capitalizing on products to be developed by another subsidiary, JetBlue Travel Products.[24] This subsidiary developed a travel website, called Paisly, that not only helps travelers book related products (hotel, car rentals, etc.) but also makes recommendations based on the itinerary of the traveler.[25] AirAsia has already announced its plans to expand its services "beyond its core airlines-to-cargo delivery and fintech services." The airline is extending the applications of its super-app by launching, for example, *AirAsia Ride*, a ride-hailing service that focuses "primarily on airport transportation for flight passengers." Can a single app meet the varying needs of all its customers? Breeze Airways states: "Breeze is a technology company that just happens to fly airplanes." David Neeleman, Breeze's CEO, gives an example of the use of technology in which passengers can get their issues resolved using text/messaging within an average of 15 and 20 minutes.[26]

The key is to take a much deeper dive (into waters that are becoming increasingly deeper!) into the unmet needs of customers and employees, based on their changing behaviors and preferences, and to develop game-changing strategies based, on breakthrough thinking. Consider, for example, how the developers of mobile phones have been developing product features to meet the changing lifestyles of users—text message and email capabilities, a camera to take photos and videos, a broad spectrum of apps, access to the internet, screen size and resolution, and built-in security. What more could the airline industry do? How about, finally, door-to-door travel services? The concept is not new, but the challenge has been related to both the logistics and the development of game-changing strategies. Modern retailer/supplier schemes introduced by IATA, as part of its vision for offers and orders, would make a significant contribution. And, as with a premium for an environmentally-based experience for renting cars, what if air travelers were willing to pay higher fares to book on airlines that not just comply with environmental government rules and regulations but also develop and implement sustainability-focused visions and purposes? Some companies are already beginning to insist on buying "green" tickets.

Make no mistake about it. Airlines know that they need to go through a major transformation. And it is not that they do not want to transform. The challenge is twofold: (1) how to identify big disruptions and (2) how to transform, given the complexities of the business. For the first challenge, some business researchers suggest that management look at small data to identify big disruptions. Martin Schwirn, for example, points out that "[s]mall data is where every big disruption started. Filter small data from the sea of data. Identify the weak signals of change."[27] Here is just an example of small data that could represent a big disruption. The concept of door-to-door service has been discussed by airlines for years. However, Sun Country Airlines (a small airline, based in Minneapolis, Minnesota, USA), actually announced the implementation of the concept.[28] See Chapters 2 and 4 for more details on this announcement. For the second part of the challenge, according to Delta's CEO, the transformation can be achieved within the framework of three pillars, attitude, purpose, and teamwork.[29] While many airlines have developed innovation labs, the labs are still looking into making incremental improvements, as opposed to transformational improvements.

Outline of chapters

- Chapter 1, an introduction, asks the question, What if airlines adapted to the prevailing social changes, resulting from the convergence and intersection of major global trends? If yes, then how would the basic product be transformed to make shopping and travel easier, more convenient, and consistent, attributes requiring airlines to extend the boundaries of their businesses by, for example, collaborating within the ecosystems, not an easy concept. Of course, before making significant changes, airlines need to ensure they get the basics right. Once they are able to consider a transformation, then they can extend the boundaries of their business.
- Chapter 2 asks the question, What if an airline's network and schedule (the heart and soul of an airline's product), could be totally reengineered, with the ability to make changes in almost real time? The object would be to start developing, with agility, networks and schedules that are economically much more viable but operationally much more robust in the near term. Solutions would be based on the use of new data (e.g., shopping data), new techniques (e.g., dynamic scheduling), and new technologies (e.g., machine learning). The midterm goal could be to develop new products, such as viable nonstop services in low-density markets, door-to-door services, new forms of cost-effective urban air mobility, and intermodal transportation. The long-term goal could be the evaluation of the technical and economic viability of supersonic aircraft, Hyperloop systems, and hydrogen-powered aircraft.
- Chapter 3 asks the questions, What if airlines could reimagine different approaches to generating revenue, for example, by customizing and managing offers in real time? and How about using new pricing and revenue management techniques such as dynamic pricing and ways to optimize revenue from the sale of ancillary products and services? Three key requirements are (1) selling differently, (2) managing revenue in almost real time, and (3) integrating far more effectively network planning and revenue management.

10 *What if airlines adapted to consumer lifestyle changes?*

- Chapter 4 asks the questions, What if an airline could change its customer experience from an incremental to transformative level, not just to meet but to exceed customer expectations of targeted segments as well? and What if an airline could step up from offering a mediocre level of customer service and customer experience, or at least a hit-or-miss one, to a level that converts customers into promoters through the use of effective personalization processes? What if airlines could develop more effective strategies to win digital customers based on the experience of other businesses? What if airlines could seize opportunities to develop into lifestyle brands, based on the experience of, for example, such brands as Amazon and the DBS Bank?
- Chapter 5 asks the question, What if skies can be cleaned up strategically and cost-effectively? Airlines are clearly developing strategies to comply, cost-effectively, with government regulations, for example, through a commitment to reach "net-zero carbon emissions by 2050." What are the implications for airlines of the net-zero-by-2050 scenario? What is the future of sustainable aviation fuels? What if one airline made sustainability a major competitive advantage, by deploying advanced technologies and collaborating within the ecosystem, for example, with technology businesses and with partners, such as airports?
- Chapter 6 asks the question, What if airlines found new ways to do more with less by (1) collaborating by design, (2) building digital resiliency capabilities, and (3) strategizing for positional superiority? These opportunities can be seized by (1) leading with data to measure changes in behaviors, preferences, and expectations, as well as to get more intelligence on the market and the internal business, using leading and lagging measures; (2) collaborating in value-adding ecosystems; (3) deploying digital platforms to create superior end-to-end customer experience, at scale; (4) investing in employees and their work experience, by focusing on people strategy; (5) developing effective partnerships between legacy airlines and innovative start-ups; and (6) dealing with the ongoing problem of execution.[30]
- Chapter 7 asks the questions, What if a new airline, with an ecosystem-based lifestyle brand, let us call it, Agility Airlines, emerged to compete with the existing major players, for example, with a new large network, using all the assets of existing airlines, to compete with American, Delta, and United in the US? And what if Agility designed a lifestyle brand based on insights from Amazon, the DBS Bank, and Nike and developed the capability to achieve marketing and scheduling innovation by implementing dynamic scheduling and dynamic pricing? What if Agility Airlines developed new customer-centric products, such as point-to-point services (even in long-haul international markets) by operating single-aisle aircraft only, even across the Atlantic and the Pacific?

As others in this series, this book discusses, first, some best practices in the business world, identified by some accomplished business researchers—retailers and banks, for example. According to input provided by readers, this attribute of the series continues to provide valuable insights for airlines. Think about the rise and fall of Nokia, a business that was mentioned briefly in the previous book in this series.[31] For more details, the reader is now referred to an article by Kenji on "What Happened to Nokia?" In the summary, the writer, Kenji, makes two key points: Customers expect innovation, and businesses need to embrace new ideas.[32] And make no mistake about it. There are examples of best practices coming from the airline industry too. How about Southwest Airlines' success with "Hire for Attitude, Train for Skill."[33] Second, again, based on input from readers, this book also contains multiple forewords (at the front of the book) and thought leadership pieces (in Chapter 8). The diversity of the forewords provides readers some global perspectives from a wider angle on the book's theme, and the thought leadership pieces provide global perspectives from narrower, but detailed, viewpoints on the subject matter.

This book is primarily aimed at high-level practitioners within the airline industry, professionals engaged in innovation and development of new technologies, financial investors, non-airline businesses interested in entering the air transport market, and students of business studies in a wider context.

Notes

1 Jonathan E. Hillman, *The Digital Silk Road: China's Quest to Wire the World and Win the Future* (New York: HarperCollins, 2021), inside front flap.
2 Fareed Zakaria, Opinion in *The Washington Post*, "Politics is Trumping Economics. It Might End Badly," January 13, 2022. https://www.washingtonpost.com/opinions/2022/01/13/politics-is-trumping-economics-it-might-end-badly/
3 Ro Khanna, *Dignity in a Digital Age: Making Tech Work for All of Us* (New York: Simon & Schuster, 2022), p. 15.
4 "Q&A: EURAIL ON ITS DIGITAL-FIRST REBRAND," *PhocusWire*, March 17, 2022. https://www.phocuswire.com/eurail-on-its-digital-first-rebrand.
5 Raj Venkatesan and Jim Lecinski, *The AI Marketing Canvas: A Five-Stage Road Map to Implementing Artificial Intelligence in Marketing* (Stanford, CA: Stanford Business Books, 2021), p. 4.
6 Shameen Prashantham, *Gorillas Can Dance: Lessons from Microsoft and Other Corporations on Partnering with Startups* (Hoboken, NJ: Wiley, 2022).
7 "Omicron: Cathay Pacific at 2% of 2019 Passenger Capacity," CAPA Centre for Aviation, January 8, 2022.
8 Don Yaeger, "Delta Air Lines CEO Ed Bastian: 'We Keep Climbing,'" January 14, 2022. https://chiefexecutive.net/delta-air-lines-ceo-ed-bastain-we-keep-climbing/#:~:text=From%20labor%20shortages%20to%20supply,is%20all%20that%E2%80%94and%20more.
9 Rashmi Bhaskar Mukherjee and Ashok Khris, "5 Ways the COVID-19 Pandemic Is Changing the Role of Leaders," October 4, 2021. https://www.weforum.org/agenda/2021/10/5-ways-the-pandemic-is-changing-the-role-of-leaders/.
10 Differences between the Salient (1928–1945), the Baby Boomers (1946–1964), the Gen X (1965–1980), the millennials (1981–1995), the Gen Z (1996–2010), and the Generation Alpha (2011+) generations.
11 Howard Tiersky, *Winning Digital Customers: The Antidote to Irrelevance* (Houston, TX: Cranberry Press, 2021), p. 17.
12 John A. List, *The Voltage Effect: How to Make Good Ideas Great and Great Ideas Scale* (New York: Currency, 2022), front jacket flap.

12 *What if airlines adapted to consumer lifestyle changes?*
13 Cyril Bouquet, Jean-Louis Barsoux, and Michael Wade, *A.L.I.E.N. Thinking: The Unconventional Path to Breakthrough Ideas* (New York: PublicAffairs, 2021).
14 Cyril Bouquet, Jean-Louis Barsoux, and Michael Wade, *A.L.I.E.N. Thinking: The Unconventional Path to Breakthrough Ideas* (New York: PublicAffairs, 2021), titles and subtitles of the book.
15 Brant Cooper, *Disruption Proof: Empower People, Create Value, Drive Change* (New York: Grand Central, 2021), p. 67.
16 Ron Adner, *Winning the Right Game: How to Disrupt, Defend, and Deliver in a Changing World* (Cambridge, MA: MIT Press, 2021).
17 Ron Adner, *Winning the Right Game: How to Disrupt, Defend, and Deliver in a Changing World* (Cambridge, MA: MIT Press, 2021), pp. 43–44.
18 Ron Adner, *Winning the Right Game: How to Disrupt, Defend, and Deliver in a Changing World* (Cambridge, MA: MIT Press, 2021), pp. 58–69.
19 Colin Bryar and Bill Carr, *Working Backwards: Insights, Stories, and Secrets from Inside Amazon* (New York: St. Martin's Press, 2021).
20 Nawal K. Taneja, *Airlines in a Post-Pandemic World: Preparing for Constant Turbulence Ahead* (London, UK: Routledge, 2021), p. xx.
21 *Aviation Strategy*, Issue Number 265, December 2021, p. 4.
22 Alfred Chua, "Cargo-Centric Strategy Reaps Record Revenue for China Airlines," January 10, 2022. https://www.flightglobal.com/strategy/cargo-centric-strategy-reaps-record-revenue-for-china-airlines/147063.article.
23 Interview of Robin Hayes (CEO of JetBlue) by Graham Newton, "Understanding the Future of Travel," *Airlines*, IATA Corporate Communications, 2021-03, pp. 19–21.
24 Sean O'Neill, "The Aspirations of JetBlue to Be a Travel Tech Company," *Skift*, March 4, 2021.
25 http://mediaroom.jetblue.com/investor-relations/press-releases/2021/03-25-2021-140214502
26 Mitra Sorrells, "In the Big Chair – David Neeleman of Breeze Airways," *A PhocusWire* Interview, February 8, 2022. https://www.phocuswire.com/ceo-interview-breeze-airways-david-neeleman.
27 Martin Schwirn, *Small Data, Big Disruptions: How to Spot Signals of Change and Manage Uncertainty* (Newburyport, MA: Career Press, 2021), p. 11.
28 "SUN COUNTRY AIRLINES BRINGS THE AIRPORT TO YOUR DOORSTEP WITH NEW DOOR-TO-DOOR SERVICE," Media Contact: Sun Country Airlines, mediarelations@suncountry.com, September 28, 2021. https://ir.suncountry.com/static-files/6997f726-96ee-4919-a95a-31db9e1ce857.
29 Don Yaeger, "Delta Air Lines CEO Ed Bastian: 'We Keep Climbing,'" January 14, 2022. https://chiefexecutive.net/delta-air-lines-ceo-ed-bastian-we-keep-climbing/#:~:text=From%20labor%20shortages%20to%20supply,is%20all%20that%E2%80%94and%20more.
30 Chris McChesney, Sean Covey, and Jim Huling, *The 4 Disciplines of Execution: Achieving Wildly Important Goals*, 2nd ed. (New York: Simon & Schuster, 2021), ch. 1.
31 Nawal K. Taneja, *Airlines in a Post-Pandemic World: Preparing for Constant Turbulence Ahead* (London, UK: Routledge, 2021), pp. 65–66.
32 https://medium.com/swlh/what-happened-to-nokia-2a920b622d52.
33 Peter Carbonara, "Hire for Attitude, Train for Skill," *Fast Company*, August 31, 1996. https://www.fastcompany.com/26996/hire-attitude-train-skill-2.

2 What if airline products were reengineered?

A critical function in any company in any industry is to define and design the core product or service being offered. Automobile manufacturers spend hundreds of millions of dollars in deciding what kind of car to build and sell. Software companies go to great lengths to understand market needs and design software products to meet those needs. Getting the core product right often means the difference between business success and failure.

What is the core product of an airline? In its simplest terms, the core product of an airline has been a flight from point A to point B. It has been the basic unit of airline travel being offered and consumed. More generally, the core product of an airline could also be composed of the following attributes:

- starting airport and ending airport of the airline part of the journey
- type of service offered, for example, nonstop, connections, one-stop directs, and the like
- total journey time, including time spent at a connecting airport
- departure and arrival times, also departure and arrival days
- type of aircraft used in the journey—for example, wide-body aircraft, single-aisle aircraft, turboprop aircraft, and so on

Of course, there are other aspects of the airline product. One example is the cabin: airlines do a good job of segmenting their customers according to their preferences for first-class versus business-class versus premium-class versus economy-class travel. And many ancillary services, such as premium processing at the airport and bag transportation are also offered. And, more importantly, of course, an important aspect of the airline product is the brand equity associated with the airline itself. There is no doubt that many customers distinguish between different airlines when choosing their flights, even after accounting for some types of airlines (for example, ultra-low-cost carriers) that consistently offer lower fares than other airlines. This preference may be due to differences between loyalty programs, the airline's relationship with travel agents, and its reputation for superior service. Building and offering a strong brand loyalty is, of course, an important part of an airline's success, a topic discussed in more detail in previous books in this

DOI: 10.4324/9781003332824-2

series. It is also the theme of a thought leadership piece by Evert de Boer in Chapter 8. But at its core, the airline product can be represented by its published schedule. Failure to get the core product right will result in a loss of profitability, no matter how advanced an airline's loyalty, revenue management, distribution, or commercial strategies.

Notice that the starting and ending airport defines the market being served. For example, passengers wishing to fly from JFK Airport in New York City to LAX Airport in Los Angeles will consider all itineraries offered between these two airports. This airport pair can be described as one market. One interesting aspect about defining the airline product, that is, developing the airline schedule, is that services to many such markets are simultaneously defined. That is, decisions on service between airport A to airport B and airport B to airport C will determine connecting opportunities between airport A and airport C. As such, airline schedulers consider many such airport pairs at the same time; for a large airline, for example, American, Delta, or United, the number of relevant airport pair combinations to explicitly consider in their scheduling process can easily exceed 20,000.

Before discussing ways to improve the core product of an airline, it would make sense to point out (1) airlines are evolving from the core product to offers, discussed in the next chapter, and (2) the distinction between the core product and the full product. The full product would contain an offer (that would include conditions, such as re-bookability, refundability, bags, and so forth; mile accruals, including services such as meals and media/movies; and ancillary services), not to mention, full travel experience. Getting back to answering the question about how to improve the airline's core product, one must consider how customers value the product today. The following statements can be made about how customers generally regard the attributes mentioned earlier:

- Customers prefer nonstop service to direct (one-stop) or connecting flights, not just because of the time savings (although this is significant) but also because of less potential for disruption. Customers also prefer connections on the same airline to connections between different airlines also because of the potential for less disruption. But if the two airlines are engaged in a codeshare relationship, then customers will take that into account and not penalize that service as much.
- Beyond the type of service (e.g., nonstops versus connections), customers value itineraries with less total journey time. Consequently, time spent at connecting airports is a factor for customers. However, customers may penalize connections with very short connecting times at connecting airports if they perceive there is potential for disruption.
- Customers value leaving and arriving at favorable times of day, for example, leaving at 9:00 a.m. on Monday for a business trip and returning on Friday at 5:00 p.m. Given the different characteristics of different markets defined by airport pairs, these preferences could greatly vary between markets. For example, departing from DFW Airport at 9:00 a.m. to London would mean arriving at midnight local time, a situation not likely to be preferred.

- Customers have historically shown a preference for wide-body jet aircraft over single-aisle jet aircraft and jet aircraft over turboprop aircraft. This effect can be difficult to discern in the data, given that wide-body aircraft carry more passengers and, on average, offer lower fares, but it is present, nonetheless. Studies have shown that wide-body aircraft are preferred by 15% over single-aisle. As an example, some passengers were impressed the first time they flew a Boeing 787: the quiet ride, the superior air filtration, and the ability of windows to limit outside light, made for a superior experience. Customer views towards different and newer aircraft types are available from the Quality-of-Service Index (QSI) tables that airlines can access. Information in QSI tables relates not only the comparison of type of aircraft (wide-body at one end to turboprops at the other end) but also the desirability of nonstops versus connections, intra-line connections versus inter-line connections, and travel on full-service carriers versus low-cost carriers versus ultra-low-cost carriers. See Table 2.1.

Of course, different customers in different markets will value these attributes differently. For example, customers flying in short-haul markets may be less sensitive to departure times and total journey times than customers flying in long-haul markets. Business travelers may be more sensitive to timings than leisure customers, and customers booking three months in advance are usually less sensitive to timings than customers booking one day in advance. Understanding the relative preferences for different kinds of customers is an important part of being able to construct a profitable core product. Table 2.1 shows some representative values for the customer preferences. It should be noted that the figures indicate, for example, that nonstop flights are preferred over one-stop direct flights by a factor of roughly 6:1.

These general preferences described above have been stable for many years, even decades. It is fair to say, for example, that customers have always preferred nonstops to equivalent connections, other things being equal. However,

Table 2.1 Recent calibration of airline customer preferences

Effect	Quality of Service (QSI) Points	Effect	QSI Points
Nonstop	1.00	Widebody	1.22
One-Stop Direct	0.17	Narrowbody	1.00
Single connect	0.09	Regional Jet	0.84
Double connect	0.01	Turbo	0.74
Interline penalty	17%		
Codeshare penalty	54%	Legacy airline	1.00
		LCC airline	0.90
Elapsed time (versus fastest connect)	EXP(−0.65*hr)	ULCC airline	0.80

Source: Amadeus data, U.S. domestic one-way flights. March 2021.

Note: $N = 430{,}000$. All effects are significant.

one interesting question is whether the COVID-19 pandemic has changed anything regarding these preferences. And, clearly, the answer is that the COVID-19 pandemic has had an effect. There is a different mix of customer types flying in 2022 than in 2019 and customers treat the prospect of travel with less certainty than before. For example, customers are more likely to cancel or change their plans for a variety of reasons, including changes in government mandates. Understanding changes in customer attitudes towards travel considering the COVID-19 pandemic is a key part of positioning an airline for success. The key is to understand what customers really want, as captured and measured from their actual purchase decisions.

What if an airline improved its core product, for example, its flight schedule, differently in different time frames? In the short term (e.g., next five years), it can be assumed that today's aviation environment will remain largely the same. That is, the model of flying largely between airport pairs, using current types of aircraft will remain intact. In that sense, improvements in the airline's core product—its schedule—will come from more efficiently deploying its available assets in the current environment. There would be some exceptions, such as Qantas's decision to fly nonstop between Sydney and London and between Sydney and New York using the new Airbus 350-1000. The 19-hour flight between Sydney and London is expected to be about 5 hours less than the current almost 24-hour one-stop flight with a stop in Darwin. In the long term (e.g., beyond five years), however, new types of aircraft will be available that will change the current operating model. In addition, new technologies will be available that will challenge the paradigm of travel exclusively between airports. As such, in the long term, there will be many exciting possibilities to greatly extend an airline's core product.

Short-term improvements in the core product

As mentioned earlier, short-term improvements in the core airline product—the flight schedule—will come from more efficiently utilizing available corporate assets like fleet, gates, and slots, to develop a more profitable schedule. However, from an end-customer perspective, a most profitable schedule does not mean necessarily better products or more value. In some cases, it could mean worse products (e.g., a flight schedule that is not convenient for travelers or has a higher fare). Profitability will be a consequence of better meeting customer needs, instead of starting from profitability targets. New companies that have disrupted markets (Amazon, Uber, and so forth) lost money for a long time but focused on delivering superior customer value. This strategy gave them ultimately a near-monopoly position with huge profits.

To better understand how to build a more profitable schedule, it might be helpful to understand the scheduling business problem. This problem is easy to state but hard to solve, namely, finding the maximally profitable schedule that is also operationally feasible. This deceptively simple objective is complicated by several factors:

- *Endless scheduling possibilities.* Given traffic rights, airlines have the freedom to carry passengers between the airports they serve. The more airports an airline serves, the more routes—or airport pairs—that are possible. The number can get very large. For example, as Renzo Vaccari points out in his thought leadership piece in Chapter 8, an airline that flies to 100 airports has the possibility of flying almost 5,000 routes. Considering that an airline can schedule flights any day of the week and any time of the day, with any available aircraft type in its fleet, the decision space becomes unimaginably immense.
- *Complexity of operational feasibility.* All schedules must satisfy numerous operational constraints—aircraft count, block times, ground times, crew, maintenance, gates, slots, curfews and many more—to be "flyable." Many of these constraints are complex. Yet, accounting for all the dimensions of operational feasibility is critical to ensure that schedules can be flown.
- *Different airline passenger types.* Considering flight connections, especially between alliance partners, large international airlines serve up to 100,000 origin–destination markets (O&Ds). Within all these O&Ds, there are differences among passenger types. For example, some fly for business, some fly for leisure, and some for those visiting friends and relatives (VFR). Or, some passengers book flights months in advance, while others book the day before travel. Proposed schedules must be attractive to all targeted customers to maximize profitability.
- *Uncertain future environment.* Schedules must be finalized and available for sale months in advance of their eventual operations. As such, assumptions need to be made about other factors that are now changing in almost real time—competitors' schedules, expected traffic volumes, and available resources. And now, the even more dynamic nature of the airline operating environment means that changes often must be made after the schedule is available for sale but before the flights depart.
- *Quality and timeliness of data.* The quality of a proposed schedule is directly related to the quality of the input data used to develop it. While airlines can be reasonably confident of some input data, such as airport locations or internal cost structure, other key data are now becoming much more difficult to determine. For example, there is no single, accurate source of industry-wide origin-destination traffic volumes, and no airline can be 100% confident that this essential data for developing schedules is accurate.

To make it more manageable, airlines typically have solved their scheduling business problem—the need to create profitable but operationally feasible, schedules—by breaking the problem into separate sub-problems and solving each sequentially. These processes were often performed on a cyclical basis when many different schedules were in different phases of development at the same time. Consider the process to develop an operating schedule. There are typically six to eight steps, beginning with ensuring that the schedule is consistent with an airline's corporate strategy, and ending with handing over the control of the schedule to the airline's operations control center. While each step is commercially oriented, the focus is on making sure that all known operational constraints are accounted for and the schedule correctly reflects changes in resources (e.g., new aircraft entering service) across its entire effective period. As such, at different times, the schedule gets sent to various other internal stakeholders at the airline, for example, operations planning, crew management, maintenance, and catering departments for review and analysis. The key point to note is that these steps are taken in a sequence and often conducted manually with the goal of making the schedule "work" without significantly diminishing schedule profitability. And airlines have applied a combination of data, models and algorithms, and manual activities to perform each step, in sequence. As such, each step has been individually optimized to the extent possible, given the technologies available. What if the coordination process could be performed simultaneously as the schedule is being developed?

The definition of how an airline's corporate strategy should inform its scheduling practices has been subjective and has been an ad hoc one. There is no specific model that has been used to perform this step. Each airline determined its own set of guidelines for its scheduling practices to follow, based on its underlying business model and marketing priorities. Regarding the route development step, there has been no common way of performing this function across different airlines. Some airlines took priorities from a marketing planning function based on individual route analyses and grouped them together in a larger plan. Other airlines attempted to solve this problem in a systematic way, while still others performed it in a much more ad hoc and subjective manner.

Even now, it is well accepted that the schedule planning step can and should be performed via a fleet assignment model and a schedule forecasting model. Such models are used to determine passenger demand for proposed markets and routes and then determine fleet assignments that best match aircraft capacity to those flights to maximize airline profitability while satisfying operational constraints. Traditional schedule forecasting models are used to build connections across the airline and its competing network, estimate market shares by O&D, according to a simple QSI model, and reflect airline management practices by applying spill and recapture techniques. (For a discussion on the QSI model, going forward, read the thought leadership piece by Jim Barlow in Chapter 8.) Of course, in this step, a significant amount of manual intervention is still required to review model results. A schedule editor is used to make manual edits to the schedule and gets especially heavy usage during the schedule development and schedule finalization steps. This tool permits graphical views, reporting, validity checks, editing, and communication of proposed and historical schedules.

Airlines have often used a special tool to distribute the schedule and afterward check to see if it has been correctly interpreted by each receiving party. After publication, schedule changes have been managed in a similar manner.

What if airline products were reengineered? 19

It should be noted that some airlines have performed a short-term check to see if feasible "swaps" of crew-compatible aircraft rotations can be made to improve profitability. These airlines have typically used a highly constrained version of their fleet assignment model to perform this function using revenue management data. These weaknesses are not new; airlines and their technology providers have attempted to address these weaknesses over the past several years and have largely been unsuccessful. However, because of recent trends in technology and trends in the airline industry itself, it is now possible to offer a more modern approach to solving the airline scheduling problem.

What if an airline performed these processes in a much more effective way? While the traditional solution approach has been in place for many years, there are, at least four, weaknesses with it:

- *Suboptimization by separating key decisions in a sequence.* Breaking down a complex process into a series of sequential steps inevitably meant that some information got lost. For example, rather than adjusting the schedule later in the process to account for the needs of other departments (e.g., crew, maintenance, ground operations), suppose those needs could be well understood and considered in the optimization in the first place. Or rather than sequentially deciding fleet assignments, then timings, then aircraft rotations, suppose these steps could be performed simultaneously. Going forward, solving a more holistic problem in one step will produce a more profitable, operationally feasible schedule.
- *Overall process is manually intensive with significant time pressure.* The amount of time taken during one schedule development cycle has varied among airlines. Typically, this period has ranged from less than one month to about six months. During this period, a significant amount of data has been gathered, many other departments involved, and a significant number of manual activities performed. No airline has been content with the time available to it and there has been a widespread belief that the quality of the eventual product has suffered due to the lack of time to identify and evaluate different scheduling scenarios. It has often been difficult enough to just develop one feasible schedule, let alone develop many schedules and choose the best one. This time limitation has led to a series of shortcuts, such as beginning the schedule development cycle by using, as a starting point, the schedule published during the same schedule period for the previous year.
- *Forecasts are not acceptably accurate.* Reliable traffic, revenue, and cost forecasts are critical in identifying the maximally profitable schedule, yet many airlines have been uncomfortable with the accuracy of their forecasts or, worse yet, were even unaware of how accurate their forecasts were. Key reasons for this inaccuracy are the quality of input data, the difficulty with calibrating traditional forecasting models, the difficulty with which traditional forecasting models represent an airline's revenue management practices, the cost of maintaining a model calibration team, and the immaturity of forecast accuracy metrics.

20 *What if airline products were reengineered?*

- *Opportunity to perform an optimization across all steps in the process.* While the principle of performing an optimization has been well accepted in the schedule planning step, there are opportunities to apply this principle at all other steps in the process. In particular, the route development, schedule development, schedule finalization, and schedule adaptation steps would benefit from applying more advanced optimization technologies to them. It is a weakness of the traditional solution approach as so much is expected of airline schedulers.

As stated before, these weaknesses are not new, and airlines and their technology providers have attempted to address these weaknesses over the past several years but without much success. However, because of recent trends in technology and trends in the airline industry itself, what if an airline now used a more modern approach to solving the airline scheduling problem to develop its basic product?

The following trends in technology and the changes in the marketplace affecting the airline industry are now enabling airlines to offer a new, modern solution approach to the airline scheduling problem.

- *More data processing power.* With more data processing power, the technology to optimize a proposed schedule can now consider more factors than ever, such as explicitly considering detailed crew and operations constraints in schedule planning. In addition, alliance and partner schedules can be considered in the optimization that allows and even encourages alliance- or partner-friendly schedule changes. Finally, this extra processing capacity can be used to automate key scheduling tasks more quickly to reduce schedulers' time and allow more schedule scenarios to be considered.
- *Machine learning/artificial intelligence (AI).* The use of machine learning and AI algorithms allows forecasts to be more accurate. It can also reduce the burden of performing forecast calibration work to the point that the solution itself can be "auto-calibrated." Keep in mind that these techniques need to supplement existing knowledge about schedule forecasts and not become a kind of "black box," providing schedulers an intuitive understanding of the forecasting process. In addition, the increased use of these techniques can contribute to better forecast accuracy measurement and monitoring.
- *Shopping and booking data.* New shopping and booking data from key distribution channels are now available. The new data give airlines insight into their passengers' shopping requests, what was displayed to them, and what they ultimately chose. With this information, airlines can infer the choice behavior of their and their competitors' passengers and calibrate a much more precise QSI model. Shopping data also gives a much more precise sense of the days and times that passengers prefer to depart by market than is possible from only examining internal data and market information data tapes.

What if airline products were reengineered? 21

- *Importance of reliability in schedule planning.* As the worldwide aviation infrastructure is requiring airlines to handle more flights and undergoing even more strain, airlines are increasingly looking to address this problem in the schedule itself, by improving how operational problems can be handled on the day of departure. As such, schedulers are now under more pressure than ever to play a major role in addressing an airline's on-time performance issues, without significantly affecting schedule profitability.
- *Employee turnover and new scheduler profiles.* As airlines experience turnover in their scheduling departments, they can no longer afford the long lead time for new schedulers to learn how to manage complexity and become highly specialized experts. Instead, new ways are needed to quickly develop new schedulers and look to technology to perform detailed tasks that before were handled manually. In addition, younger, digitally savvy schedulers who grew up using technology expect to be given scheduling solutions that reflect their own technology knowledge.
- *New view of the scheduling function.* In the past, a reasonably clear division of responsibilities existed. Schedulers developed schedules, and then other commercial areas priced them and sold them. With the introduction of offer optimization—needing a more integrated approach to how offers are constructed, priced, and distributed—airlines now need scheduling solutions to be integrated with revenue management, pricing, shopping, and other commercial solutions.
- *COVID-19.* The uncertainty caused by COVID-19, such as border closures, limited crew availability, and disrupting historical demand patterns will likely remain with the airline industry for some time. As such, airlines will need to transform their existing business processes and technology solutions to deal with this disruption. See the thought leadership piece by Philippe Puech in Chapter 8.

Accounting for the new trends in technology—and in the airline industry itself—to address the known weaknesses of the traditional scheduling approach, what if an airline used five new scheduling techniques to develop its basic product? Applying any or all five of the following techniques will allow an airline to improve its core product in the short term:

1 Clean-sheet scheduling
2 Scheduling for profitability *and* reliability
3 Producing operations-friendly schedules
4 Improving forecast accuracy
5 Dynamic scheduling

Clean-sheet scheduling

As discussed earlier, the business problem of airline scheduling is extremely complex. There are clearly many, many possibilities, considering all the combinations of where to fly, when to fly, and which aircraft to fly, resulting in an unimaginably large number. Building a schedule attractive to customers means understanding in detail where customers are, what they value, and how much they will contribute. The problem is highly interactive—the value of putting a flight from, say, A to B, depends on whether there is a flight from, say, B to C, so that connections can be made. And there are so many dimensions of operational feasibility to account for—gates, slots, maintenance, crew, curfews, aircraft constraints, partners' schedules, and so forth. In the new environment that involves much greater uncertainty, how can an airline now reliably find the schedule which is both operationally feasible and maximally profitable?

As stated earlier, airlines typically start their schedule development processes using the same seasonal schedule flown the previous year as a starting point. In a stable world, this was a reasonable assumption. Once an airline found patterns of service for a specific season that performed well, it made sense to start with that schedule and then fine tune it. This assumption worked well in the past but will not work going forward. The marketplace is no longer stable and probably, will not be going forward. Too much is changing—customer demand is now highly variable, passengers' willingness to pay is different, and even their preferences for different times of the day and days of the week are not necessarily stable anymore. And competitors' schedules are changing. If a competitor leaves an interesting market, then that is an opportunity. And the assets of an airline itself are changing, for example, there may not be enough crew to fly the whole schedule. In that case, what does an optimal schedule, utilizing 90% of the aircraft, look like?

What can and should an airline do? What if an airline developed a new practice to build a new schedule from scratch based on what an airline knows about customer demand, competitors, and its own assets? The airline cannot assume that patterns from previous schedules will apply, requiring these hypotheses to be tested. Then, an automated, optimizing system can produce an optimal schedule, based on underlying route economics, geography, and airline resources. An airline can identify what has changed and then use technology to obtain a better starting point. Of course, any schedule derived through an automated and optimizing process will still need to be manually reviewed and fine-tuned. But the starting point would be much better, meaning the resulting schedule would also be much better.

This approach can be called clean-sheet scheduling since it starts with zero assumptions about the schedule. Although any airline can benefit from this approach, it would be particularly beneficial for airlines facing large strategic questions after the closure of operations because of COVID-19. Think of Cathay Pacific, which went down to 2% of its 2019 capacity. Think of airlines restructuring their networks after declaring bankruptcy, Avianca, for example. Think of Air New Zealand launching nonstop flights to New York, after the pandemic, to fulfill the airline's ultra-long-haul ambitions. As these airlines decide how to come back, they cannot rely on their 2019 schedules as guides, and they will need to build new schedules based on 2022, and forward, with assumptions, based on new opportunities. Think about South

African Airways, which is thinking about working with Kenya Airways to become a pan-African airline. There is no historical schedule that would be of any guide for such an entity and using an optimization solution to find the best combined schedule should drive a lot of value. Think about Air India. A strong international airline, based in India, could and should do well, but how to structure it to make the most of the many opportunities with large demand to/from India? Think about Alaska Airlines, American, and JetBlue developing partnerships in different markets. How would they combine their networks to optimize the combined schedule? What possibilities there could be in the realignment of hubs? Think about ITA Airways, a re-formed Alitalia. Should it compete with the two major European low-cost airlines (Ryanair and EasyJet) on price, or transform fundamentally its network and services to become an effective competitor and from Italy, a major European market? There are two steps for developing clean-sheet schedules. See a thought leadership piece by Renzo Vaccari in Chapter 8.

Clean-sheet scheduling is now possible for two reasons. First, there is the underlying optimization technology. Clean-sheet scheduling means being willing to consider many, many different scheduling possibilities beyond what airline schedulers would typically consider in the limited time available to them. If an airline scheduler is going to look for an optimization solution to find the best schedule out of all possible schedules, then the underlying search technique will need to be exceptionally efficient, and work at scale. One technology to do this has only become available recently, thus allowing the analyses of large strategic questions, like the ones mentioned earlier, to be done in days, not weeks or months. By the way, it can account for all the constraints with which schedulers work. In fact, clean-sheet scheduling, if done properly, accounts for all the constraints, such as fleet, crews, maintenance, gates, slots, and so forth. The basic idea is to become aware of new ways of flying the schedules that are operationally feasible, not just swapping aircraft or making minor changes to times. Without a clean-sheet scheduling approach, airlines become too incremental in their thinking. Second, clean-sheet scheduling needs data of sufficient volume and quality. For example, good estimates of industry O&D travel volume are required in a timely manner and processing these data can be complex and difficult. More important, reliable data on customer schedule preferences are needed. The best source for this information comes from analyzing customer shopping requests and resulting bookings. These data—actual shopping requests merged with actual bookings—have only recently become available.

Scheduling for profitability and reliability

Think about poor travel experiences during recent periods and the need for airline schedule reliability. Of course, unexpected events happen—weather problems, aircraft problems, crew issues—and no airline can ever be perfectly reliable. But notice a distinct difference in on-time reliability between some airlines and others and how some airlines recover from problems much quicker and better than others. What is needed is for an airline to build greater reliability into its schedules in the first place. When developing schedules and before publishing them, an airline can do things to make it easier for it to successfully operate these schedules. Some airlines already decide on block time standards, select to add in ground time where needed, plan on crews following aircraft routings, take advantage of spare aircraft, and so forth. However, there are more potential levers in building a schedule that can yield good on-time performance.

Think about the contemporary implementation of a QSI model that can give an airline much more confidence that its proposed schedule would be as profitable as possible. However, think also about how so much attention is paid to forecasting schedule profitability in the schedule development process with relatively little attention paid to simulating on-time performance. At the margin, it seems that there is an inherent trade-off between profitability and reliability. But airlines need better data and solutions to understand this trade-off. Is there a way to improve on-time performance without hurting profitability or to improve profitability without affecting on-time performance?

Many schedulers do not forecast on-time performance explicitly when they build their schedules. They expect their block time standards, ground time rules, fleet assignment algorithms, and so forth to produce a schedule with acceptable on-time performance. What if an airline were to routinely simulate the operation of a proposed schedule before the schedule is finalized and published? Think about how manufacturers simulate the performance of an aircraft before building it and how pilots "fly" simulators before flying certain aircraft. Could the same process be used in developing schedules? That way, once the schedule has been simulated, a scheduler can explicitly make trade-offs between profitability and reliability when finalizing the schedule. Too often, airline schedulers just consider profitability, and that would be like "trying to clap with just one hand." In the past, it might have been said that the technology was not there to be able to properly simulate on-time performance. But this is not the case. The technology exists to make a profit versus on-time trade-offs. It is now possible to simulate on-time performance and use that information to develop schedules that would reduce poor traveling experiences.

Producing operations-friendly schedules

One major feature of modern scheduling solutions is that they can reflect the needs of departments like operations planning, crew, and maintenance into the schedule development process. This feature produces schedules that take into consideration aspects essential to these critical departments. Less rework is needed once these affected departments review the schedule and provide their feedback, reducing schedule development time and improving quality. One example of this effect relates to the determination of flight rotations—or aircraft routings—during the schedule development process. With the traditional approach, a flight scheduler could propose rotations based purely on scheduling constraints and may not be aware that the resulting rotations could produce inefficient crew pairings. Once a proposed schedule is reviewed by an airline's crew planning department, these inefficiencies would likely be noted, and requests made for changes. But by this point, a significant amount of time may elapse. What if an airline could use modern scheduling solutions to address this problem by clearly including crew-friendly rules in the process of determining aircraft rotations? These rules can reflect well-known crew planning practices.

Other examples of operational-friendly schedules include increasing out and back flights to the crew base which reduces overnight/hotel costs for the airline. The additional benefit is that the crew spends more time at home, which provides a better quality of life. Another example of operational-friendly schedules is the capability of incorporating route-based maintenance. This functionality avoids the schedule having locked rotations and ensures that aircraft are landing at maintenance bases after an aircraft reaches the required interval of cycles, flight/block hours, or total time. Producing operational-friendly schedules earlier in the schedule development process supports the trend toward the blurring of the lines between the numerous process steps described earlier. In the future, distinctions between the major scheduling steps become less apparent, and a new modern schedule development process is more of a continuum.

Improving forecast accuracy

As with traditional approaches, modern scheduling solutions will continue to have a schedule forecasting module, but this module will be auto-calibrated based on state-of-the-art machine learning and AI algorithms. This aspect leads to a more complete and accurate treatment of passenger choice behavior. In addition, airlines can expect to lower the cost of maintaining staff to calibrate this module. In a modern scheduling solution, forecast accuracy will be automatically measured, monitored, and reported to schedulers so they can understand the effectiveness of the solutions they are using. In addition, modern solutions can diagnose causes of error as part of prioritizing future research. Reducing forecast error can generate significant benefits. Simulation studies have shown that a 20% improvement in forecast accuracy (i.e., from 15% error to 12%), can improve top-line revenue by up to 1% through better route selection, fleet assignment, and timings.[1] One way to reduce forecast errors is to use new sources of data. For example, curves depicting passengers' preferred time of departure are a key input into schedule forecasting solutions. These preferences can vary by market, even by the direction of the market.

Historically, deriving such curves has been a challenge, given the nature of available data. Data showing strong customer preference around, for example, a 10:00 a.m. departure may only be due to the lack of alternative flight options. This inherent bias makes it difficult for schedulers to predict customer reactions to new flight times. What if an airline used new data, which have now become available, based on actual shopping requests made by customers? These data can show when customers prefer to fly and provide a new way to produce those preferred time-of-day curves. Moreover, these data provide a window into the overall customer choice process, beyond the ability to produce time-of-day curves. These data can provide an excellent source for the machine learning algorithms, embedded within the auto-calibration routines, to learn from, further improving the calibration of the forecasting model and accuracy.

Dynamic scheduling

During 2020 and 2021, worldwide commerce was disrupted, including how businesses related to their customers and to each other. In the airline industry, COVID-19 caused great disruption on both the *demand* side and the *supply* side. On the demand side, the number of passengers willing and interested in flying became much more variable than before, with this effect often being different in different markets. Competitor volatility became a factor as well—competitors began to enter and leave markets much more frequently, causing both opportunities and challenges for all. And customer willingness to pay changed as the mix of customer segments changed, for example, a decline in business travel. On the supply side, government mandates, relating to COVID-19 quarantines, began to quickly shut down available travel. And the volatility in crew availability, due to uncertainty in COVID-19 cases, began to limit, at the last minute, the number of aircraft an airline could operate. It became more and more difficult for airlines to rely on their ability to operate a proposed schedule.

As a result, some airlines have begun to use an approach called dynamic scheduling to partially address the demand–supply variation. Dynamic scheduling is the practice of continuously and systematically reviewing an airline's schedule, after publication, in an automated and optimizing manner to identify and execute profitable and operationally feasible changes to the schedule. Traditionally, airlines finalized their schedules 6 to 12 months before eventual operation. While the schedule reflected known market conditions at the point of publication, it was not at all unusual for the new market conditions, as described before, to arise after publication that would cause the schedule to be suboptimal. Historically, airlines have been reluctant to change their schedules for the fear of creating disruptions, thus missing revenue opportunities. However, with COVID-19, the negative consequences of changing the schedule after publication are now a risk worth taking.

What kinds of schedule changes could be considered by practicing dynamic scheduling? Conceptually, many kinds of schedules could be considered, such as adding or deleting flights, adding, or deleting aircraft, changing aircraft type assignments, and changing flight times (e.g., departure times, ground times, or block times). One specific kind of change is swapping two aircraft routings (the sequence of flights flown by a specific aircraft), especially when both aircraft are from the same crew-compatible family. Another change is to plan on the same flight schedule across all days of the week and then selectively change schedules on weekends, given the difference in demand patterns during weekends. The principles behind dynamic scheduling are not new. Some readers may recall the idea of Demand-Driven Dispatch (D^3) promoted by Boeing in the 1990s. In D^3, schedule changes being considered were specific to equipment reassignment. This approach can be a subset of what is now called dynamic scheduling, which considers more types of changes.

What if an airline did dynamic scheduling but in a more effective manner that requires access to three things?

> *A schedule optimizer.* This would provide an automated solution to hold schedule and operational data and identify the set of scheduling changes that are both maximally profitable and operationally feasible. The scale of most medium-sized to large airlines is such that an advanced optimizer will be required.
>
> *Market data.* This requires the use of reliable and accurate data on bookings and revenue. Given the short-term orientation of dynamic scheduling, the source for these data is a revenue management system.
>
> *Operational constraints.* There is a need to understand all dimensions of operational feasibility to ensure that the resulting recommended schedule changes can be implemented. In turn, this need requires robust and complete information on how any airline determines operational feasibility.

One critical aspect of practicing dynamic scheduling is to avoid unnecessary churn. There is value in having consistency between schedules from different periods. It does not make sense for a dynamic scheduling solution to chase a few dollars in extra profit, as the potential disruption from any one schedule change could cost more than that amount. As such, the optimizer should penalize any possible schedule changes so that only the changes that meet an acceptable threshold of additional profitability will be recommended. This penalty, or "continuity factor," can be manually calibrated to be consistent with each airline's tolerance for change.

Interestingly, the scope of changes considered by dynamic scheduling can be increased or decreased. One approach is to commit the entire fleet to a published schedule and then only make changes in the context of that commitment. For example, one could schedule all available aircraft and then, if it is determined to be profitable, add a new flight, but then an old one would need to be canceled. Alternatively, one could commit only a portion, say, 90%, of all available fleet to a published schedule and then selectively add the remaining 10%, as opportunities become available. What is the value of dynamic scheduling? Of course, benefits from this practice depend on the degree to which changes can be accommodated. Studies have estimated an additional 1% to 3% in revenue from undertaking dynamic scheduling, depending on the degree to which it is exercised. Once profitable schedule changes have been identified, they will then need to be implemented. Meeting this need requires advanced schedule load capabilities offered by modern passenger service systems and advanced passenger re-accommodation solutions. Going forward, undoubtedly, there will be a need to process more and more schedule changes.

Medium-term improvements in the core product

In the medium term (e.g., three to five years), new technologies will become available to challenge the existing paradigm of air travel exclusively between airports. Clearly, from customers' viewpoints, they do not necessarily wish to travel between airports. They have a preferred pickup point to start their journey, presumably their home or office, and wish to travel to another specific place, such as a hotel or another residence. And there is the burden of having to book services from different providers on different systems to meet travelers' door-to-door needs. Moreover, travelers may have to book some transportation services once they reach their destination airports, wasting a lot of time. If they could avoid the monetary and time expense of traveling to and from airports, then they would. Airports have been an efficient way to provide air travel but not because passengers prefer to travel to them. To adapt to the emerging expectations of consumers, leading airports will become mobility hubs. See the thought leadership piece in Chapter 8 by Michaela Schultheiß-Münch and Jennifer Berz with the Fraport AG.

One example of this effect is considering intermodal travel, such as integrated travel involving both trains and aircraft. In France, a passenger may take a high-speed train from the center of Lyon to Paris Charles de Gaulle Airport (CDG) and then board an aircraft. In contrast to air travel from Lyon to Paris CDG, the train service has several important advantages.

The comparison of experience between train and flight is interesting (e.g., for domestic leisure travel). End-to-end travel by train is much easier and frictionless than in flights. There is no need to stand in lines for check-in, security check, and baggage drop-off, and there is no need to arrive a long time in advance to perform these steps. Additionally, trains usually arrive in city centers, not requiring significant additional transportation. However, the train cannot compete with aircraft for travel beyond 1,000 kilometers.

More important, from a sustainability perspective (discussed in Chapter 5), high-speed train service uses less fossil fuel per person-mile carried and is thus much more sustainable. Of course, it takes special types of markets to have high-speed train service. High-speed rail service is already linked with many airports today, especially in Europe and Japan. One key lesson is that the geography and demographics of candidate markets must justify their large setup cost. But, in the interests of sustainability, it is easy to imagine that more markets will be given high-speed rail service than before. And, in many of these markets, the high-speed rail service will link to airports, thus allowing much more intermodal services to be offered in the future. What if an airline evolved its core product to offer travel from many more initial starting points? What if the airline designed the intermodal service to be not only integrated but also seamless and digitally manageable by travelers? With respect to the last point, think about passengers being able to manage every aspect and every step of the trip using their mobile devices, for example, using biometric technology to board different vehicles at different places and to pass through controls at borders.

Related to the point of more intermodal travel is the opportunity to offer greater end-to-end services and door-to-door travel (discussed later) for customers. What do customers want? Again, they want to leave from their own personalized starting points and arrive at their own personalized ending points. They would like all modes of transport to be integrated into their reservations with all aspects of managing their journey handled by their providers. As an example, customers would like to be picked up at their starting points and then have their bags delivered to them at their end points, without any intervention on their part. That is, once they have been authenticated at their starting points, they would like to leave their bags to the supplier providing the first mode of transport and then be confident the bags will eventually be delivered to them at their ending points. Of course, rules for international travel require passengers to clear international customs with their bags, but it is easy to imagine this service becoming more common in several years. What if an airline were to provide such end-to-end services?

Door-to-door travel

What if an airline could develop and implement comprehensively a game-changing strategy for providing door-to-door travel with structured input from all stakeholders and not just by the C-suite? The key stakeholders are customers, employees, and suppliers. In the past, airlines have generally used their C-suite executives to plan their major strategies, with some airlines relying heavily on consultants. Most of the time, airlines have shied away from getting different stakeholders involved in any proactive or structured manner. The main category of stakeholders left out has been the employees. The rationale seems to have been, presumably, that strategies discussed and implemented needed to be kept confidential or that the employees were likely to suggest unconventional strategies or that the employees may not have had a full comprehension of the dynamics of the marketplace. This type of thinking is unfortunate as different stakeholders, especially employees, can, in fact, generate innovative ideas through nonconventional thinking. In fact, some employees may be in a better position to recognize the potential threats in the marketplace and the changing dynamics of the marketplace. And they are more likely to be able to identify the unmet needs of customers than the executives in the C-suite. In any case, senior executives may not be willing to take the risk involving the development of unconventional strategies, the very strategies needed to cater to the unmet needs of customers. Consequently, it is the involvement of employees that will help an airline to get the nonconventional strategies executed.

The concept of door-to-door service is not new. The challenge, however, has been to develop innovative solutions and not get hung up in the logistics.

Christian Stadler et al. provide numerous examples of well-known businesses that were not able to think through innovative strategies by not using an "open strategy."[2] In the case of airlines, in some cases, even when a CEO might be open to transformative strategies, the C-suite team may not be willing to deviate significantly from conventional thinking. The team may be willing to deviate a little to extend the boundaries of the airline business but generally may not be willing to go beyond the core competencies of the airline business. The key is to be open to discussing nonconventional concepts and nontraditional ways of execution, collaborating in the ecosystem, and being willing to experiment. In the case of door-to-door travel, there could be numerous new stakeholders whose opinions and participation could lead to viable solutions. The challenge is to find effective ways to get the proactive participation of all stakeholders, for example, the size and number of groups and their goals, the ideal communication platforms, and different ways to present the problem. It is also necessary to answer questions about the concerns, for example, the confidentiality of the strategy, motivating and incentivizing the stakeholders, and the time scope for the strategy—short term, midterm, or long term. As stated in Chapter 6, one goal could even be for an internal group to destruct the business before a competitor does it.

Within the context of air travel, end-to-end travel and door-to-door travel would mean providing the capability to make reservations at one place. The IATA vision for offers and order and the modern retail/supplier scheme (combined with a platform approach), could help support this capability in an efficient way. An important point would also be for each provider of services in the chain to recognize a customer and provide relevant offers and deliver hassle-free services. As mentioned in previous books in this series, a platform can be used to enable different third parties as well as partners to work together. In the past, airlines working in an alliance did produce some benefits, although not as many as planned. But the comprehensive use of a platform could mean the delivery of end-to-end and door-to-door services much more consistently and seamlessly. For example, in the case of a flight arriving late, the hotel would be notified so that the room is not canceled or that the limo pickup service driver does not leave but waits outside the terminal that has been changed.

Small electric aircraft

Aircraft technology has been a game-changer since the beginning of the aviation industry. Think about the contributions made by just the following aircraft: the 1909 Bleriot X, the 1935 Douglas DC-3, the 1952 de Havilland Comet, the 1987 Airbus A320, and the 2009 Boeing 787. Think about the first 17-kilometer nonstop flight between St. Petersburg and Tampa, Florida, in 1914. Compare this with the first 15,353-kilometer nonstop flight between Singapore and New York. And in the not-too-distant future, aircraft technology will change the game again by flying small electric aircraft at mid-range distances (i.e., less than 1,000 miles). In addition to being sustainable, these aircraft will likely generate lower costs, thus making them attractive for long, thin routes. Given that one of the core attributes of the airline product is nonstop service, the ability to offer more nonstop service on many new routes constitutes a real improvement in the airline product.

Consider Heart Aerospace—based in Gothenburg, Sweden—that is developing a 19-seater (ES-19), an all-electric (battery-powered) fly-by-wire regional aircraft. The key is the economics of the aircraft and its zero-emission capability. The attractive economics appear to be the result of lower operating costs of electric motors and lower maintenance costs. It is reported that the aircraft could be in service by 2026. The challenge is for the batteries onboard to power the entire aircraft, including all systems onboard—avionics and cabin, for example. The manufacturer will, obviously, work within the regulatory limits of the takeoff weight of aircraft in its category (under 20,000 pounds). Keep in mind that the takeoff and the landing weight are the same since the aircraft is powered by batteries, unlike conventional fuel that reduces the weight of the aircraft as the fuel onboard is used. The range, determined by the batteries, is expected to be up to 250 miles, depending on the expected improvements in the density of the batteries, a development that could also increase the capacity of the aircraft. Think about the value of cost-effective electric aircraft in high-density markets, such Boston-New York, Rio-São Paulo, and Osaka-Tokyo. How about high-density markets that involve crossing a body of water, for example London-Dublin, London-Amsterdam, and Seoul-Jeju?

Air taxis

The technology to offer air-taxi services for limited distances already exists, but it is easy to imagine the technology evolving to the point that this kind of service could become viable for short-range distances. As such, air travel on an almost personalized, and on-demand, basis could become possible. As a result, a new airline, or a division of an existing airline, could eventually become, at least for short-range distances, a kind of "Uber of the Air." Related to this point is the prospect of unmanned vehicles whose costs could make personalized service to specific starting and ending points much more attractive. The key point to keep in mind is the increase in urbanization based, presumably, on the increase in household incomes. According to one set of figures, 16% of the world's population lived in urban areas in 1900. The percentage increased to 30% in 1950 and to 50% in 2007 and is expected to increase to 68% by 2050.[3] Consequently, with a growth in populations, urbanization, and congestion, the concept of urban air mobility has always made sense. However, the technology, namely, conventional helicopters, was not cost-effective. Now, with the availability of electric propulsion, the urban air mobility concept is becoming much more plausible in a sizable market, estimated to be about $30 billion by 2030.[4] Think about the VX4, being developed by Vertical Aerospace. See Figure 2.1. It is being designed to be "faster, quieter, greener, and cheaper." According to the planners, it is being

32 *What if airline products were reengineered?*

Figure 2.1 The Vertical Aerospace VX4
Copyright Vertical Aerospace 2022, used with permission

designed to fly over 200 mph, produce virtually no noise when in flight, produce zero emissions, and have a lower cost per passenger transported. The aircraft is expected to carry four passengers and a pilot and have an initial range of 100 miles, with a lower cost per passenger transported. Vehicles such as these would be game-changers in urban air mobility.[5]

And let us not overlook the value of autonomous drones to fly packages of different weights. Think about the value 42air maritime drone delivery company, based in Berkeley, with its operations anywhere in the Mississippi River below Baton Rouge, Louisiana. It has been delivering items like urgent documents, favorite local pastries, or coffee to ships using its current DJI M600 drone (Figure 2.2), equipped with a high-tech winch, engineered and manufactured by 42air engineers, enabling the drone to lower cargo to the deck or bridge wing of a vessel—without having to land. Each drone can carry up to 7 pounds of cargo, as of now, but the payload capability will gradually grow in the near future. Currently the drones can only deliver to ships that are stationary. However, the company's engineers are working on a system that will enable deliveries to be made to moving vessels in a near future. There are also second-generation drones, such as Korea's Doosan Mobility Innovation (DMI), emerging in the industry. DMI's hydrogen

What if airline products were reengineered? 33

Figure 2.2 DJI M600 drone, operated by 42air

drone can fly for more than two hours and has low noise and vibration, making it suitable for tasks, such as parcel deliveries, reconnaissance, and monitoring. Think also about the possibility of larger electric vertical take-off and landing, for example, the Elroy Air's Chaparral, being developed with a hybrid-electric system and an in-flight rechargeable lithium battery. The vehicle is envisioned to be able to carry cargo weighing up to 500 pounds and flying distances up to 300 miles.

Long-term improvements in the core product

In the long term (e.g., five years or more), there is an additional way in which the core airline product will improve, using new technology and new types of aircraft. Some examples of new aircraft technologies that will be available in the next several years and how they might disrupt the core airline product follow.

Supersonic aircraft

As mentioned at the beginning of this chapter, one important attribute of the core airline product is total journey times. Aircraft flying faster than the speed of sound will offer dramatically lower total journey times to customers. In turn, such services will be quite attractive and are likely to justify large revenue premiums. A new supersonic aircraft, such as Overture by Boom, cannot be compared with the Concorde, which had limited commercial success. Boom Technology's Overtures are expected to have better economics due primarily to an improvement in propulsion technology. See Chapter 5.

To start with the aircraft will have two engines compared to the Concorde, which had four. It will also not have an afterburner. Next, it could operate on a slightly lower cruising speed, for example, around Mach 1.7 rather than Mach 2. Moreover, what if Overture's engines operated on 100% sustainable aviation fuels? Finally, the main question would not be if Overture's fuel consumption per passenger transported would be less than the Concorde, but could it be less than a subsonic jet? What if airlines that have already ordered this aircraft, for example, Japan Airlines and United Airlines, used different network analyses and scheduling processes to meet customer needs and make a profit? What if these airlines used new techniques, new data available (discussed in this chapter), and smart platforms to engage much more comprehensively with customers?

Hyperloop vehicles

These vehicles are expected to provide ultra-fast travel not only in selected high-density markets (e.g., SFO–LAX) but also between nearby airports (e.g., those located within the greater Los Angeles area). Could John Wayne, Hollywood Burbank, Ontario International, Long Beach, and San Bernardino International become as they were different terminals of the Los Angeles International Airport? The Hyperloop service could simply transport passengers from each of these five airports in a few minutes to LAX, in fact, in less time than it currently takes to go from one existing terminal to another one in the LAX Airport!

Hydrogen-powered aircraft

As discussed in Chapter 5, hydrogen-powered aircraft are expected to provide a lot of value from the sustainability perspective, but they are not expected to be available for at least 10 years. Airbus has already announced its plan to build the world's first zero-emission commercial aircraft to run on hydrogen. The estimated time frame is 2035. See Figure 5.1 in Chapter 5, which shows the development of three hydrogen-powered airplanes. The hydrogen plane with a totally new design is being explored to have a blended wing, shaped like a large triangle. This shape would allow the aircraft to carry more fuel. In addition to the design of the aircraft, a real challenge would be the infrastructure to produce, transport, and store hydrogen.

These vehicles, with advanced technology embedded in them, will change the core products of airlines and their broader networks, fleet, and scheduling processes. Where would the data come from to determine their cost-effectiveness, and what new data would be generated by them? How could the network, fleet, and schedule processes, discussed in this chapter, be changed, and integrated with the new processes to generate more revenue, the subject of the next chapter?

Highlights

- To answer the question about how to improve the airline's core product—flight schedule—one must consider how customers value the product today and how their preferences will change with changes in their lifestyles.
- The scheduling function in airlines is extremely complex due to, for example, endless scheduling possibilities, complexity of operational feasibility, multiple segments of targeted customers with enormous differences in preferences and willingness to pay, and uncertainty of the future environment, not to mention the quantity and quality of the available data.
- In the medium term (e.g., three to five years), new technologies will become available to challenge the existing paradigm of air travel exclusively between airports. Two potential areas for improvement are the availability of more intermodal travel, and the opportunity to offer greater end-to-end services to customers.
- In the long term (e.g., five years or more), there is an opportunity to improve the core airline product using new technology and new types of aircraft: small electric aircraft, supersonic aircraft, and hyperloop vehicles.

The traditional approach to solving the airline scheduling business problem is to work in a sequential manner, from route development to the publication of a schedule. This process has several weaknesses, such as suboptimizations by separating key decisions in a sequence. The known weaknesses in the traditional scheduling approach can be addressed by using five new scheduling techniques: clean-sheet scheduling, scheduling for profitability and reliability, producing operations-friendly schedules, improving forecast accuracy, and scheduling dynamically.

Notes

1. Amadeus research studies—2018.
2. Christian Stadler, Julia Hautz, Kurt Matzler, and Stephan Friedrich von den Eichen, *Open Strategy: Mastering Disruption from Outside the C-Suite* (Cambridge, MA: MIT Press, 2021), ch. 1.
3. "eVTOLs: Upwardly Urban Mobility," *Aviation Strategy*, Issue No. 266, February/March 2022, p. 16.
4. Tim Robinson, "Vertical Dreams Are Made of These," *Aerospace*, February 2022, p. 20.
5. https://vertical-aerospace.com/vx4/.

3 What if airlines rethought their revenue approach?

Traditional revenue approach

In an industry with relatively low margins, like the airline industry, the search for more revenue is paramount. The ability to generate new sources of revenue can often make the difference between success and failure. However, for many customers, airline travel is seen as a commodity, and in such markets, it is difficult to sustain long-term profits. Airlines will need to strategize differently to significantly distinguish themselves from their peers to generate larger revenue margins. In addition, airlines operate in an environment that limits their ability to creatively access new sources of revenue. To be sure, some airlines can overcome some of these limitations to generate more revenue, but the industry has yet to move away from the traditional approach to selling and pricing air travel. This traditional approach is characterized by the following weaknesses:

Focus on seats. As mentioned in Chapter 2, the core product sold by airlines is a seat from point A to point B. Yet, airlines today sell many things besides their core product, including services like transporting baggage, changing reservations, having priority screening/boarding, and so forth. These additional services—called ancillaries—have been generating significant amounts of additional revenue for airlines. Some airlines have reflected the importance of this additional revenue by implementing programs to optimally price their ancillary services. However, it is reasonable to assume that the science behind optimally pricing these services is not as advanced as the science in pricing the core product, that is, traditional revenue management. Could one reason be that scheduling and revenue managers do not think of the inventory of ancillary products as constraints (except for some specific ancillaries, for example, lounges)? As such, is it possible that the managers of ancillary products and services do not feel the need to have sophisticated science techniques for revenue management? However, when arranging their travel, customers typically buy more than just the core product and a few services. They also often purchase hotel accommodations, car rentals, and other travel products. The totality of a customer's travel purchase—core airline product, airline services, other travel purchases—would now be an offer. This provides an immense opportunity for an airline that can optimally construct and price this combination. See Chapter 7, for an example.

Pricing set at predefined price points. Current airline pricing and revenue management practices typically follow processes developed many years ago. For example, airlines still file fares that are statements of rules and conditions for carriage at set price points. The collection of all fares, in each market, is a fare structure and illustrates how airlines intend to vary their price points by, say, days before departure, stays during Saturday nights, or other rules. The availability of these fares is then managed minute by minute by the process of revenue management, determining the set of controls to be applied in an airline's inventory system. The number of price points that can be offered is influenced by several legacy assumptions; for example, each booking class is assigned a letter of the Western alphabet. How many modern retailers use such practices? Instead, price can be determined as the provider wishes on a continuous scale.

Inability to practice brand differentiation in legacy distribution. As mentioned earlier, it is difficult to make higher-than-normal profits in a commodity industry. See the discussion on the existence of commoditization by Glenn Hollister in Chapter 8. To generate significant profit potential, one airline must demonstrate it provides more value than its competitors. Once this value has been demonstrated, customers can purchase products and services from the superior provider, for example, via brand identification. However, in the airline industry, it can be difficult for customers to distinguish true brand differentiation in the indirect or travel agency channel. Of course, attributes of the core product, as described in Chapter 2, are easily identified (e.g., type of service, departure/arrival times, total journey time, and aircraft type). However, it is not as obvious how to show the differentiating services between airlines in travel agency displays. An airline that can properly represent itself the way it wishes to be represented in all selling channels will have a major advantage over competitors that are not able to do so.

Slow implementation of product/pricing decisions. Marketing is about giving the customer the right product at the right price at the right time. But what happens if market conditions change, and the product needs to change? Or if pricing needs to change? Clearly, there must be a process of learning and adapting, but in the airline industry, the process of determining available fare products and related services is set months ahead of the purchase. And while airlines monitor their competitive pricing positions, there is a lag between receiving signals of new market information and acting on them. What if an airline could react instantly to any new information about the market to keep its products and services always current? This capability would mean the ability to define products and services as well as to price them in near real time.

Relative lack of personalization. Beyond the core product, discussed in Chapter 2, airlines can offer a relatively wide collection of ancillaries, non-air content, and other services. Yet, as discussed in the next chapter, it is rare that this collection of services is personalized to form a curated and unique offer for a specific customer. Why? Clearly, airlines know a lot about their customers, given, for example, that they invented loyalty programs. A significant amount of data is collected on passengers' previous trips. But how much information is collected on their purchasing experiences? When booking flights, it should be noted that the same offer keeps coming up—after 18 booking sessions without choosing trip insurance, for example, an airline should think about other services. The ability to understand unique customer needs (and preferences based on purchase history) and offer a personalized and curated offer present a massive opportunity to drive more revenue as well as increase customer satisfaction.

Focus on prebooking optimization. A significant amount of effort is spent in the commercial planning process before any booking is made. By this point, the schedule has been optimized, an appropriate fare structure has been determined, and fare inventory controls have been optimized. At that point, planners have managed to bring data and science together to maximize the revenue from bookings. However, after the booking is made, there are still opportunities to drive more revenue. Examples include running upgrade campaigns much more effectively, selling additional services, and possibly re-accommodating passengers to take other flights if a passenger is willing, and it is profitable to do so. To be sure, many airlines perform some of these post-booking activities today, but experience shows these activities do not get the attention they deserve. Additional focus on revenue opportunities, after the booking, is a source of great opportunity.

Inherent complexity and restrictions. Airlines continue to operate in an environment characterized by business processes created decades ago. Why is there a separate booking and ticket? Why are airlines limited to 26 booking classes, the number of letters in the Western alphabet? What exactly is an Electronic Miscellaneous Document, and why do we need one? Why do airlines file fares the way they do? In any other retail industry, sellers are free to define their products, price them the way they wish, and sell them in any channel according to how they want the product to be presented. What if an airline could simplify the process of implementing its revenue strategy to drive more revenue as the airline's employees cease performing unproductive clerical tasks and focus more on revenue opportunities?

Sequential decision-making. Most airlines define and price their products according to a sequential process: (1) decide the flight schedule including markets to serve, as discussed in the previous chapter, (2) make decisions on fare products and related services to offer, (3) file fares, and (4) determine fare availability. Clearly, some of the sequential nature of these processes makes sense— to file fares, an airline needs to know which markets it participates in and a sense of the competitiveness of its schedule. And fare availability cannot be determined optimally without knowing specific fare levels. Yet, there is little integration and feedback from one process to another. For example, when planning the schedule, assumptions need to be made on how it will be revenue-managed. And understanding the impact of schedule changes is important in the practice of managing revenue. A significant amount of revenue leakage occurs because these activities are not coordinated. Conversely, there are real revenue opportunities for airlines that can perform these functions in a synchronized and integrated manner by sharing data, models, and assumptions.

Relatively little innovation in the selling process. When examining different selling channels that airlines participate in, either their direct airline.com sites or global distribution system (GDS) channels, it seems that the same kinds of products and services have been sold in basically the same way for many years. Yet other retailers, with amazon.com being one of the best examples, have identified and implemented effective ways to offer and sell content. Even though no airline can operate at the scale and method of amazon.com, lessons can be learned from many of Amazon's practices (e.g., product recommendation). Being able to offer more content and sell in different ways will drive significantly more revenue.

What if an airline addressed these weaknesses to generate significantly more revenue? One way to address many of these weaknesses, simultaneously and quickly, is to use new technology, called an offer management system.

Offer management

To address the weaknesses described earlier, leading airlines are beginning to think holistically of the totality of products and services offered to customers. As mentioned, the totality of these services—called an *offer*—is composed of the core airline product; any special fare rules; any additional services; non-air content, such as hotel accommodations and rental cars; and any special reward recognition. The principle of offer management is to consider all aspects of an offer together and construct, price, and distribute the offer to any customer at any available touch point.

An important part of offer management is the ability to personalize this process to the extent possible. Data on customer behavior and experiences are recorded, and once a customer is identified and authenticated, then these data are used to create the most appropriate offer for a customer. At its limit, this personalization could theoretically be performed at an individual level, but the process can work at finer and more granular levels of customer segmentation, as well. See the discussion on personalization in the next chapter. Another important aspect of offer management is that the construction and pricing of the offer can be performed in near real time. That is to say, the latest information on market conditions can be used to ensure that the offer is constructed and priced in an optimal way. As such, a significant amount of flexibility in defining the offer and pricing is required.

The principles of offer management can be deployed using an offer management system. This system orchestrates the process of defining, pricing, and distributing the offer. It is triggered by a shopping request made by a customer or when an agent collects relevant pricing information and invokes a module to construct the best combination of products and services for that customer; optimizes a holistic price based on the latest market conditions; presents the offer in the most appealing form, according to the relevant touch point; and structures the results so that, once selected, the offer can be easily converted into an order. The key steps are to (1) determine the content to be considered in response to the traveler's request, (2) confirm the available relevant offers, (3) optimize offers, and (4) sell the offer to the customer and convert it into an order. An offer management system has two main functions, a planning module, and an execution module. Both modules call for the use and control of a lot of data, the use of scientific techniques, and significant collaboration and integration within the ecosystem.

In the planning module, available products, and rules, governing how to construct these products, are stored. A wide variety of products can be deployed, so airlines using traditional fare products, à la carte ancillaries, and bundled fare families can all benefit from an offer management system. There are links to flight inventory to ensure compatibility with existing revenue management controls. In this context, seat inventory has been generalized to offer inventory. Links also exist to network planning solutions to ensure consistency between a proposed schedule and proposed offers. Schedules are built according to customer demand and revenue forecasts, and it is important for an offer management system to use this information. Finally, data and techniques for valuing offers need to be stored to ensure the pricing of these offers is truly optimized. And plans must be developed to market these offers in optimal ways, for example, by running proactive marketing campaigns, rather than just responding to shopping requests.

In the execution module, offers are dynamically constructed and priced according to user-defined rules and the principles of mathematical optimization. This process considers the context of the offer, including personalization and various aspects of the offer experience as well as the distribution channel. Once read, the offer is then communicated to appropriate distribution channels for presentation to the customer. The entire planning and execution process is governed by various control mechanisms. All data necessary to perform offer management are held within the system, and connections are made to appropriate channels. Particularly, modern offer management systems are backward-compatible to existing assets used by airlines today. So, if an airline is satisfied with its current revenue management system, for example, then a new offer management system can be integrated with this asset. It is not necessary for airlines to purchase entirely new technologies to move towards the principles of offer management.

Offer management can provide significant benefits to airlines. It addresses some of the weaknesses mentioned earlier, for example, the focus on seats versus a holistic view of all products and services purchased by the customer, the relative lack of personalization, and slow decision-making. Technology is now available to perform offer management effectively, but the challenge is to adopt this technology. Admittedly, moving to an offer management system is not easy and is best described as a journey and not just flipping an "on/off" switch. What if an airline were to manage its offer much more effectively, using, for example, the following points:

- Airlines need to continue to work for a while with the existing legacy systems, involving the use of booking classes and revenue accounting, and so forth, as well as other limitations, such as changing prices in

specific intervals in the Airline Tariff Publication Company framework. The necessary support structure, to properly perform offer management, will come in stages, so airlines can take steps to move into offer management, rather than imagine a kind of "big bang" cutover.
- The journey has begun, facilitated by using IATA's New Distribution Capability (NDC)—enabling airlines to respond to contemporary shopping requests. However, different airlines are evolving at a different pace, in this journey, to locate themselves at different points in IATA's "Dynamic Offers Maturity Model Matrix," based on their capabilities. The dynamic framework is mapped across two axes: price and product/content.
- While historical data are not relevant for forecasting future demand, airlines can use the limited current data that is available to forecast demand, but with a sophisticated feedback loop, with the feedback based on the difference between advanced bookings and actual loads. Moreover, going forward, it should also be possible to improve forecasts even more with the use of predictive analytics.
- New types of data are available, not just shopping data but also data on price elasticities of demand, not just by segment and by market but also by product attribute, such as an itinerary, to implement effective dynamic pricing.
- Airlines need to decide on their approach to dynamic pricing. It is no longer a question of if, but of when each airline will do this. Dynamic pricing means setting prices on a continuous scale and optimizing the price levels as close to, as possible, the time of presenting offers. This approach should be performed for both seats and ancillaries. This point is further discussed later in this chapter.
- Airlines should be able to sell a wider set of ancillary products and services offered by third parties through partners and by using platforms. There is a great opportunity here to be creative. Consider, for example, Hopper, where customers can lock in, for a fee, the price of an airline booking or a hotel booking. If the price goes down, the customer pays the new lower price.
- Using machine learning, it is now possible to make much more personalized offers that are contextualized. A key area of the value provided by machine learning is a better understanding of what a customer is willing to pay and a customer's changing priorities and preferences.
- Offer management systems are beginning to evolve, enabling airlines to manage their content (seat plus ancillaries), based on different segments (behavior, expectation, willingness to pay, willingness to buy), and with the use of contemporary retailing strategies—personalized recommendations, promotions, and so forth.
- New generations of customer engagement platforms—embedded with AI and machine learning technologies—are available to help airlines collect and analyze large quantities of data with the use of smart analytics and algorithms. The information coming from these platforms can be used not only to manage dynamic offers but also to optimize them.

42 *What if airlines rethought their revenue approach?*

- There is now a greater need to develop partnerships to obtain data. Strategic partners, for example, distributors, not only have a lot of data, but they also have been experimenting with new ways to use existing and new data.

The dynamic offer management journey is just beginning. New data, new technologies, and new modeling processes (for example, consumer choice, not to mention the use of simulations) are now available to make offer management not just conceptual but also implementable to benefit customers, airlines, and their partners, distributors. More relevant offers have a higher likelihood of being accepted, leading to an increase in customer experience and, in turn, customer loyalty. Whether it is in the context of implementing an offer management system, or something separate from that, there are still ways of improving revenue, by practicing more modern pricing and revenue management techniques. What if an airline could find ways to improve its revenue position, based on an understanding of new pricing/revenue management techniques?

New pricing/revenue management techniques

To understand a few new pricing/revenue management techniques, it might be helpful to understand what sorts of new techniques are now available. Figure 3.1 shows two ladders that provide examples of pricing/revenue management techniques that are available today, or soon will be available. These capabilities are depicted in increasing order of complexity and value on the ladders. Note that this discussion takes place within the existing pricing-revenue management infrastructure, not new pricing schemes that are further discussed later in this chapter. Of course, many of these capabilities are already well accepted and understood. For example, airlines that practice origin–destination revenue management can now control their inventory in that manner. See the steps in the left-hand ladder. As such, these basic capabilities do not require further discussion. However, more advanced capabilities are shown in the second ladder in Figure 3.1 and discussed individually in the following sections.

Seat buy-back

Imagine that, one week prior to departure, a flight is sold out, and thus, there is no opportunity to sell additional seats. This situation represents a lost revenue opportunity to sell full-fare tickets to late-arriving customers. Is there any way to recover this situation? Seat buy-back is the process of offering customers, on full flights, the chance to re-accommodate to other, less full flights. If needed, customers can be offered incentives to make this change, if the value of the incentive is less than the value of the full-fare tickets. Notice that the change would happen days before flight operation without any disruption at the airport. If any customer is willing to make this change, then that represents

What if airlines rethought their revenue approach? 43

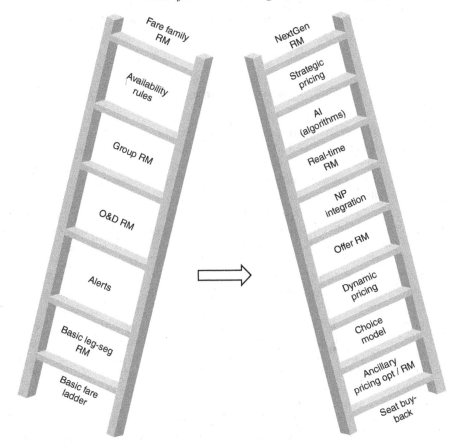

Figure 3.1 Pricing/revenue management capabilities ladders

incremental revenue to the airline. Some airlines are already doing this, but the process can be personalized. For example, some airlines are offering miles or coupons with funds that can be used for future travel. If a particular passenger has not accepted either of these offers for four times in a row on the same route, how about a more personalized offer? Suppose this passenger has requested an upgrade in a particular market and did not get it just prior to boarding on four consecutive trips, how about offering a positive space upgrade at the time of booking if the passenger is willing to take the next flight?

Of course, if revenue management is done perfectly, then this situation should not occur in the first place. Yet revenue management systems are not perfect; they rely on forecasts of uncertain demand in which there is a certain degree of error. And, with COVID-19 and its aftermath, there is more uncertainty in customer demand than before the pandemic. It is not at all unusual for airlines to under-forecast the available demand for a flight and thus fill it up prematurely. Technology now exists to identify such revenue opportunities, contact the associated customers, offer them an incentive to change flights, and automatically perform the re-accommodation when needed. This process is not invasive and often results in a net increase in customer satisfaction.

Ancillary pricing optimization/revenue management

In the context of offer management, as described earlier, individual ancillaries can be bundled into a holistic personalized offer whose price is then optimized. For those airlines not able to make a commitment to offer management yet, there is an opportunity to apply the same degree of optimization science to the ancillary prices as is done with the seat itself. Many airlines currently perform this optimization, especially those whose business model is heavily reliant on ancillary revenue. This is an opportunity for those airlines that do not perform this optimization effectively. To perform ancillary price optimization, analysts need to gather historical data on ancillary prices and demand and derive a response curve showing how changes in ancillary prices drive changes in ancillary demand. To perform this analysis effectively, there must be some degree of variation in the ancillary prices themselves. Think about offering trip insurance or baggage transportation, for example, at different prices to derive a response function. To gain a good perspective of the value of ancillary revenues, see the thought leadership piece in Chapter 8 by Peter Glade in which he points out how cinemas make huge profits not from the sale of movie tickets but from the sale of food, such as candies, sodas, and popcorn.

Once the relationship between prices and demand for all ancillaries offered by an airline has been established, then an optimization algorithm can be run to identify the price point for the ancillaries consistent with maximum revenue to the airline. This price point can then be published in all selling channels. Experience has shown that the best way to implement ancillary price optimization is to create an environment of experimentation and learning. There is, of course, not a "perfect" price for every ancillary or even if one existed, that this price point could then be used forever. Continuous monitoring and analyses are required to ensure that any optimized price point stays relevant. For capacity-constrained ancillaries, such as premium seats, the principles of revenue management can be invoked. That is, the pricing for these ancillaries could vary depending on the extent to which demand becomes close to capacity. It is easy to imagine revenue management systems for ancillaries operating in much the same way as traditional revenue management does today for seats. To emphasize, technology to perform ancillary pricing optimization now exists. Any airline that derives a reasonable fraction of its revenue from ancillaries, say, greater than 2% of total revenue, could and should benefit from implementing this technology.

Customer choice model

Is there a more important question in any industry than understanding how customers choose one product or service over another? What if an airline could gain much more insights into the process of how customers gather information about available alternatives and how they make their eventual selection? What attributes of the product or service do they value most? Do these preferences significantly change by customer segment? The model that captures how customers make their purchase selection is referred to as a customer choice model. This model attempts to predict the probability that a customer will choose one alternative over another, based on the customer's underlying preferences. See the discussion in Jim Barlow's thought leadership piece in Chapter 8. In the airline industry, these preferences relate to aspects of the core product described in Chapter 2, the price itself, and airline preference. Understanding the degree to which different customers value these attributes allows for better scheduling and pricing decisions.

Table 2.1 in Chapter 2 illustrated these preferences in the context of customer preferences for different aspects of the core product (e.g., nonstop service, total journey time, and so forth). In Table 3.1 below, containing the same information as in Table 2.1, there is now an additional price variable (at the bottom, on the left-hand box) that shows customer sensitivity to prices.

Why are customer choice models useful in pricing and revenue management? To start with, they can be used to estimate price elasticities which are crucial inputs when making pricing/revenue management decisions. There are estimates of price elasticities for those visiting friends and relatives (VFR)/leisure travel in the −2.0 to −3.0 range, while price elasticities for business travel are often in the −0.3 to −0.7 range. Generally speaking, demand for an economy-class seat is more elastic than for a business-class seat and demand for, say, travel more than 90 days away is more elastic than travel only two days before departure. Price elasticities can also vary widely between markets and even between seasons, for example, holiday travel.

What is the best way to determine price elasticity through the calibration of a customer choice model? To derive price elasticities effectively, information is needed on how people choose flights, but that information lets an

Table 3.1 Preferences from a customer choice model with a price variable

Effect	QSI Points	Effect	QSI Points
Nonstop	1.00	Widebody	1.22
One-Stop Direct	0.17	Narrowbody	1.00
Single connect	0.09	Regional Jet	0.84
Double connect	0.01	Turbo	0.74
Interline penalty	17%		
Codeshare penalty	54%	Legacy airline	1.00
		LCC airline	0.90
Elapsed time (versus fastest connect)	EXP(−0.65*hr)	ULCC airline	0.80
Price	EXP(−1.83*$100s)		

Source: Amadeus data, U.S. domestic one-way flights. March 2021.

Note: $N = 430,000$. All effects are significant. QSI = Quality-of-Service Index.

analyst focus on the demand side of the equation. The best source of this information is shopping data. What if an airline could look at detailed transactions of what customers were looking for, what was available to them, and what they chose? Through an analysis of shopping data that are now available, these elasticities can be estimated and made available to analysts. These elasticities can be estimated by market and number of days prior to departure. For one market, the value could range from −0.5 on the day of departure to −2.0 for 30 or more days prior to departure. For a different market, the same numbers could vary from −0.2 to −1.6.

This information can be analyzed to detect patterns and give guidance toward pricing/revenue management decisions. If, in a market, prices are consistently inelastic for all days before departure, then that indicates an opportunity to raise prices (by definition, revenue from inelastic demand can be increased by raising prices until the underlying price elasticity equals −1.0). Pockets of inelasticity and elasticity indicate an opportunity to consider changing revenue management controls. Understanding future prevailing market conditions, such as available flights and fares offered by competitors, in the context of underlying price elasticities, gives substantial insights as to future actions.

Beyond the ability to generate and use price elasticities, customer choice models can be used in revenue management systems to forecast passenger demand more accurately and thus provide better revenue management controls. Think about the value of the use of customer choice model in determining the price of premium economy-class seats on intercontinental flights. Finnair, for example, recently announced an upgraded version of seats in its premium cabins.[1] Would this cabin attract some passengers from the economy-class cabins or dilute revenue from the decision of some passengers to move down from higher-fare business-class cabins, or a combination of both? This effect can be evaluated from the process of integrating network planning and revenue management.

Dynamic pricing

What if an airline could improve its revenue, a topic that has been discussed a lot recently, by pricing its products dynamically using more relevant data and new techniques? By dynamic pricing, two things are typically meant: (1) that airline prices are to be determined on a continuous scale rather than limited to predefined price points, such as from a set of filed fares, and (2) that these prices can be determined dynamically in near real time according to market conditions and customer segmentation. It is worth noting that the practice of "value pricing" deployed decades ago, is different from dynamic pricing, currently under discussion. In "value pricing," the intention was to compete on a few price points and differentiate one airline from another based on other attributes. In dynamic pricing, the intention is to use the full spectrum of available price points. One approach is based on intentionally using a few price points while the other uses practically an infinite number of price points.

A dynamic pricing solution has three main components. The first component is to collect data on market dynamics, such as competitive schedules and fares. These data should be updated as frequently as possible to ensure they are current. The second component determines, for any market-day-itinerary combination, the preferred price on the continuous scale at which an airline intends to sell, depending on customer segmentation. This determination could be made based on an underlying mathematical model, such as a customer choice model described above, calibrated, and optimized using AI, leveraging machine learning models (i.e., the ability to see patterns in the data), or on the basis of business rules (or a combination). The third component then applies this information into the current selling ecosystem so that all shopping inquiries reflect the latest price.

Quite clearly, the application of dynamic pricing will provide numerous benefits for airlines. First, why should airlines be restricted in any way to predefined price points? In virtually any other industry, especially modern industries that sell online in large volumes, providers can set their prices whenever and however they wish. The fact that airlines need to file fares in advance to set predefined price points is a remnant of an old way of doing business that will soon disappear. And who can argue against the ability to use the latest information on bookings versus capacity and competitor fares in deciding pricing decisions? These benefits are so large that dynamic pricing will eventually become standard within the airline industry. It is a question of when and not if. Any airline that does not practice dynamic pricing will be at a competitive disadvantage. One MIT/PODS study concluded that early adopters could expect revenue benefits of 6% and all airlines can expect revenue benefits of 3% once all airlines adopt this technology.[2] And this capability will apply to all kinds of fares: bundled, unbundled, and so forth.

As with applying any new technology, there are some concerns about introducing the capability to perform dynamic pricing. Specifically, there seem to be two kinds of concerns. One is that this capability would set off a downward spiral of price reductions. So, the theory goes, one airline would use this capability to increase market share by lowering its prices, and then a competitor would respond by lowering its prices, in turn. Eventually airlines would reach a point of low and unsustainable prices. However, this concern can be addressed by airlines having the discipline to impose guardrails on the kinds of reductions they would be willing to make by relying, for instance, on the bid price computed by revenue management systems that account for long-term flight profitability. To those who claim that airlines don't have discipline, it could be pointed out that airlines today generally find points of sustainable equilibrium in today's pricing world. The new world of dynamic pricing would be qualitatively similar, even if the volume of pricing changes would be much higher.

Another concern has to do with the mechanics of accounting for dynamic pricing in today's world of coupons and fares. However, the basic framework is in place to properly account for dynamic price changes. For example, a fare can be filed as a kind of base fare with the understanding that its level could be changed dynamically. Any change would be recorded in the coupon/order and thus properly accounted for. There is a legitimate concern, however, that relates to the availability of proper data and technology to implement dynamic pricing correctly. Some dynamic pricing solutions are explicitly based on an understanding of the responsiveness of customer demand to price changes, that is, the underlying price elasticity. Other solutions, based on business rules, may not explicitly use an estimate of price elasticities. Knowing the right price elasticity to use in each situation is critical to determining an optimal price.

It might be helpful to keep the following principles in mind:

- *Adopt a phased approach.* A full dynamic pricing solution should not be implemented immediately. Instead, steps can be taken toward that goal. One example of a first phase is to implement the mechanics of calculating a dynamically produced price but not actually use it in production. Rather, just report on what was calculated and compare it to what was shown (sometimes called the "silent mode"). An analyst first needs to feel comfortable with what the solution would have done. Then a test can be adopted to refine the approach, perhaps by rolling out dynamic pricing by route/market or by departure day.
- *Ensure consistency.* Prices can be changed dynamically only when there is a reason to do so. Unnecessary churn should be avoided. Dynamic pricing should be adopted in all channels, including conventional, airport, and NDC channels, not just the airline.com channel, to produce consistency across channels.
- *Create guardrails.* As mentioned previously, good estimates of price elasticities are critical, again whether or not the solution explicitly uses them. But in cases of occasional "bad data," it will be important to not let any bad data cause bad decisions. One obvious and important guardrail is to ensure any proposed price is not less than the associated "bid price," or the value of a seat on a specific flight, as determined by revenue management.
- *Develop appropriate skill sets for personnel.* To properly apply dynamic pricing principles, members of the pricing department will need to become more comfortable with the underlying economics of price elasticities. Satisfying this need will require more training. In addition, manual oversight of the dynamic pricing solution will also be required.
- *Degree of personalization.* Current technology performs dynamic pricing by customer segmentation with the definition of customer segmentation becoming more and more granular, leading to hyper-personalization. At the limit, it is technically possible to perform dynamic pricing at a personal level, once the customer has been properly identified and authenticated. However, conducting dynamic pricing, at an individual level, could be discriminatory and unfair with the potential for fraud.
- *Pick the right technology and data partner.* The state-of-the-art process in dynamic pricing is to work with an organization that can provide a leading technology solution. Ideally the technology solution can scale well,

including being able to operate in the cloud. In addition, every airline will need access to shopping data that are only available from limited sources. The science behind any solution provider is critical, given that the dynamic pricing solution is only as good as the science behind it. Increasingly, providers of these solutions will compete on the quality of their science. Choosing the right partner based on the quality of the solution, and level of support, is critical in being successful at implementing dynamic pricing.

Offer revenue management

The principles of offer management were discussed earlier in this chapter. In this context, offer revenue management is important in two ways. One is to ensure any offer construction and pricing respects an airline's process of revenue management. Tight linkages must be available between an offer management system and an airline's revenue management system to ensure revenue management controls are respected. In addition, to the extent that other features of the offer are capacity controlled, then standard revenue management practices of accommodating demand relative to capacity to these other features can be applied. In this sense, there may be a limited number of available offers, so the value of limited capacity should be applied when deriving the optimal price of the associated offer.

Network planning/revenue management integration

As discussed earlier, most airlines perform the functions of schedule planning and revenue management in a sequential way, by first developing the flight schedule, then filing fares, and then deciding fare availability. The sequential nature of most airlines' business processes misses opportunities to perform these functions better by doing them together.

One simple example can illustrate this point. In this example, one airline was looking to act on an underperforming route. The scheduling department looked at this situation and then decided to downgrade the equipment, thus lowering capacity and improving load factors. The pricing department responded by lowering fares. And the revenue management department decided to open availability for the lowest booking classes. The result was that the route was filled with low-yield traffic and thus continued to underperform.

It is easy to suggest that these functions work together, but it can be hard in practice to ensure that happens. Following are some practical suggestions for ensuring that the network planning and revenue management departments work well together, typically by sharing their underlying technologies, data, and assumptions. Taken together, these suggestions should not be interpreted as implying that no airline performs these functions well together. Of course, some do. But experience has shown that, taken together, many airlines do not perform these functions well, especially in real time, and could benefit from considering the following list:

- *Build cross-functional teams.* Every major decision taken by an airline—new routes, new hub orientations, changes to the fare structure, new fleet, new partnerships, and so forth—should be evaluated by cross-functional teams much more effectively.
- *Use network planning data in revenue management solutions.* Network planning solutions are adept at forecasting passenger demand as a function of a proposed flight schedule. If there have been any schedule changes, either by the host airline or competitors, then associated changes in demand can be easily predicted. This information should be transmitted to revenue management solutions so they can account for changes in demand as part of optimally determining inventory controls. To be sure, the forecasting algorithms in the revenue management solution will eventually catch up to the reality of any schedule changes, but why wait when that information can be used now? The technology is now available from leading providers of revenue management systems to account for this effect.
- *Use revenue management assumptions when planning the schedule.* One key assumption when planning the schedule is understanding the relationship between adding extra capacity and the effect it has on revenue. As capacity is added, then revenue should increase at a declining rate ultimately, converging to the maximum. Revenue management can squeeze out more revenue per capacity unit than most scheduling solutions give it credit for, since most scheduling solutions do not account for the total number of available price points in the market. Understanding the true relationship between revenue and capacity will allow more accurate forecasting and thus more profitable schedules to be built. Another revenue management assumption worth noting is that, when planning the schedule, data on ancillary revenue should also be used as well as seat revenue to give a full picture of revenue contribution from passengers. Yet, another key revenue management assumption is that display and screen presence matter—the way flights are shown to customers can affect an airline's market share. Studies have shown that flights displayed on the first line or the first screen receive a disproportionate share. This effect should be considered when planning the schedule.
- *Use revenue management data for short-term scheduling decisions.* In the discussion on dynamic scheduling in Chapter 2, it was mentioned that there were many profitable opportunities for changing the schedule after it was published. For all the focus on optimizing the schedule before it is published, there is relatively little focus on optimizing the schedule afterward. Opportunities to improve the schedule closer to the day of operation would rely on commercial data coming from a revenue management system, so an automated and optimization process using these data will add a lot of value. Technology to perform this optimization already exists.
- *Use a revenue management system to provide signals about changes in passenger mix.* Schedules are typically built according to assumptions about

traffic mix based on historical averages. However, these assumptions may change, and revenue management systems are in an ideal position to alert network planning systems to changes in the passenger mix so that these changes could be considered when planning the schedule. For example, there is strong evidence that leisure travel has rebounded to a much greater extent than business travel in the US. Furthermore, there is more business travel coming from small and medium-sized businesses, and these passengers may behave differently than passengers from large corporations. This effect should be monitored by revenue management systems and communicated to scheduling systems.

- *Building connections.* As part of evaluating a proposed schedule, scheduling systems simulate the generation of possible connections according to a series of rules, using data, such as minimum connect times, circuity limits, and so forth. Similar rules are used in GDSs, NDC, and direct channels. One possible source of inconsistency in planning a proposed schedule and selling it is that these rules may be different. There is significant value in planning and selling connections according to the same exact set of rules.
- *Accounting for disruption in schedule planning.* Chapter 2 presented the principle of building schedules accounting for both profitability and reliability. As part of this process, when accounting for the cost of disruptions when planning the schedule, information on change fees and other disruption costs, available from revenue management, should be considered.
- *Common forecasting logic.* Both the scheduling and revenue management business problems are characterized by forecasting passenger demand. In the scheduling sense, this demand occurs over an extended future period covered by the effective and discontinue dates of a proposed schedule. In the revenue management sense, this demand occurs for a specific flight in a specific market on a specific future travel date. Nevertheless, there are many similarities in performing both types of forecasts, including using an underlying customer choice model that reflects customer behavior to scheduling and pricing effects. Using common logic reflecting this choice model in both the scheduling and revenue management areas will improve forecast accuracy and will enforce a certain sense of consistency. Less revenue leakage will occur if the schedule is being built according to the same way in which revenue is managed. In the future, it is easy to imagine forecasting being done on a continuum by days before departure, where forecasts from both scheduling models and revenue management models are shared and weighted.

Real-time revenue management

Historically, the business process of revenue management at airlines follows a standard human-machine interface. Revenue management controls are derived from a revenue management system each night and then presented for user review the next morning. Revenue management analysts then review these controls and ultimately decide to accept, change, or reject them. In exceptional cases, some controls could be re-optimized during the day, if needed. In obvious cases, the controls may be automatically uploaded into an airline's inventory control system, but the state-of-the-art process is for most markets to go through a manual review.

Of course, this process takes time, especially in the manual review of the proposed controls. Instead, some airlines have promoted the sense of real-time revenue management to continuously adapt revenue management controls as new signals of changes are received regarding customer demand, capacity, and an airline's competitive position. In this sense, revenue management controls are always fresh and there is little lag between receiving market information and determining appropriate inventory controls. To ensure this process is performed quickly and continuously, the process of user review needs to be automated, requiring revenue management analysts to express the nature of their manual reviews via a series of rules that can be automated. Although the technology to perform real-time revenue management is now available, the question is whether these automated, user-oriented rules can be implemented.

AI (algorithms)

The application of artificial intelligence to business problems represents a huge opportunity. These algorithms, including machine learning, can detect important patterns and trends in the data that are not discernible by traditional methods. Applying newly discovered patterns and trends into revenue models can provide airlines with a large strategic advantage.

In the context of pricing and revenue management, the principles of artificial intelligence can be used to generate more accurate forecasts. In addition, these principles can also be used to derive better controls than those derived from solving the traditional revenue management problems. Possible benefits from the application of artificial intelligence in this way are so large that airlines cannot ignore them. Given the availability of this technology, there is an opportunity for those airlines with the resources and interest to pursue the use of these techniques. However, caution needs to be exercised. There is great potential in applying artificial intelligence and its associated algorithms via a large "black box." It is often not immediately obvious how these algorithms work. One advantage of traditional revenue management models is that it is usually clear why a possibly anomalous result was derived the way it was. Perhaps a low demand forecast was used. Or an inadvertently high fare was assumed. Or one type of demand was competing for space with another demand that was more valuable. Applying artificial intelligence so that most users easily understand its results is still very much a work in progress. The key, according to Jason Kelly, in his thought leadership piece in Chapter 8, is to enhance the effectiveness of revenue management analysts through "human–machine symbiosis."

Strategic pricing

Opportunities for dynamic pricing were discussed earlier. One analog to dynamic pricing, or determining prices in near real time, is an opportunity to strategically set up and optimize a fare structure in the first place. What if an airline could do this? Most airlines have mastered the process of building a logical and rational fare ladder. However, there are opportunities now to further optimize this ladder by considering the following kinds of effects:

- Additional fares in the ladder, including sell-up fares
- How fares compare to fares from other airlines according to a customer choice model
- How competitors react to strategic fare changes
- How fares are revenue-managed

Note that with dynamic pricing, prices are determined for a specific flight on a specific future travel date for a specific point in time. There is little time in this process for game theory effects. However, with strategic pricing, the opportunity is to determine a stable equilibrium of fares over an extended period so that the market can be led to this point. In this sense, game theory effects do matter. It is easy to imagine building an optimization model considering an initial proposed fare structure, an airline's schedule, competitive schedules, competitive fares, assumptions about customer choice behavior, game theory effects from competitors responding to fare changes, and revenue management effects. The purpose of this model would be to identify and propose appropriate changes to any designated market fare structure. Based on practices within the industry, it is not clear that such a model exists yet. However, currently airlines seem to evaluate and decide fare structures according to their own processes. It is quite likely that adding more information to this process, along with using optimization technology, could provide better results than just following a purely manual process alone. From this point of view, there is an opportunity in examining the potential for reinventing the process to determine an airline's strategic fare structure.

What if an airline were to integrate much more effectively four basic considerations in developing and implementing pricing strategies? As shown in Figure 3.2, from the point of view of an airline, the two major considerations are an airline's costs and its competitors. From the point of view of a customer, the two major considerations are the perceived value of the product/service, and the customer's willingness to pay for the product/service. Then there are two common considerations, loyalty, and the brand. As with the scheduling process described earlier, decisions have tended to be made at suboptimal levels relating to all these considerations. There is a need to make decisions at an optimal level, with input combined from all four considerations. The optimization would then take into consideration both the revenue aspect and the profit aspect. This optimization also calls for the use of behavioral economics. As business researcher Gerald Smith points out, pricing

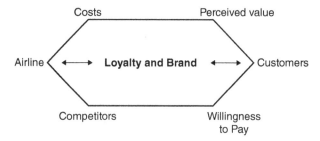

Figure 3.2 Pricing strategy considerations

decisions must take into consideration not only economics and business aspects but also "psychology—the behavioral side of human decision-making." Within this framework, Gerald Smith discusses how pricing decisions are made and how they should be made. Pricing analysts tend to have good analytical skills to make pricing decisions. What is needed, according to the author, is "soft behavioral price-setting skills."[3]

Next-generation revenue management

Finally, it is appearing that the science of airline pricing and revenue management has not been completely mastered yet. Over the last several decades, more and more techniques have come into play. Airlines today generally are practicing pricing and revenue management at higher levels than before, but more improvements can still be made. Some "next generation" ideas proposed for better pricing/revenue management include the following:

- Accounting for the interaction effects between flights, for example, spill and recapture between different flights, when determining prices and revenue management controls. Currently, controls for each flight are solved individually, even though there is a greater benefit in considering all flights together, even recognizing that this is a very large challenge.
- In addition to the goal of maximizing revenue on its own flights, an airline can also have the goal of supporting partners' flights. Communicating bid prices between partners is a simple way to encourage alliance-friendly behavior, although it is easier to imagine the pricing and revenue management functions for an alliance being performed at an alliance level.
- Simulating the revenue management function of competitors, to identify revenue opportunities from spilled customers on competitive flights.
- Optimizing network planning, pricing, and revenue management decisions together in a large mathematical model rather than treating the decisions independently and sequentially.

To be sure, technologies for these effects are still under development. The purpose to discuss them now, however, is to encourage airlines to become interested in pursuing new research directions for what is possible. In addition to applying new pricing/revenue management techniques, as appropriate, there are also revenue benefits from selling more and different content or even changing the way in which sales are made in the future. Think about the concept under discussion that enables travelers to buy, trade, or resell their tickets from the creation of a secondary market. In this sense, the principle of "selling differently" will provide new opportunities for airlines.

Selling differently

"Selling differently" simply means selling more content in new and different ways. There are many examples of these kinds of possibilities, including the examples that follow.

Selling more products on airline.com as a natural retail channel

The direct distribution channel, that is, airline.com, is a natural touch point for selling different travel-related services, and content available for sale in this channel can be expanded. This channel should be able to generate new streams of revenue from third parties that can create more value for travelers. One example is destination-related content. By working more closely with online travel agents and providers of content at destinations (beyond the conventional tours and activities), based on customers' profiles, airlines should be able to expand the content from which they can generate revenue. Other types of content include becoming more creative with products and services relating to the trip itself. For example, some customers may be interested in purchasing an on-time guarantee relating to their travel. For an extra fee, they could receive a refund in the event the flight was, for instance, 30 minutes late. Technology exists to offer and fulfill this kind of product.

In addition to the airline.com site itself, airlines could capitalize on the use of mobile applications to connect customers with personalized activities. These applications would not only provide a communication channel with customers during trips but also show the location of customers within the itineraries (e.g., arrival and departure dates) as well as specific touch points.

New pricing schemes

Customers may be interested in pursuing new and different kinds of pricing schemes. Innovative airlines can test such schemes and learn from experiences as they implement these schemes to find an additional source of competitive advantage. Examples of these schemes include

- time-based subscriptions (a fixed price for up to a certain number of trips),
- membership models (along the lines of Amazon Prime) with exclusive privileges, and

- meeting the travel needs of distributed teams to meet even at higher prices, keeping in mind that some businesses would have saved money through the elimination of office space

Subscription pricing, again, not a new concept, is beginning to generate interest. Examples of airlines testing the market include Alaska Airlines (based in the US), Volaris (a low-cost airline, based in Mexico), and FlySafair (a low-cost airline, based in South Africa). There are several reasons for the renewed interest in subscription travel. First, there is the growing trend that people can work from almost anywhere. Second, in the past the concept was of some interest to a segment of business travelers who could save money and have greater convenience. Now, some leisure travelers have become interested, depending on the conditions and restrictions of subscription models. Third, given that airlines have begun to implement dynamic pricing that can produce large swings in fares, subscription models can provide a piece of mind. Fourth, given the very limited success of brand differentiation in the past, subscription pricing may enable an airline to increase its market share in certain markets.

Better shopping displays

Whether an airline sells directly or through a third party, the content options offered need to be easy to display, painless to search, and easy to compare, for example, through a well-defined rating system based on relevant attributes. The result of this display should encourage customers to book their preferred options by accurately highlighting preferred options. There is a need for consistency in the display of offerings by multiple airlines. What do "economy plus" or "premium" mean for different airlines? How much does the seat recline, and what is the seat pitch? Shopping displays in indirect channels need to permit easy comparisons. With the rich content available through the NDC, this comparison should be much better in the future. Keep in mind that the meaningful adoption of the NDC, ONE Order, and digital transformation in general, still faces many challenges. The key is the implementation of effective ways to interact with consumers. Remember, NDC is not a plug-and-play system or application. There is a need to think through how the NDC platform can be used to modernize the retailing process in a meaningful way—win–win for customers, suppliers, and intermediaries in terms of simplicity, costs, and experience.

Improvements in shopping displays can come from greater personalization. Once customers have been identified and authenticated, and relevant customer history applied, then more relevant flight choices can be offered. Moreover, additional improvements can be made in future shopping technologies using voice recognition as well as interactive shopping displays, allowing customers to further refine and reorient their searches.

In-flight shopping

There are significant opportunities to expand in-flight shopping by monetizing upon high-speed, high-capacity, and robust in-flight connectivity and in-flight entertainment systems. Traditionally, in-flight purchases have been in two areas—perfumes and alcohol. Moreover, space in the cabin has been limited to offer a much broader spectrum of products. Weights of the products and carts are a cost burden, not to mention shopping from paper catalogs is unappealing. Now, the vast improvements in in-flight connectivity are changing the game by offering the convenience of digital retail, greater personalization, and a much higher level of customer experience. While an effective strategy to increase in-flight sales will depend on the use of large amounts of data, this avenue will also provide new data for airlines to use in other areas for developing and offering personalized products and services and possibly, even helping to change customer behavior.[4]

NDC and distribution

Airlines have been trying to increase the control of their customers, redefine their working relationship with GDSs, and, in some cases, reduce the influence of third parties. The object, presumably, is not to try to eliminate third parties, as they do add value. It is worth noting that airlines clearly saw the value of GDSs when they created computer reservation systems that later became GDSs. Then IATA introduced the NDC, a way for airlines to go direct and be in control of the offers they market. However, while the NDC enables airlines to go direct for some segments, it can also enable third parties to add value by aggregating content. The purpose of the NDC was not to eliminate third parties but simply to allow airlines to have more control of their offers to meet the specific needs of a customer—a specific seat, access to Wi-Fi, access to a lounge in an itinerary with a long layover, fast-track through security, and so forth. Such offers cannot be made easily using third parties. This direct linkage between customers and airlines is a win–win situation for both parties for some customer segments. However, there is a large segment of customers, of the order of about 50%, that does not go through direct channels. Some customers, for example, the leisure segment, may prefer to use travel agents, taking advantage of tour packages. Moreover, a specific segment of corporate travelers may not be able to use the direct channel due to corporate travel policies. In such cases, the NDC can also enable third parties to add value, based on their areas of expertise, thereby benefiting both airlines and customers. Delta is an example of an airline that has shown its willingness to partner with third parties so that each party can focus on its core competencies.

Marketing is not just about giving the right customer the right product at the right price and at the right time. According to some analysts, customers' selection of flights used to be usually based on two criteria: itinerary and price. Now they seem to be itinerary and brand that relates to reputation. And that is about customer experience and branding, the subject of the next chapter, both can be vital components of competitive advantage.

Highlights

- Airlines have focused on the sale of their core product, a seat from point A to point B. Yet, airlines today sell many ancillary products and services to generate significant amounts of additional revenue—a business practice that can now be optimized using advanced techniques used in revenue management.
- The benefits of dynamic pricing are so large that the practice will eventually become standard within the airline industry. It is a question of when, not if.
- One way to enhance revenue is to sell the product differently. An example would be to sell more products on an airline's website as a natural retail channel.
- There are significant opportunities to expand in-flight shopping by leveraging high-speed, high-capacity, and robust in-flight connectivity and in-flight entertainment systems.
- The purpose of the NDC was not to eliminate third parties but simply to allow airlines to have more control of their offers to meet the specific needs of a customer.

Customers now want simplicity in their shopping processes. Airlines need to think holistically of the totality of products and services offered to customers, in a personalized way and with the use of offer management systems that orchestrate the process of defining, pricing, and distributing the offer. Through an analysis of shopping data, which is now available, patterns can be detected, patterns that can provide guidance towards pricing/revenue management decisions. A full dynamic pricing solution shows a huge potential, but it should only be implemented in steps.

Notes

1 Linda Blachly, Alan Dron, and Kurt Hofmann, "A Premium Experience," *Air Transport World*, April 2022, pp. 10–17.
2 Emmanuel Carrier and Larry Weatherford, "Implementation of MNL Choice Models in the Passenger Origin-Destination Simulator (PODS)," *Journal of Revenue and Pricing Management*, Number 14, pp. 400–407 (2015).
3 Gerald Smith, *Getting Price Right: The Behavioral Economics of Profitable Pricing* (New York: Columbia University Press, 2021), pp. 9–10.
4 "The Future of Inflight Retail," Inmarsat. https://www.inmarsat.com/en/insights/aviation/2017/the-future-of-inflight-retail.html.

4 What if airlines reimagined and redefined customer experience?

Why is customer service mediocre or, at least, a hit-or-miss experience? Is it because

- travel is complex, from shopping to collecting baggage, or
- airline partnerships (e.g., codeshares) and change of equipment and or change of schedule after booking can be confusing for the end customer or
- there is insufficient understanding of customer behavior, despite the availability of volumes of data and analytics, or
- every customer interaction does not get considered to provide a personalized service or
- expectations set tend to be too high or
- the value proposition is not clear as to whether an airline is portraying itself to be a Ritz-Carlton or a McDonald's or
- customer experience tends to be viewed from the perspective of airlines more than from the perspective of customers or
- confusion tends to exist between customer service and customer experience or
- confusion exists as to who the customer, the traveler, the distributor, or the frontline employee is or
- there is a lack of consistency among channels, for example, a customer's interaction that is physical (with a gate agent or a flight attendant) or digital (on a website of an airline or in a post on social media), or
- airlines do not consider end-to-end customer journey experience (total travel experience) from inspiration for travel to post-travel or
- there is not sufficient understanding of human psychology?

Customer service versus customer experience

Sometimes, there is confusion between the concepts of customer service and customer experience, and they are often used interchangeably. Customer service is part of customer experience but just the experience at one touch point in the purchase or use of a product or service or the help required to solve a particular problem. Customer experience, on the other hand, includes experience

DOI: 10.4324/9781003332824-4

during all interactions during the entire journey, from the general awareness of an airline's brand to the purchase of a ticket, to the services provided at the airport and in flight. Travel experience refers to a holistic approach. In addition, customer service is reactive in that a customer initiates an interaction, for example, a call for some service or to resolve an issue to which an airline responds, for example, a customer's call to a service center. Customer experience, on the other hand, is proactive in the sense that an airline needs to anticipate a customer's needs and then respond to such needs without being provoked. It involves all interactions. In some ways, customer service relates to responding to a question raised by a customer and providing assistance, and it tends to be quantifiable. Customer experience, on the other hand, relates to building a relationship and tends to be less quantifiable.

A common measurement of loyalty used by airlines is the Net Promoter Score (NPS) to see how they are evaluated by their customers. The developer of the NPS, Fred Reichheld, has come up with a new version (NPS 3.0) to help businesses improve the effectiveness of their loyalty programs. The author has created a new measure called *Earned Growth Rate*, which measures the revenue growth generated by existing customers and their friends. He gives an example of a bank that managed to achieve high-quality growth without risk. This growth was generated by the bank's existing customers who were known quite well to the bank. However, the author points out that to achieve earned growth, a business would need to upgrade its accounting process, to develop a customer-based accounting capability that is already being used by such businesses as Amazon.[1]

Even though some airlines claim that they do, but they really need to put the customer at the center of their thinking process. What if an airline used a digital platform approach that has made the digital platform operators, such as Netflix, Uber, and Airbnb, so successful? What if an airline were to revisit the entire traveler journey from a customer's perspective (considering all the steps from leaving home, parking, checking-in, dropping off baggage, going through security, waiting for gate display, going to gate, boarding, landing, collecting luggage, going through customs and immigration, and taking ground transportation to the final destination)? Think also about the time between all these steps—waiting, walking, lining up, and waiting again. All these steps could transform a less than two-hour flight into an exhausting 5-hour, door-to-door experience. Airlines can leverage advancing technology to remove friction, improve experience, and reduce waiting/wasted time throughout this process.

Think about when a passenger calls the customer service center to ask a question about the booked itinerary. The automated telephone menu tree offers numerous options about the nature of the call, and none of the options meets the needs of the passenger. Eventually the automated service answers saying that all agents are tied up with other customers and that the customer can wait or be called back between 57 and 72 minutes. What kind of impression does that leave about the brand of an airline? Consequently, both customer service and customer experience need to work together to serve customers.

What if airlines reimagined and redefined customer experience? 61

Airlines have clearly tried to improve the level of service provided. Take, for example, JetBlue, which visualized its vision of "bring humanity back to air travel." Alaska Airlines developed its "20 Minute Baggage Guarantee." Delta developed its "PARALLEL REALITY" applications for passengers to receive personalized information in preferred languages. American adopted Google Assistant's Interpreter to develop a frictionless travel experience for non-English speakers. AirAsia developed its "Superapp," a travel and lifestyle mobile app that makes booking flights, hotels, and a variety of activities, including shopping for deals, easier, and "BigPay" to make payment much easier. Singapore Airlines is experimenting with using blockchain technology to enable its passengers to maximize their loyalty points in new ways. Vietnam Airlines is using an advanced technology experience management platform to "capture and respond" to customer feedback in real time, while also increasing the volume of customer engagement captured.

How about Sun Country Airlines, a small US airline that has begun to offer door-to-door service, through a partnership with Landline, to pick up a passenger at their home for transportation to the airport. The pickup is timed for the passenger's flight. During the drive to the airport, the passenger can "settle in and enjoy the free Wi-Fi, onboard entertainment, refreshments and hassle-free experience." With this service, "travelers don't have to worry about getting to the airport on time, navigating parking ramps or waiting in lines at the check-in counter or security." Initially, the door-to-door service is limited to customers living within 30 miles of the Minneapolis–St. Paul International Airport.[2] American Airlines has started to offer ground services between small airports near its major hub at Philadelphia Airport to Philadelphia Airport (PHL). Consider, for example, Lehigh Valley International Airport (ABE), previously known as Allentown–Bethlehem–Easton International Airport. Passengers can check in at ABE twice a day and take a Landline bus (that can accommodate up to 35 persons) to PHL. Passengers can clear security at ABE, check their luggage, board a bus, and then disembark in an area post-security clearance at PHL.[3]

Airlines have clearly tried to improve customer experience. During the pandemic, for example, airlines eliminated some charges and fees relating to changes in reservations and some airlines even kept the middle seats open for a while. As a result, according to a J.D. Power's "North America Airline Satisfaction Study," the passenger satisfaction index increased.[4] The question is, How to take customer experience to the next level? Is it by "becoming a detective to solve the mystery of customer behavior?"[5] From this perspective, it would take a different approach to engage with customers to learn why customers do what they do, even though it may not make sense. Would it require redesigning internal functions to make the customer experience seamless? Would it require airlines to go beyond incremental improvement initiatives implemented by them, for example, by

- handling more complex situations relating to itineraries, disruptions, and the services required at destinations;

- engaging with customers much more effectively by focusing on every interaction through any channel (text/SMS, emails, chats, voice over internet protocol) virtually and with humans to resolve issues;
- scaling customer-care initiatives to solve problems of all customers, not just those in the top-tier status;
- suggesting ideas and making offers proactively via any digital device (e.g., a mobile phone) that knows its user;
- capitalizing on the trend to "transform customer experience for an on-screen world";[6] or
- changing the purpose of the airline to "enrich the lives of its customers"?[7]

Clearly, airlines need to figure out how to improve the lives of their customers. While this is not a new concept, how to do it effectively remains a mystery. Traditional ways of doing market research and the use of big data and data science can help. But people's lives are changing at a faster rate not just by the expanding use of social media but also the influence of the digital revolution and hyper-connectivity. In addition to using big data, there could also be much value in using small data to "see" signals of change and to "see" emerging patterns to "see" the emerging needs of customers.[8] The key to understanding customer behavior, customer expectations, and customer needs is to identify the "important, unsatisfied 'jobs' they are looking to get done."[9] Could an airline gain some insights from the best practices of leading businesses to make customers and employees supporters?

Two insightful examples

Amazon

Think about the customer experience provided by Amazon. What if an airline provided an effortless shopping and travel experience along the lines of the customer experience provided by, for example, Amazon:

- Amazon's 1-Click Button
- Amazon's convenient process to return items with painless effort relating both to physical aspects as well as mental aspects
- Amazon's Dash Buttons, connected wirelessly to products, to order products simply by pushing the buttons
- Amazon's Firefly visual recognition software designed to identify and, presumably, buy, items that a consumer sees in the real world
- Amazon's Alexa, with the capability to order through spoken words
- Amazon's Go Store—walk in, pick up the items, and walk out, with charges made automatically for the items picked up for purchase
- Amazon Prime, a paid subscription program that provides valuable services, such as fast delivery and streaming of music, videos, and e-books, at no additional costs[10]

Think about how Amazon has made it easy for a shopper to find a product, purchase it, and, if necessary, return it. Purchasing it involves not just selecting the product and paying for it. It also involves understanding the terms and agreements. The interactions need to be effortless. Again, think about Amazon's 1-Click feature, the Dash Buttons, the Firefly visual recognition software, and the artificial intelligence (AI)–powered Alexa virtual assistant.[11]

Amazon is known for providing exceptional customer experience. One could ask about Amazon's secret. According to two business writers who worked for many years for Amazon, the secret lies in "Working Backwards: Starting with the Desired Customer Experience," the title of Chapter 5 of their book, with the same title.[12] The authors provide a tool, called "writing the press release and FAQs before you build the product." The authors also provide a detailed example of a press release and a comprehensive list of FAQs for an imaginary company and an imaginary product. This is an incredibly valuable tool that could be used by airlines before new products are introduced.

DBS Bank

Think about how DBS Bank, based in Singapore, transformed itself to take customer experience to a new level. It transformed itself from being a standard bank into a technology company to target the digital segment of the customer base that had a much lower cost-to-income ratio than the traditional segment.[13] DBS, with a motto, "Live more, Bank less," is a multinational financial services group. It is an example of an organization that has gone through a major digital transformation to provide its customers a simple and seamless experience. Jason Bloomberg, a Forbes contributor, provides some insights based on his communications with Paul Cobban, chief operating officer, technology and operations, for DBS Bank, about how the bank went from being the worst in 2009 to being the best:[14]

- First was the decision on the type of services to be provided, to be "*respectful, easy to deal with*, and *dependable*"—an "acronym 'RED,' an adjective that became part of the corporate vocabulary."
- Second was the establishment of cross-functional workshops to find different ways to eliminate waste, relating to the waste of customers' time.
- Third was to call some customers and learn about their problems. Consider an example provided in which a person loses their credit and debit cards that were in their wallet. There are three immediate concerns: being able to get cash to get home, someone using the stolen cards, and getting the person's life straightened out.
- Fourth was to use technology "to make banking joyful, (and) make the banking part invisible." Management is reported to encourage employees to think like not just "techies" but customer-focused techies, like Amazon. In fact, the bank has espoused the phrase "What would Jeff (Bezos) do?"

- Fifth was to work with partners in the ecosystem, possibly even to control the ecosystem. For example, the bank partnered with the fintech company, Doxa, to provide an automated payment solution for the construction industry in Singapore.
- Sixth was the ways to identify "blockers" of change and introduce "enablers" of change.
- Seventh was to recognize that innovation is all about culture and behavior, and as such, the decision was made to take "leaders and put them in 'hackathons' with start-ups."

According to author Ram Charan, the CEO of DBS, Piyush Gupta, saw its bank becoming a technology business instead of a financial business. The CEO is reported to have said that he does not see banks, such as Citigroup and Bank of America as competitors. Instead, he sees Google, Amazon, Alibaba, and Tencent, as competitors.[15] Ask the question, How many airlines see other airlines as competitors instead of these high-tech companies?

According to *Euromoney*, a leading industry publication, the DBS Bank has been named as the "world's best bank" for the fourth year in a row. Moreover, it has also been recognized as the "world's best digital bank."[16] One key element of its success has been for management to recognize the need and preferences of the new generation of customers, along the lines of tech start-ups using new technologies to make banking hassle-free. It has also taken initiatives relating to new online exchanges for blockchain-based fundraising and carbon credit trading.

Personalization

The concept of airlines developing strategies centered on personalization, with a seamless and omnichannel experience, is not new. The challenge has been to collect and deploy the relevant data at scale to effectively implement the strategies. Personalization is, however, much more than referring to customers by their names. It involves providing customized solutions whether the customer is communicating with a call center or is on the website of the airline. Personalization means more relevance for the end customer, resulting in improved experience and expected improved brand loyalty, NPS, and revenue opportunity for an airline. This is where AI can play an important role in enhancing the experience with the brand. The idea is to provide relevant data to empower staff (within a call center, at an airport check-in counter, in an airport lounge, or in the aircraft) as well as within systems (websites, apps, and so forth). In both cases, the object is for customers to be provided with personalized solutions to achieve their goals. Personalization can be at an inspiration stage (before booking) as well as during post-travel. This can be via a direct channel (airline.com, email, SMS, notification, chat, and so forth), but it can also include personalized ads/recommendations on their channels (sponsored ads on Facebook or any other website).

Challenges

There are numerous challenges:

- monitoring and capturing granular data on a customer's interactions in real time and at every touch point and through every channel
- keeping the history of a customer's interactions to determine the customer's preferences (or inferred preferences!)
- generating a 360-degree view of a customer by connecting data coming from different sources, including the value of purchasing data from external sources, such as Facebook and LinkedIn
- providing personalized solutions to meet the end-to-end needs within the context of a customer
- scaling the provision of personalized experiences for all customers

These challenges exist due to the

- inadequacy of organizational structures (silos), systems, and processes,
- unavailability of relevant and timely data,
- insufficient use of analytics embedded in the platforms, and
- greater focus on products than customers.

Opportunities

Some business researchers suggest the use of AI. For example, Edelman and Abraham, suggest the use of *intelligent experience engines* to develop and deliver personalization at scale.[17] These authors say that intelligent experience engines can be developed using machine learning algorithms with focus on "microgoals—positive individual moments that compose the total experience—and ensure that all those goals get stitched together."

The key is to monitor the behavior of a customer at every touch point (online, call center, airport check-in, lounge, and on an aircraft). It is the data derived from these sources that can be used to provide personalized services. The challenges, however, are how to collect these data, how to analyze it using analytics and algorithms, and how to create a real-time engagement and interactions. Examples could include a recommendation for making a booking or a resolution on the phone with a call center, such as which connecting flight based on the situation, what time to leave for the airport, which lounge to visit at the airport. How about an airline building a relationship with a broad spectrum of retailers to enhance the attractiveness of its loyalty programs? Some airlines have done that, but are they effective in the sense, do they take into consideration a customer's preferences? An airline could develop an effective loyalty platform that helps develop a relationship with each customer based on the individual behavior, individual preferences, and individual context of each customer across each channel, not on the ability to cross-sell products and services. Relating to loyalty, for example, some customers may want rewards, and some may want offers. Some may want points and some cash back, as in the case of some credit cards. With respect to payments, some may want to buy now and pay later, and some may want to use "digital wallets." The use of digital wallets means much more than just making payments with mobile phones. It also means that consumers are getting interested in aggregating their digital assets—credit cards, gift cards, loyalty points, and so forth. Such a platform would enable a small airline to compete with much larger airlines, JetBlue for example, with American, British Airways, Delta, United, and Virgin Atlantic across the Atlantic. The effectiveness of the loyalty programs can be increased through ongoing experimentation with feedback.

The booking part of the trip is an important experience, especially now with the extensive need and capability to make changes. Should airlines think about providing a limited choice and letting customers decide on the degree of personalization? Personalization requires not only capturing of information but also providing employees with access to the information. As for capturing the information, Picoult uses the phrase "Radar on: Antenna up."[18] This aspect clearly applies to gate agents, flight attendants, call center agents, and customer service staff in airport lounges. Think about the value of information from the itineraries browsed by customers online. Some airlines send emails if no purchase is made, saying, something like "fares as low as ..." Would it be better if the email asked how the airline could help?

Let us not forget about customer experience during recovery. First, there needs to be a sense of urgency. Second, the staff needs to be empowered to resolve a customer's problems. And the problem needs to be looked at from a customer's perspective. A missed connection means a missed business opportunity, not just a late arrival at the destination. Third, changes in the behavior and expectations of employees are part and parcel of the provision of good customer experience. Not only customers but employees also are realigning life priorities. Think about the old priorities of a quest for wealth and the accompanying "rat race" and "burnout." The key to employee acquisition and retention is not just about wages, benefits, and training but also about effective engagement and meaningful experience relating to the changes in their lifestyles, given now the increasing link between work lives and personal lives. There is a need relating to stress, trust, flexibility, and social issues for both customers and employees.

Finally, it is interesting that the word *hyper-personalization* has now begun to be used, given that many airlines are still a long way from providing even basic personalized information. Would it make sense, first, to let passengers reveal the degree of personalization they desire, including their need for privacy of the data provided? Second, an airline needs to be clear on its value proposition. Think about a visit to Costco. The store is a warehouse, and it is even called by that name. The value proposition is not a great shopping experience in the warehouse. It is simply low prices. What lessons are there for ultra-low-cost airlines? Is an airline aiming to be the Ritz-Carlton or the McDonald's of the airline industry?

Consumers want personalized services, with or without human involvement. Personalized services can be provided by self-service systems and processes if the back-end processes have been transformed to not only make self-service systems more efficient but also with the possibility of having human interactions become available when necessary. The point is that human intervention should be there for an airline to handle the unusual and complex situations, not just to deal with the airline's poor back-end systems and processes. The experience during the pandemic has caused consumers to accept digital and virtual interactions, such as telemedicine instead of personal visits to doctors' offices, particularly for follow-up visits. In fact, in some cases, customers may even pay a premium for self-services and digital services due to their convenience. The question then is, What is the right combination of human interaction and self-service?

The key point is that an airline's interactions with its customers need to be not only instantaneous but also continuous to build deep relationships. Think about it. Why would an airline interact with a customer only when the customer is shopping or traveling? Think about the value provided by a car insurance company that interacts with a customer not only during the purchase of insurance or at a renewal time or in a situation involving an accident but on an ongoing basis as well. The insurance company can install sensors in the vehicle that can monitor the driving behavior and provide feedback, including reductions in premium, based on good driving habits. What about items that people could wear to monitor their vital systems that would provide vital information to healthcare providers, enabling them to make helpful recommendations on an ongoing basis, instead of during the office visits, when there are specific problems? Of course, there would be some consumers who do not want personal data collected on them and be made available to outsiders or be interacted with by providers on a continuous basis, unless consumers could be assured that the data collected was going to be used to understand the pain points and to reduce friction.

How about creating an app for customers to provide instant feedback and have relevant systems and processes in place to analyze the feedback and act, based on the feedback, in almost real-time? Let us say that a passenger receives poor service in some area during a long-haul outbound flight and reports it using the app at the time the poor service is received. Would the airline have the systems and processes in place to act and take care of the problem on the long-haul inbound flight? Systems are needed to recognize problems based on the feedback, take action to correct the problems, and respond to customers. Can chatbots facilitate this process?

The composition of travel segments is changing, both for the business segment as well as for the leisure and the visiting family and relatives (VFR) segments. This variation in the mix is changing the requirements of travelers in all segments, meaning not only a change in the products but also in other areas, such as loyalty programs. Revenue- and point-based systems may not work going forward. See the thought leadership piece by Evert de Boer in Chapter 8. As for customer experiences, different marketing techniques are needed to facilitate the development of a framework to improve customer experience. There are obviously challenges faced by the marketing departments that cannot be dealt with using the currently available data and conventional mindsets. New data, new technologies, new analytics, new experimentation techniques, and nonconventional mindsets are needed to deal with the ongoing challenges. New types of data, for example, location intelligence, are needed to identify consumer interests. It is one thing to know a shopper's age, gender, and past shopping history. It is another thing to understand a consumer's hobbies, a serious interest in healthy food, and some knowledge of brand affinity. Next, we have new technologies, such as AI, to help an airline compete in the digital area. How about using customer experience analytics to scrutinize customer journeys and experiment, using a contemporary marketing canvas, the value of different options? The object is not only to experiment smarter but also to gain insights faster to win a broad spectrum of customers, not just digital customers. The main point is to question the status quo.

For an airline, one way to extend the boundaries of its business would be to work on a platform. The subject of platforms has been discussed extensively in previous books in this series.[19] However, the point is to go much further than just bringing together several buyers and sellers. The major benefit of a platform is the availability of data that each seller has on its customers that can be used by different sellers to provide personalized products and services. Think of the global platforms (e.g., Google, Facebook, and WeChat) and the benefit of leveraging their user bases. Add to that the role AI is playing in networks, such as Google search. Think about how Google is adding new features to Google Flights to help travelers search for information to plan their trips. For example, users can now track fares in a market for travel three to six months ahead and be informed of "a lower-than-typical fare." In the previous version of the systems, fare alerts could only be enabled for travel on specific dates. What if additional features could be added, related to, for example, lower-priced hotel rooms (or upgrades to airline cabins and hotel rooms) or sports events, around the lower airfares alerts, in other words, alerts on bundled products and services?

While the value of a platform increases with the number of sellers, the increase in value can be even higher from the value of the data that each seller brings on its customers. Next, value can be increased even further using algorithms, facilitated using AI and machine learning technologies (discussed later in this chapter), to make personalized recommendations. Keep in mind that just as AI is enabling network platforms to improve their functionality, travel platforms can do the same thing. The AI-enabled travel platforms can look at all the attributes of a traveler's profile and preferences and determine the offers that are relevant at the time. However, while the benefit is clear, the challenge is to persuade each seller on the platform to share the data collected by each seller. Large airlines can develop their own platforms while smaller airlines can join the platforms of large airlines or the platforms of other parties in the ecosystem, such as airports. Think about an important area through which passenger experience could be improved significantly—the development and operation of efficient multimodal and intermodal hubs that provide physical and digital connectivity. As discussed by Michaela Schultheiß-Münch and Jennifer Berz in their thought leadership piece in Chapter 8, Frankfurt Airport is already on its way to becoming such a mobility hub.

During the pandemic, many aspects of consumer behavior have changed, for example, the movement toward digital and e-commerce, instead of going to brick-and-mortar stores and restaurants. Two thoughts. First, it is possible that even after the pandemic some consumers might continue to use digital and e-commerce. Second, even if service providers do increase their focus on digital and e-commerce initiatives, it is important to develop new ways of interacting with customers to improve their experience even when purchases are made through digital channels. Leslie Zane, a branding expert, calls this phenomenon, "digital humanization" that can be achieved by "using technologies to offer what feels like white-glove concierge services."[20] Just as brand-name stores can help customers find the exact products they are looking for, airlines should also be able to help customers find the desired itineraries online without hassles and frustration. Think about how some retailers have found ways to use technologies that enable customers to try on clothes virtually. Zane also provides an insightful example of a business that provides a positive brand connection in customers' "unconscious minds." The footwear company, Allbirds, not only produces extremely comfortable and stylish shoes, but it is also committed to sustainability and transparency. It discusses, for example, how the use of wool makes its sneakers lightweight, breathable, cool in the heat, warm in the cold, and odor-resistant for those who do not want to wear socks.[21]

Some experts are suggesting that psychology needs to be considered when exploring different ways to improve customer experience. Rory Sutherland, Ogilvy's vice chairman and behavioral science researcher, says part of the problem is that most travel systems seem to be designed by people who are driven by rational decisions and measurable outcomes. What seems to be missing is psychology, an understanding of how humans make decisions. There is a need to look at travel differently, ways that take into consideration "the messiness of human decision-making as opposed to the neatness of business decision-making." Sutherland provides Eurostar as an example. Eurostar invested £6 billion in 2007 to build new tracks between London and Paris to reduce the trip time. But "it was actually the addition of Wi-Fi several years later that gave Eurostar a stronger advantage over air travel." Sutherland provides another thought-provocative example: "About 20% of people would be motivated to go on a later flight if all you put on the website was this is the least crowded flight of the day."[22]

As Jordie Knoppers, with KLM, explains in his thought leadership piece in Chapter 8, airline customers are now not making their choices based on itineraries, followed by price, but on itineraries, followed by the brand and reputation. What if an airline could position itself to derive a competitive advantage by redeveloping its brand? Think about the competitive positioning of companies such as Apple, Chanel, Gucci, IKEA, Mercedes-Benz, Nescafé, Nike, Samsung, YouTube, and Zara.

70　What if airlines reimagined and redefined customer experience?

Think about Nike for a minute. What made Nike a truly global brand? Is it its tagline, "Just do it," or the iconic "Swoosh" logo or the endorsements of famous athletes and celebrities? While all of these have played important roles, there is a lot more to Nike's marketing strategies, for example, the creation of Nike's value proposition. According to Indika Bandara, a digital marketing expert, Nike's value proposition has four major components—accessibility, customization, innovation, and brand/status.[23] While the brand/status does relate to partnerships with top leagues and athletes, the other three components cannot be underestimated. Take customization, for example. Nike allows customers to customize their shoes either online or through physical studios. And according to one analyst, Nike has almost become "the definition of sports themselves." Nike has transitioned from "just another shoe company to an athletic and fitness lifestyle brand."[24] Nike created the brand from its value proposition and has managed to keep it visible. Could an airline transition itself from just another airline to a travel lifestyle brand?

Businesses that have positioned themselves for competitive advantage, have generated higher revenue and market value, and achieved a higher market share. According to one business researcher, Kimberly Whitler, this did not happen by luck. It is the result of specific consumer-based and science-backed tools and techniques to create and communicate key features of a brand. These skill-building tools are in three categories: "marketing strategy, bridging, and planning."[25] These tools can help an airline to achieve positional superiority by identifying, developing, and testing a unique position that is relevant to targeted consumers and provides meaningful value for them. The challenge for airlines has not been what to do but how to do it with clarity.

Many travelers find the planning process of trips, especially for leisure travel, to be quite stressful, especially during the pandemic, producing a need for empathy. An effective delivery of empathy, geared at the specific needs of each customer, would undoubtedly lead to an increase in their loyalty. Technology can help customers obtain positive and streamlined experiences. If travelers feel that they are taken care of during their end-to-end journey, they are more likely to become loyal customers. The barrier to the provision of empathy is the challenge to scale it. This is where collaboration within the ecosystem can play a major role. How about communicating with passengers with a well-developed strategy and in their native language? The key is to have an effective and proactive communication strategy—as chatbots are already quickly providing text messages to acknowledge a situation and a process to provide a solution—from the starting point at the origin to the end point at the destination and back to the point of origin. What if an airline collected and reviewed feedback from customers at each touch point to identify the root causes of problems and worked with cross-functional teams to find solutions? Remember the goal is to respond to every customer, at any location, at any time, and through any device. Every customer needs to be treated with empathy. Chatbots have begun to help as they "learn" from human-provided interventions through the machine learning processes. Readers can obtain insightful information on the role of robots in a book by Martin Ford.[26]

Digital experience

The conclusion that airlines need to produce a compelling experience is hardly a new concept. Yet, according to some experts with experience in the airline industry, airlines continue to be obsessed with "product and price" that "has created a culture of customer experience mediocracy." See the thought leadership piece by Kerstin Lomb in Chapter 8. According to her, what is needed is the creation of "unexpected compelling experiences to increase bookings and ancillary revenues." Moreover, according to her, "today's customers want not just a good experience, but a good 'digital' experience."

Digital experience is an important part of customers' desire, over and above the features of the product. This—a seamless experience throughout the journey—is especially true post-COVID. A lack of digital experience could easily affect the loyalty of customers. While the desire for seamless travel has always been there, it has now become more important. However, while it appears that more customers prefer digital interactions as opposed to face-to-face interactions, these digital interactions need to be efficient and user-friendly, based on a comprehensive understanding of digital customer behavior, based, in turn, on meaningful consumer profiles. Could an airline make these interactions much more effective and create an opportunity to generate more revenue through selling digitally new services—seat upgrades, priority boarding, and services to help with tight connections, for example? Ancillary products and services can also be sold that are offered by third parties, for example, at destinations. And information obtained through digital interactions can be helpful in realigning loyalty programs.

The key is to do a "forensic" mapping of the customer journey, both current and in the future, to reduce pain.[27] Howard Tiersky defines two kinds of pain, blame pain and accepted pain. He explains the two kinds of pain as a visit to two kinds of stores. In the first case, it takes 30 minutes to check out of a standard store. This is blame pain. In another case, a customer can go to the Amazon Go store, where there is no checkout line and purchases are automatically charged to a customer's account as the customer picks up the items. However, it takes some time to drive to the Amazon Go store that is located at some distance. That is accepted pain. The conclusion, drawn by Tiersky, is that finding ways to relieve blame pain avoids negative emotions while helping to relieve accepted pain creates positive emotions. What if an airline developed systems and processes to relieve both kinds of pain, relating to current journey maps, and future journey maps (that involve travel restrictions and cancelation policies) to meet the changing needs of customers, current and future customers, and particularly digital customers? Airlines need to provide digital (e.g., mobile-first) solutions that are user-friendly (less complex) to manage their travel experiences.

There is also now some discussion about metaverse and its role in providing a digital experience. The technology behind the metaverse has been available for many years. Think about pilots using simulators and retailers using the technology to have a shopper try on a dress, without physically trying on the item. And, given that the technology has advanced, the use of metaverse does show numerous opportunities to improve customer experience, for example, allowing a customer to see how they would feel seated in a particular seat on a long-haul flight and the potential to sell ancillary products and services to customize a trip. How about the opportunity to engage with a customer interactively to sell an upgrade to a premium-economy seat? Then there are the opportunities to market some unique aspects of destinations to inspire purchases of travel. However, there are also several questions about the use of metaverse. First, when will it be available for use by average consumers? Second, will consumers be inspired to travel to destinations or simply enjoy the destination without traveling? Third, how much control would technology companies have over the use of the technology?

AI and machine learning

While customer relationship management (CRM) is not a new concept, there are two other value-adding initiatives that can help an airline to take the CRM concept to a new level. The first one is to use platforms that not only bring buyers and sellers together but also enable sellers to engage effectively with customers. Sophisticated platforms have algorithms embedded in them to increase the connectedness with customers, thereby increasing further the amount of data available. The second aspect is the ability to implement AI in marketing initiatives. Two business researchers, Raj Venkatesan and Jim Lecinski, provide a road map on how to implement AI (and machine learning) in marketing, from developing pilots to scaling the initiatives and effective implementation. They illustrate the use of their concepts with insightful examples from Google, Starbucks, and Coca-Cola.[28]

An airline can use machine learning to identify its best customers, relevant messages for each one, and the best communication channel for each one. While these steps are the basics of traditional marketing, technology now enables the marketing initiatives to move up to the next stage to make an airline better understand its customer base and how to develop, and market, personalized offers to improve customer experience. In addition to machine learning, there are other technologies, for example, natural language processing, that can help. The point is that while some airlines are beginning to think about end-to-end customer journeys, the customer experience does not begin just on an airline's website. Kerstin Lomb with IBM points this out in Chapter 8 in her thought leadership piece.

How about the use of computer vision, which can help identify specific objects? Think about the value of this technology to recognize an image of a traveler and assign the profile of a traveler to specific products and services.

Keep in mind that machine learning is simply the capability of a machine to take in and process large quantities of data and provide insights that can be used to make predictions. The learning part relates, in simple terms, to the use of new data to update insights and predictions. The necessity is the availability of clean data, collected by the original organization (sometimes called the first-party data). Data need to be comprehensive in that it needs to relate both to transactions and behavior. In addition, the data collected should be in the structured category as well as in the unstructured category. The value of machine learning is to take the comprehensive data and generate comprehensive views of each customer. However, the data collected by airlines (coming from loyalty programs and website cookies) are not likely to be sufficient. It needs to be complemented by data collected by other organizations, such as hotels before it is input into the machine systems to adapt to customer behavior, preferences, and expectations. To be effective, data needs to be collected on each customer, not by category, such as passengers or sales by region; domestic versus international; by market, transatlantic versus transpacific; by city, New York versus Miami; or even by company, IBM, versus P&G versus Ford. In fact, even when data are collected on each customer, it needs to be connected in that a hotel partner of an airline tracking a customer needs to verify that it is the same customer that is being tracked by the airline.

Airlines obviously capture data on what is being purchased by customers (itineraries), when, and how far ahead the purchase was made before the actual travel. How long was the customer on the website before the purchase was made? Did the customer make the purchase on the first visit to the website or after multiple visits? Which payment system was used? Was the connection offered by an airline to a website of a hotel or a car-rental company made? These are the types of data that can be analyzed to detect patterns to suggest personalized offers. If a passenger did not check a bag during past three-day trips to and from a same destination, then why offer a bundle that contains a feature that offers not only the first bag checked for free but also a second?

If a customer does not book on the website, was it because the fare was too high or because the schedule (outbound and or inbound) was not appropriate? Or was the passenger waiting to see if the fare would drop? Would an offer be attractive if the airline communicated a feature that if the fare drops, the customer would be contacted and given a credit? Or, if the customer purchased a high-fare aisle seat and if seats were available, the middle seat would be kept open for this passenger? A customer can be offered an upgrade to first class with the difference in the fare based on the customer and the situation, or how full the economy section is. What if the passenger upgrades for three trips in a row in the specific market in a specific time by paying an upgrade fee, could the fourth upgrade be free, even if the passenger is not in a loyalty program? None of these ideas is new, but the point is that AI and machine learning technologies are now available to help airlines make predictions and learn from carefully controlled experimentation. Clearly some airlines are investing in start-up companies that are researching the use of world-class technologies. Not only can these technologies be used by the airlines making the investments, but they can also monetize on these investments by making the technologies available to other airlines.

AI and machine learning technologies can also be used to reduce tasks that customer-contact staff do on a repetitive basis. Think about flight attendants, gate agents, and call center agents. These categories of staff can then engage with customers to handle special situations. An important question relating to the use of AI and machine learning is, Do marketers really understand what AI and machine learning are and how and why these technologies need to be used right now? These technologies can be leveraged if an airline wants to get laser-focused on its customers and find effective ways to connect with them and to make personalized offers.

Although the key value of AI and machine learning lies in the technology's capability to recognize patterns, in recent years the value of this technology has increased enormously as machines are able to learn by themselves without human intervention to upload the necessary data to start the training process. Kissinger, Schmidt, and Huttenlocher provide three examples. First, the AlphaZero chess program, developed by Google DeepMind in late 2017, proved to be superior to the Stockfish chess program, as it had no human input relating to past experience or strategy. The human input related only to the rules of the chess game and the object to maximize the number of wins compared to losses. The second example relates to the research conducted at the Massachusetts Institute of Technology to predict the antibacterial properties of molecules to identify potential new antibiotics. The third example relates to the machine's capability to "generate humanlike text." For example, if a machine is given a partial phrase, it can produce meaningful completions.[29]

Think about AI's ability to put a customer's search into the context of a real world surrounding and circumstances (that are likely to be dynamic), for example, search for an airline ticket and a hotel, with the embedded algorithms to produce improvements by learning through experience. Add to this capability the ability to translate languages and to recognize objects. Now think about being able to recognize a customer from an image. Let us go further and consider the capability not just to translate text but to finish a text. Just as a machine can generate text to finish a sentence, it can also produce an offer based on partial preferences selected by a customer. Again, while some airlines are clearly beginning to think about end-to-end customer journeys, customer experience does not begin just on an airline's website. Kerstin Lomb with IBM distinctly points this out in Chapter 8 in her thought leadership piece.

How about the use of algorithms to identify groups of customers with similar behavior and preferences to identify and develop relevant offers? Keep in mind that machine learning can detect patterns better than humans because the technology can analyze much larger quantities of data to improve predictions. Keep also in mind that it is not just the ability of the machine to take in large amounts of data with instantaneous access but also the multidimensional aspects of data, coming from direct and indirect sources, given the computation power of machines, algorithms, and training methods.

Just as an airline can use AI and machine learning to develop a competitive advantage, an airline can also use the increased focus on sustainability to develop a compelling competitive advantage. How would an airline make the net-zero transition to gain the trust and brand loyalty of its targeted customer? This is the subject of the next chapter.

Highlights

- The challenge relating to personalization (with or without human involvement) relates to the collection and deployment of relevant data at scale to effectively implement effective strategies. The data collected by airlines (coming from loyalty programs and website cookies) is not likely to be sufficient. Not only big data but also small data can provide important information on the changing behavior and expectations of customers—all customers, not just digital customers.
- The major benefit of a platform is the availability of data that each seller has on its customers that can be used by different sellers to provide personalized products and services.
- With the availability of enormously large quantities of data (made available by the internet and social media) and with the use of AI (particularly, deep learning), airline marketers can identify quickly patterns based on multiple sources of data, derived from the use of platforms.
- The vast quantity of data collected and analyzed can be used to create an offer at the individual level and to communicate it through multiple channels in response to modern search engines, also enabled by AI. Think about travelers searching for, and receiving, relevant and real-time offers through Amazon Alexa, Google Home, and Apple Siri.
- Airlines can position themselves to derive a competitive advantage by redeveloping their brands. The process requires the use of specific consumer-based and science-backed tools and techniques.

Customer service tends to be mediocre, or at least a hit-or-miss experience. To start with, there tends to be confusion between customer service and customer experience. The key is to monitor the behavior of a customer at every touch point. And interactions with customers need to be not only instantaneous but also continuous to build deep relationships. Think about the customer service and customer experience provided by Amazon and the DBS Bank and the insights for airlines.

Notes

1 Fred Reichheld, *Winning on Purpose: The Unbeatable Strategy of Loving Customers* (Boston, MA: Harvard Business Review Press, 2021), pp. 107–110.
2 "SUN COUNTRY AIRLINES BRINGS THE AIRPORT TO YOUR DOORSTEP WITH NEW DOOR-TO-DOOR SERVICE," Media Contact: Sun Country Airlines, mediarelations@suncountry.com, September 28, 2021. https://ir.suncountry.com/static-files/6997f726-96ee-4919-a95a-31db9e1ce857.
3 Jonathan Hendry, "American Airlines Uses Secure Airside Bus Services to Connect Local Airports," *Simple Flying*, April 7, 2022. https://simpleflying.com/american-airlines-secure-local-airport-transfer-bus/
4 https://www.jdpower.com/business/press-releases/2021-north-america-airline-satisfaction-study.
5 David Scott Duncan, *The Secret Lives of Customers: A Detective Story about Solving the Mystery of Customer Behavior* (New York: PublicAffairs, 2021).

6 Rick Delisi and Dan Michaeli, *Digital Customer Service: Transforming Customer Experience for an On-Screen World* (New York: Wiley, 2021).
7 Fred Reichheld, *Winning on Purpose: The Unbeatable Strategy of Loving Customers* (Boston, MA: Harvard Business Review Press, 2021).
8 Martin Schwirn, *Small Data, Big Disruptions: How to Spot Signals of Change and Manage Uncertainty* (Newburyport, MA: Career Press, 2021).
9 David Scott Duncan, *The Secret Lives of Customers: A Detective Story about Solving the Mystery of Customer Behavior* (New York: PublicAffairs, 2021), p. 2.
10 Jon Picoult, *From Impressed to Obsessed: 12 Principles for Turning Customers and Employees into Lifelong Fans* (New York: McGraw-Hill, 2021), pp. 71–75.
11 Jon Picoult, *From Impressed to Obsessed: 12 Principles for Turning Customers and Employees into Lifelong Fans* (New York: McGraw-Hill, 2021), pp. 74 and 75.
12 Colin Bryar and Bill Carr, *Working Backwards: Insights, Stories, and Secrets from Inside Amazon* (New York: St. Martin's Press, 2021).
13 https://www.mckinsey.com/industries/financial-services/our-insights/banking-matters/becoming-more-than-a-bank-digital-transformation-at-dbs.
14 Jason Bloomberg, "How DBS Bank Became the Best Digital Bank in the World by Becoming Invisible," Forbes.com, December 23, 2016. https://www.forbes.com/sites/jasonbloomberg/2016/12/23/how-dbs-bank-became-the-best-digital-bank-in-the-world-by-becoming-invisible/?sh=198165863061.
15 Ram Charan and Geri Willigan, *Rethinking Competitive Advantage: New Rules for the Digital Age* (New York: Currency, 2021), pp. 57–58.
16 Vinika D. Rao, INSEAD Emerging Markets Institute, and Robin Speculand, Bridges Business Consultancy Int., "How DBS Became the 'World's Best Bank'," November 15, 2021. https://knowledge.insead.edu/blog/insead-blog/how-dbs-became-the-worlds-best-bank-17671.
17 David C. Edelman and Mark Abraham, "Customer Experience in the Age of AI: The Case for Building 'Intelligent Experience Engines'," *Harvard Business Review*, March-April 2022.
18 Jon Picoult, *From Impressed to Obsessed: 12 Principles for Turning Customers and Employees into Lifelong Fans* (New York: McGraw-Hill, 2021), p. 179.
19 Nawal K. Taneja, *Re-Platforming the Airline Business: To Meet Travelers' Total Mobility Needs* (London, UK: Routledge, 2019).
20 Leslie Zane, "Humanizing the Digital Experience in a Post-Pandemic Era," *MIT Sloan Management Review*, January 6, 2022.
21 https://www.insider.com/guides/style/allbirds-wool-runners-review.
22 Mitra Sorrells, "Psychology, Emotion Hold Key to Extraordinary Travel Experiences," PhocusWire?, March 31, 2022. https://www.phocuswire.com/psychology-emotion-hold-key-to-creating-extraordinary-experiences-for-travelers?utm_source=eNL&utm_medium=email&utm_campaign=Daily&oly_enc_id=1138E4720701F5U.
23 Indika Bandara, "What Can We Learn from Mike's Business Model," *ECOMHustler*. https://ecomhustler.com/nike-value-proposition/.
24 "How Nike Re-Defined the Power of Brand Image," *ConceptDrop*. https://conceptdrop.com/blog/27-the-importance-of-branding-how-nike-re-defined-the-power-of-brand-image/#:~:text=Nike%20has%20created%20superior%20marketing,brand%20more%20desirable%20and%20valuable.
25 Kimberly A. Whitler, *Positioning for Advantage: Techniques and Strategies to Grow Brand Value* (New York: Columbia University Press, 2021), p. 11.
26 Martin Ford, *Rule of the Robots: How Artificial Intelligence Will Transform Everything* (New York: Basic Books, 2021).
27 Howard Tiersky, *Winning Digital Customers: The Antidote to Irrelevance* (San Antonio, TX: Cranberry Press, 2021), chs. 10 and 11.

28 Raj Venkatesan and Jim Lecinski, *The AI Marketing Canvas: A Five-Stage Road Map to Implementing Artificial Intelligence in Marketing* (Stanford, CA: Stanford Business Books, 2021), ch. 5.
29 Henry A. Kissinger, Eric Schmidt, and Daniel Huttenlocher, *The Age of AI: And Our Human Future* (New York: Little, Brown and Co., 2021), ch. 1.

5 What if the aviation industry contributed no carbon emissions?

What would the airline sector look like if the aviation industry evolved to the point where it contributed no emissions? What would be the benefits to societies, consumers, and airlines? For context, it is estimated that air traffic is responsible for about 2.5% of the global CO_2 emissions. Some analysts point out that aviation's contribution to climate change is much higher (as much as 5%) if one "takes into account other gas emissions from the aircraft as well as the effect of vapour trails."[1] Regardless of whether 2.5% or 5% is the correct figure, or how air traffic compares to other sources of carbon emissions, the aviation industry is a more "visible" industry regarding climate change. And any reduction in carbon emissions is important. Given the huge impact that climate change has on the future of our planet for generations to come, the reduction in carbon emissions produced by the aviation industry, to the point of net-zero emissions, simply must become a priority. And it will require collaboration among all stakeholders in the aviation industry, not just the builders of aircraft and the operators of the aircraft but also government policymakers and regulators, as well as investors and travelers.

Despite the increase in concern for the environment, according to a new report by IBM's Institute for Business Value, "only 35% of companies have acted on their sustainability strategy and only 37% have aligned sustainability objectives with their business strategies."[2] Could the starting point be corporations that, in the spirit of a public–private partnership, change their goals and make net zero mandatory? In fairness, some corporations have started to play an important role. For example, Microsoft is planning to encourage its corporate staff to travel less by increasing its own carbon fee by 600%.[3] Turning to governments, what if they levied substantial taxes to protect the climate?

How could the achievement of a net-zero future happen? In the long term, as discussed in more detail later in this chapter, alternative fuels and new types of aircraft hold the promise of delivering a net-zero environment. However, actions can be taken, and are being taken, in the short term to dramatically reduce carbon emissions while the long-term technologies are put in place. What sorts of short-term actions, and their impacts, are possible? Based on the potential actions on the part of corporations and governments, could it mean a significant decrease in business travel? What decisions

DOI: 10.4324/9781003332824-5

would corporations make about the use of corporate jets, that generate a very large carbon footprint, given the few passengers onboard? Keep in mind that unlike in the commercial sector, the demand for business aviation grew during the pandemic and the trend seems to be continuing. Think about the deliveries by the OEMs and their backlogs, for example, Gulfstream's G650 and G700, Bombardier's Globals and Challengers, Textron's Citations, Embraer's Phenom and Praetor jets, and Dassault's Falcon 6X and 10X. During the pandemic, many high-net-worth buyers placed large orders for these aircraft, partly in response to the reduction in capacity during COVID-19 lockdowns in the commercial sector and partly due to the concerns of COVID-19 security.

For normal business travel, could corporations, for example, reduce the long-haul trips by their staff and ask the staff traveling on 1-hour-plus trips on regional planes to travel by trains, assuming that train travel is a viable source in a region, such as within Europe? The trend to ban short-haul flights is already on the horizon in Europe. In 2021, the French government passed a law that domestic flights on routes that can be served by a high-speed train in less than 2½ hours need to be eliminated. Air France eliminated its flights from Paris, Orly to Bordeaux, Nantes, and Lyons, for example, and is coordinating with the French national rail company, SNCF, to improve connections between the airline and trains.[4]

From another perspective, again in the short term, what if corporations start to have their staff travel less because, based on experience, virtual communications have proved to be sufficient and, certainly, less expensive? What if significant numbers of tourists also decided to change their travel behavior—travel less, travel to near tourist destinations, or take ground transportation? Decisions will, of course, vary by corporation, region, and segments of travelers, not just business versus leisure versus visiting friends and relatives (VFR), but subsegments within each of these segments. How would these developments affect airlines' networks, fleet, and schedules as well as pricing and revenue management policies? To put these questions in perspective, let us review briefly some recent developments relating to climate change that are influencing every country with significant impacts on economies and people's lives.

Developments relating to climate change

The 2015 Paris Agreement called for member countries to limit warming to 1.5-degrees Celsius to limit the impacts of climate change that has been causing sea levels to rise and creating floods, fires, and droughts. The 1.5-degree target means, presumably, that global carbon dioxide (CO_2) emissions need to decline by about 45% by 2030 (from the level in 2010) and to a net-zero level by 2050. The United Nations also set 17 Sustainable Development Goals (SDGs), such as good health and well-being (number 3), affordable and clean energy (number 7), and responsible consumption, and production (number 12).[5] The momentum, relating to the environmental, social, and governance (ESG) movement, has been increasing. These three areas are of particular interest to socially responsible investors, especially millennials. It is one measurement of a business's consciousness for social and environmental considerations. As such, the ESG movement could affect investments, for example, in the development of sustainable aviation fuels (SAFs), which could mean higher fuel prices for airlines. Next, the United Nations Climate Change Conference (COP26), held in Glasgow, Scotland, between October and November 2021, was, in some ways, also a pivotal moment for countries worldwide to reach an agreement on the urgency of how to deal with climate change.

Can effective solutions to climate change be found in a timely manner? The answer by one expert, John Doerr, is yes. According to him, "While many climate solutions are in hand, we lack the policy, investment, and global consensus to fully deploy them."[6] However, there are some examples that show that progress can be made. Until about 2008, 90% of the electricity, in the state of Hawaii, came from burning conventional oil, a source that not only produced unhealthy air and greenhouse gas emissions but was also expensive. Then Hawaii began to promote the use of solar panels and water batteries. The state set a goal of 30% clean energy by 2020, a goal that was exceeded. Now the new goals are 70% by 2030, and 100% by 2045.[7]

Within the framework of these developments, governments and leading businesses, including airlines, have already begun to develop goals to offset carbon emissions. Think about the value of collaboration in the implementation of the Carbon Offsetting and Reduction Scheme for International Aviation (CORSIA) developed by ICAO, with a goal to limit the CO_2 emissions from international aviation at the 2020 level and to deliver carbon-neutral growth, going forward after 2020. Airlines are already required to maintain accurate data on their annual CO_2 emissions and to have the numbers verified through a certification process.[8] Aviation affects climate change from the release of CO_2 emissions (from the burning of fossil fuels). The question relates to not just how to reduce emissions but also how to measure them and how to track them. Again, aviation is responsible for about 2.5% of the global CO_2 emissions. Some analysts point out that aviation's contribution to climate change is much higher (as much as 5% and as pointed out in the article by Becca Rowland).[9] Again, to emphasize one more time, according to a new report by IBM's Institute for Business Value, "only 35% of companies have acted on their sustainability strategy and only 37% have aligned sustainability objectives with their business strategies."[10]

If governments do not see significant changes in the carbon footprints, they could establish challenging quotas and carbon taxes. These decisions will have a significant impact on air travel, tourism, and the hospitality sector, as well as in their respective supply chains if climate change is to be controlled. While measuring and tracking the emissions being generated is not an easy task, some airlines have begun to think about using smart analytics and smart technologies, for example, artificial intelligence (AI), to quantify and benchmark their environmental carbon footprints. A few airlines have even begun to partner with technology companies to develop their strategies for sustainability.

Etihad Airways, for example, has reported its partnership with Microsoft to gain insights from the use of AI and advanced analytics and to measure and benchmark the airline's environmental footprint, relating both to flight operations and ground operations. It does not appear that any airline has yet set the goal to go all out, by replacing the older-generation fleet, and gaining operational efficiencies right away by using advanced planning techniques for ground operations and flight planning to minimize the CO_2 emissions.

Sustainable Aviation Fuels (SAFs)

Using conventional fuel, each airline trip generates carbon dioxide, raising an airline's carbon footprint. Compared to conventional petroleum-based jet fuel (or kerosene), SAFs can reduce greenhouse gases by large amounts without reducing performance. And SAFs can be produced in a more sustainable manner. However, there are two fundamental questions. About a decade ago, the development of SAFs was focused on agriculturally grown material for biofuels. This process leads to deforestation as more land is used to grow the needed crops. This leads to the first question about costs. Second, can such fuels be produced at scale? Waste, landfill and agriculture, for example, can be converted into synthetic gas that, in turn, can be converted into a SAF that can then be blended with fossil-derived jet fuel (e.g., 50–50) to get to similar properties to jet fuel. Other sources for producing the SAFs include oils and discarded animal fats. How fast can these fuels be produced? As for SAFs that do not need to be blended, they are still under development and the government approval process could take a long time. On top of that, some analysts are also raising a question about SAFs producing greenhouse gases in their life cycles. What about the price of SAFs? According to Air France, the price could be between four and eight times higher than the price of conventional fuel.[11]

Keeping in mind the concerns of costs, availability, and scale, some airlines have already begun to switch, on a trial basis, from traditional fossil-derived jet fuels to fuels made from renewable sources. United Airlines, for example, made a trip between Chicago and Washington in November 2021, in an aircraft (Boeing 737) fueled 100% with SAFs. However, the percentage of flights using SAFs relative to conventional jet fuel is very small (probably less than 1%). While airlines are obviously planning to increase the use of SAFs, it will take a very long time to get a percentage high enough to make a difference in lowering emissions. The important question about the use of SAFs relates, not to its value in reducing carbon emissions but to their price and their availability in quantity to meet the needs of the airline industry. What if the price and quantity available are no longer challenges because not only governments made huge investments but also large oil companies got involved in the development of SAFs?

What are some other options for fuel, given that SAFs only appear to be an interim solution? For short-haul flights and small aircraft, it is possible to use electricity. Airlines are beginning to develop an interest in the use of small regional electric aircraft. United Airlines and Mesa Airlines, for example, have signed an agreement to purchase from Heart Aerospace, a 19-seater electric aircraft to reduce the carbon emissions footprint of their operations. The viability of electric aircraft could increase in markets up to 250 miles with an increase in the density of the batteries needed for their operations. American has shown interest in the development of electric vertical take-off and landing aircraft (eVTOL) to operate the aircraft over congested cities and highway traffic.[12] Some analysts question if electric aircraft would be completely carbon-free if the electricity needed to power them were to come from fossil fuel power plants.

The challenge is for long-haul flights, leading manufacturers to look to other types of fuels that reduce the quantity of greenhouse gases emitted during the lifetime of the fuels—from production to combustion. Even though plant- and waste-based SAFs can be viable substitutes to the use of kerosene, they still produce some CO_2 emissions. On the other hand, hydrogen-powered aircraft will not produce CO_2 emissions, making hydrogen a viable option. Airbus is researching the potential use of three types of airplanes that could use hydrogen—a small turboprop aircraft for regional markets, a single-aisle turbofan for medium-sized markets, and a blended-wing body for longer-haul markets. See Figure 5.1. Hydrogen-powered aircraft could be in service by 2035, but there are three types of questions. First, could enough green hydrogen be produced to meet the needs of global fleets for commercial operations? If yes, then according to one report, hydrogen-powered aircraft could handle one-third of passenger travel.[13] The second question relates to the economic viability of hydrogen-fueled aircraft. And the third question relates to the operational and infrastructural aspects, for example, range, turnaround times (including the time to refuel), and the infrastructure required at airports.

Figure 5.1 Airbus ZEROe concept planes

Copyright Airbus 2022, used with permission

The net-zero-by-2050 scenario

Can the airline industry go carbon-neutral by 2050? While efficiencies have been increasing (due to a decrease in aircraft fuel consumption and an increase in load factors), have they been enough to offset the growth in traffic, about 5% per year between 2010 and 2019, the year before the pandemic? Think also about how much traffic growth will be fueled by the growth in the world population as well as the growth in the middle classes, especially from some highly populated countries, such as India and China. And, while building efficient light rail and electric aircraft would add much value, can they be introduced in the near term, and are they likely to be expensive? Could governments go so far as to ban flights in short-haul markets, especially in markets where train service is available? Could this happen more easily in European countries where governments have provided significant amounts of money to bail out their airlines, exemplified by the policy of the government in France? How about fast-rail service in the Boston/New York/Washington, D.C./Baltimore/Philadelphia markets or in the San Francisco/Los Angeles/San Diego markets in the US?

An important question is not just the exploration of renewable energy sources and an increase in energy efficiency, but the willingness of people to bring about a behavioral change in their lifestyles. It has been suggested that an increase in CO_2 emissions is partly the result of the low costs of flying. The proponents of this thought claim, for example, that according to the US Bureau of Transportation Statistics, the average fare in US domestic markets decreased from $510 in 1995 to $286 in 2021, adjusted for inflation (1995 dollars).[14] The promotion of this thought leadership raises the question of the potential implications of this movement not only for full-service airlines and business travel but also for low-cost carriers and tourist destinations. In some ways, the future of low-cost carriers is also connected to the emissions generated. On one hand, they carry more passengers per flight (due to higher density configuration), but they also offer lower fares that generate more demand. There is also a concern about the implications of the net-zero-by-2050 scenario on the global economy and the impact on tourism.

On the other side, what if consumers forced the travel sector to proactively tackle holistically the changing climate challenge?

- How would the sector develop and promote more sustainable types of travel?
- What role would government taxes play, for example, taxes on airline tickets and visitor taxes?
- How would airlines change their loyalty programs, for example, by moving away from rewards related to the frequency of travel?
- Can digitalization of the travel sector help?

The willingness to reduce carbon emissions seems to have increased since the emergence of the pandemic. It has been reported that a larger percentage of business travelers are willing to travel by train than before the pandemic, especially in markets where the travel times for the two modes (air and train) are similar. Of course, part of the willingness to travel by train could also be due to health reasons relating to COVID. Another reason could be the acknowledgment that travel by cars leads to a higher level of carbon than travel by trains. This development seems to be more prevalent in Europe than in North America.

While there has been a reduction in demand for air travel due to the pandemic, the question remains as to if the demand will catch up, and when, and will the pandemic bring a change in the behavior of travelers. Will people travel less or more? Have consumers gotten used to traveling less? Are they getting more concerned about the environment and therefore likely to travel less? How will businesses respond to travel by their staff? Answers will vary by region (e.g., India and China versus the US and Europe) and by type of business. One view is that travel will rise given the pent-up demand, relating both to leisure travelers as well as business travelers. Despite the increase in the price of fuel, beginning in February of 2022, airlines have managed to handle such price increases in the past, for example, the increase between 2009 and 2012. The thought is that demand will reach the 2019 level and go beyond. On the positive side, some airline executives even see a shift in consumer spending from goods and durables to services. As for technologies, according to the same executives, videoconferencing is likely to increase travel as the technology enables people to take their offices with them, enhancing mobility.[15]

Implications for airlines

At the IATA AGM in 2021, the industry committed to net-zero carbon emissions by 2050, in line with the goals of the Paris Agreement limiting global warming to 1.5-degrees Celsius. All sectors of the aviation industry are playing important roles—airlines, airports, aircraft manufacturers, and infrastructure service providers, for example. Specifically, IATA has identified four pillars for creating a sustainable aviation industry—technology, operations, infrastructure, and economic instruments. Technology can, in fact, provide benefits in both operations and infrastructure.

Consider the technology pillar and the assets of an airline. Airlines are asset-intensive businesses, not just aircraft but also maintenance, airport facilities, and staff. The object is to (1) comply with regulations, (2) reduce the costs of compliance, and (3) make sustainability a competitive advantage. Let us start with aircraft, their development, and their operations during their life cycle—operations, maintenance, upgrades, and so forth. New materials are making the aircraft lighter and more aerodynamic, not to mention requiring less maintenance. Lighter material in building aircraft (e.g., composites instead of aluminum alloy), not only reduces weight but with different types of coatings (outside and inside), parts are more resistant to wear and tear. For example, the new type of coatings applied resist rust (fuselage) and withstand high temperatures (combustion chambers). Windows can be coated to make them heat- and ultraviolet-resistant. The working systems of seats can be made to produce less friction. Lighter aircraft mean less fuel used and that means lower emissions. Composites can reduce the weight by about 20%. Newer generations of composites can be even lighter, and parts can be 3D-printed. That means less waste since parts can be produced in their exact size and shape. Let us consider the need to increase the utilization of staff. Think about some information provided by Christopher Gibbs, a former engineering director at Cathay Pacific Airways, and a Group Director at HAECO, in his thought leadership piece in Chapter 8. He says that in transit line maintenance, for example, staff utilization is rarely above 50%.

Technologies can help reduce fuel consumption and make maintenance much more efficient in other ways too. Think about the value of the greater use of digital twins, AI, the Internet of Things, geospatial and location data, computer vision, hybrid cloud, and blockchain to understand the basic cause of defects and system failures. However, there would be a need to model the entire end-to-end flow to assess the CO_2 contribution/impact of each of them.

Regarding route optimization, improvements are already being made relating to fuel efficiency by optimizing routes, flight paths, altitudes, and by reducing aircraft waiting times. For the optimization of flight operations, pilots are being given the tools to identify the most fuel-efficient procedures possible, for example, with more timely speed adjustments and optimized procedures, landing configurations, and taxiing on the ground with one engine. Now more efficient tools based on the use of AI are becoming available. While many leading airlines have already achieved successes in making operations and maintenance more efficient using traditional techniques, more can be achieved in predictive maintenance and remote sensing using digital twins and AI. How about the maintenance hangars themselves—their construction, the use of space, their operations, and their maintenance? In other words, it is not just the use of technology-driven insights (coming from the use of digital twins and AI) to improve the operation and maintenance of aircraft but also the operation and maintenance of maintenance facilities.

Blockchain is a trusted, distributed, transparent, and shared-ledger platform. Traceability is important in the real-time management of inventory and maintenance, and blockchain technology can make traceability much more effective (from records going back to the date and the place of when and where a part was manufactured). Think about the value of the right part becoming available at the right time and at the right place. Optimizations can make available not only the right parts at the right time and at the right place but also the capability to share data. The key to effective inventory management is not a new concept—having available just the right number of parts (not too many and not too little), minimizing the costs of capital tied up, and enhancing service levels. But now smart technologies are available to have the right level of inventory to help reduce the carbon footprint by optimizing the use of warehouse space.

Again, technology can add much value to the infrastructure to reduce the carbon footprint. Just think about the potential changes in navigation (to optimize the use of airspace) and airport operations, not only making the SAFs available but also making the operations of buildings themselves more efficient (building designs and usage) and vehicle operations (including hybrid towing vehicles). While the air traffic control (ATC) authorities are trying to make air navigation changes to enable more direct routes and less congestion, advancing technologies can reduce the time to achieve the results sooner. Keep in mind that the airline industry's track to net-zero does include the expected growth in travel and infrastructure, such as the development of the third runway at London's Heathrow Airport. Assumptions have, presumably, been made about the type of aircraft that will be used to enable the expansion of facilities at airports and the price to pay for the expansion of the facilities, such as the third runway at LHR. Leading airports have already started to implement AI to predict crowding in terminals, especially at security checkpoints, to improve passenger experience. Some airports have already started to think about using sophisticated models to predict passenger arrival times in parking garages and curbside, check-in counters, security lines, and concessionaire locations. Consequently, advancing technologies can facilitate the operationalization of sustainability.

IATA's Economic Investment pillar relates to carbon offsetting and carbon capture, as well as taxation that could increase airline fares and reduce demand. Offsetting is, of course, a controversial area, involving not only a price on CO_2 emissions but also the requirement to use SAFs. From the perspective of airlines, the forward-thinking airlines have already begun to use market-based strategies relating to aircraft and revenue management. Each generation of aircraft is more fuel-efficient and sophisticated revenue management techniques are being deployed to fly the aircraft with even higher load factors, leading to a significant improvement in the CO_2 emissions per passenger transported. Could passengers be incentivized to travel with less baggage? These strategies are certainly more desirable to avoid the potential impact of governments introducing a high level of taxes to reduce passenger demand. Could government-implemented taxation policies to reduce flying become a burden to the public? It would be possible if one were to assume that some people have already become used to flying less. More important would be an assumption as to if frequent flyers begin to fly less. Their decision could also impact the choice of airlines they fly, for example, airlines using older- or new-generation aircraft, seat densities, load factors, airports used, and airlines observing the use of more efficient operational practices. Could we expect that governments would tax airlines that are greener less? However, how could one measure in an accurate and an "objective" way the footprint of an airline, or a flight, and how can airlines be sure that all airlines are not taxed the same way? From another perspective, could the services offered by low-cost carriers, in some markets, be preferred as they use single-aisle aircraft that have higher seat densities, and some tend to use less congested airports? And then, there is also the concern that carbon reduction gains, made by other business sectors, may not be available to the airline sector to offset the carbon footprint in aviation.

Keep in mind that there are four key reasons for the increasing focus on sustainability: (1) some purpose-focused consumers appear to be saying that they are willing to pay more for products and services that are produced in a sustainable way, (2) some purpose-focused employees (e.g., millennials and generation Z) appear to be interested in working for businesses that are more focused on the environment, (3) some social issues–driven investors are moving toward businesses with sustainable business practices, and (4) governments are tightening the regulatory standards to protect the environment. According to Air France, one segment of passengers, namely, corporate is willing to pay a small premium to offset the cost of higher costs of sustainability. The airline thinks that it is because businesses may "mandate sustainable travel."[16]

Based on these trends, most airlines have adopted some type of sustainability initiative. However, how many airlines have developed a deep understanding of how sustainability can transform their business models to develop a competitive advantage? Can there be a win–win situation—the ability for an airline to meet its commercial goals and its social goals? It can be done through a deeper understanding of the technical aspects of sustainability and social issues and the use of designed collaboration (within public and private ecosystems). For example, the current systems and solutions used by airlines to reflect better CO_2 emission key performance indicators (KPIs or other sustainability KPIs) can be enhanced by modeling, monitoring, and improving the processes and decisions. With data, new KPIs (CO_2 emissions) can be displayed in dashboards to show all steps of the end-to-end processes. Is the goal to optimize according to CO_2 emission or, according to revenue, cost, profit, or on-time performance? The optimization process could even reflect certain specific initiatives and reporting tools (e.g., percentage of use of SAFs in cost model of network and schedule planning, the impact of waiting and taxiing at the airport, and so forth). The key is to understand how sustainable goals can be aligned with commercial goals. And let us not overlook what role branding would play, not just for millennials and generation Z but also for employees. As discussed in the next section, an airline can develop its business model around social causes.

Of the four preceding points, the key one pertains to consumers. While some consumers are saying, in surveys, that they are willing to pay more for sustainable products and services, what percentage will actually pay more? And even those who will pay more, how much more will they pay? On the part of corporate travelers, would they need to have a clear purpose for travel? Would their employers start using aviation carbon calculators to allow travelers to see a display of the specific carbon footprint for different flights, not just nonstop versus connection, but the type of aircraft? Could corporate travelers start using calculators that include some additional information not just on the type of aircraft and the itinerary (nonstop versus connecting flights) but also some useful information, such as the number of passengers and cargo onboard? Empowering a traveler is a critical success factor, for example, by providing a CO_2 calculator and giving a traveler the capability to compare easily travel options. What if a traveler could "see" the impact of her luggage weight on CO_2 emissions? What if a traveler could "see" the value of travel, relating to carbon emissions, on a different mode of transportation? What if an airline offered more miles for travel on "greener" flights?

Consequently, there are many questions before an answer can be provided about the potential to achieve the net-zero-by-2050 goal. For example, replacing older aircraft will take time and be costly. Operational areas would need to go through fundamental changes, relating to ground operations, flight operations (flight planning and onboard weight management), and ATC operations. Just think about the combination of a number of systems, processes, and organizations involved in handling an international arrival and departure of an aircraft at a gate. Think about how changes in systems and processes (the use of a smart platform and digital technology) could save costs for an airline and improve on-time performance, good for airlines and customers. The question, however, is if airlines have the tools today to measure or model the CO_2 impact of each of the processes involved in the end-to-end travel flow; how to monitor and improve each process? Similarly, performing condition-based maintenance would require changes in processes and systems. How about using computer vision to "see" and predict an emerging problem? And airlines can use smart data and advanced technologies to understand and manage their carbon footprint by using carbon calculators that can help travelers and, to some extent, employees and investors make informed decisions.

Finally, while some airlines are thinking about the use of electric aircraft, some are also thinking about the use of supersonic aircraft. Leaving aside the question of the financial viability of a supersonic aircraft, there is also the question of its carbon footprint. Boom Technology claims that its supersonic aircraft, Overture, can achieve net-zero carbon emissions and should be able to operate on 100% sustainable fuel. United has ordered 15 with options to purchase another 35. Since supersonic aircraft are expected to fly at much higher altitudes than subsonic aircraft (e.g., at about 60,000 ft compared to about 35,000 ft), there is some concern about the level of emissions generated. Although at higher altitudes the air is thinner, producing less resistance, emissions generated from the supersonic aircraft, flying at higher altitudes, could also be higher than from the subsonic aircraft flying at lower altitudes. Nevertheless, imagine, if these supersonic aircraft took a significant percentage of business passengers out of corporate jets.

Making sustainability the core of an airline's business strategy

As stated, while sustainability has been a goal for many years, the concern to protect the environment has accelerated in recent years, especially during the pandemic. Not only is there an increase in government regulations and enforcement, but there is also an increase in consumer expectations relating to sustainability. On the other hand, in a few cases, climate change initiatives of some airlines have been Band-Aid solutions, and they cannot heal the underlying condition. And while sustainability may have been an afterthought for some airlines, those that strategize to make it a competitive advantage to reduce their impact on the climate will become leaders in the minds of customers, employees, investors, and government regulators.

What if now an airline made sustainability the core of its business strategy to become a leader and a pioneer by balancing business goals and its goals to reduce carbon emissions? An airline can develop sustainability as a competitive advantage by realigning its purpose, deploying advanced technologies, and collaborating within the ecosystem and supply chain—in which members are also looking for carbon neutrality. EasyJet appears to be moving in this direction. And let us not forget the input from customers and employees and the need for rebranding. The approach needs to be holistic.

Let us start with the dual goal (a goal that is both market-based and cause-based) that makes sense relating to strategy, markets, customers, and the revenue model of the airline. Think about it from a clean-sheet perspective. However, the plan cannot just be conceptual. It needs to be practical, meaning numbers must be measurable, and actionable. What if an airline were to overcome some key challenges?

- What if travelers begin to make reservations, based on specific information on the amount of carbon emissions relating to particular flights, with the information displayed at the point of sale? Assume also that travelers will use the relevant information to choose different modes of transportation, for example, sharing cars, rail versus air, depending on destinations. What if the airline worked with different organizations within the ecosystem to develop this information and make it available at the point of sale to potential buyers of travel? What if information on each airline's sustainability initiatives was completely visible at the point of purchase?
- What if the airline were to reduce the complexity of measuring, monitoring, and reporting the information on its environmental footprint?
- What if the airline changed its organizational structure and culture of all departments in operations (flight operations, ground operations, maintenance, repair, and overhaul, as well as maintenance and engineering) not just to save costs but also to focus on sustainability?
- What if the airline clarified some of its assumptions? For example, there is a lot of discussion about frequent flyers contributing a lot to carbon emissions, given the amounts they fly. However, a very small percentage of travelers are frequent flyers, even in developed regions. Next, it is reported that customers are starting to think about making their purchase and loyalty decisions based on airline brands that align with customers' sustainability values. What if the airline was able to determine how many consumers just say that they are pro-sustainability, how many are willing to pay higher prices to travel, and how much more?

- Building upon the point raised earlier, what if travelers make reservations according to information on the amount of carbon emissions relating to particular flights, with the information displayed at the point of sale? Assume also that travelers will use the relevant information to choose different modes of transportation depending on destinations. What if the airline worked very closely within the ecosystem to identify critical information and make it available at the point of sale to potential buyers of travel including intermediaries?
- What if the airline made communities a part of its strategy? Why? Because air travel directly impacts the communities, not only destinations, infrastructure, and local workers but, in some cases, also the local economies.
- What if an airline were to run marketing campaigns, leveraging on consumer latent interest in sustainability, to make sustainability an important part of a consumer's purchase decision? What if this concept could be expanded and monitored? What if, as a result of overcoming the challenges discussed, an airline was able to make its commitment to sustainability into a competitive advantage?
- And, what if the airline found ways to make these ideas scalable?

The net-zero goal can be met even before 2050. It will require airlines to take ambitious steps to develop their strategies based on establishing the right baselines and targets to achieve stepwise goals, collaborate within ecosystems, make the necessary investments, and monitor their progress. And let us not overlook the point that while CO_2 emissions (and their contribution to climate change) is probably the main parameter relating to sustainability, there could be other aspects to consider (in term of sustainability): air quality, aircraft noise, waste, pollution at high atmosphere (impact on the ozone layer), impact of mass tourism on countries' local environment ecosystems, and biodiversity (waste, pollution).

What if one airline, say Agility Airlines, discussed in Chapter 7, found ways to make the ideas in this chapter scalable?

Highlights

- The 2015 Paris Agreement called for member countries to limit the impacts of climate change. Within this framework, governments and leading businesses, including airlines, have already begun to develop goals to offset carbon emissions. It is estimated that aviation is responsible for about 2.5% of the global CO_2 emissions. The question relates to not just how to reduce emissions but also how to measure and track them.
- Relating to the net-zero-by-2050 goal, the main question is about the willingness of people to bring about a behavioral change in their lifestyles.

- Compared to conventional petroleum-based jet fuel (or kerosene), SAFs can reduce greenhouse gases by large amounts without reducing performance. However, the use of SAFs faces two challenges, their availability in sufficient amounts and their higher prices.
- IATA has identified four pillars for creating a sustainable aviation industry—technology, operations, infrastructure, and economic instruments.
- A leading airline could make sustainability the core of its business strategy. It could transform itself not only to become resilient and adaptive but also to stay committed to its sustainability agenda.

There are four key reasons for the increasing focus on sustainability: (1) some purpose-focused consumers, (2) some purpose-focused employees, (3) some social issues–driven investors, and (4) governments tightening the regulatory standards. There are a number of ways to reduce emissions and become more sustainable: reduce volume of air travel, for example, by the greater use of high-speed trains; increase the carbon efficiency of air travel, by using SAFs, and vehicles propelled by electricity; and leverage more technology.

Notes

1. Becca Rowland, "Can Flying Ever Be Green? Towards Sustainability in Aviation," *OAG Insights*, November 25, 2021.
2. "Sustainability as a Transformation Catalyst: Trailblazers Turn Aspiration into Action," *IBM Institute for Business Value*, 2022, p. 2.
3. Matthew Parsons, "Microsoft Discourages Corporate Travel by Raising Own Carbon Fee 600 Percent," *Skift*, March 14, 2022. https://skift.com/2022/03/14/microsoft-discourages-corporate-travel-by-raising-own-carbon-fee-600-percent/.
4. Madhu Unnikrishnan, "Air France CEO Stays Upbeat on Summer Amid Global Turmoil," *Skift*, March 24, 2022. https://mopays.com/air-france-ceo-stays-upbeat-on-summer-amid-global-turmoil/.
5. https://sdgs.un.org/goals.
6. John Doerr, *Speed & Scale: An Action Plan for Solving Our Climate Crisis Now* (New York: Penguin, 2021), front flap.
7. John Doerr, *Speed & Scale: An Action Plan for Solving Our Climate Crisis Now* (New York: Penguin, 2021), pp. 43, 298, and 300.
8. https://www.icao.int/environmental-protection/CORSIA/Documents/CORSIA_Newsletter_Oct_2021_for_web.pdf.
9. Becca Rowland, "Can Flying Ever Be Green? Towards Sustainability in Aviation," *OAG Insights*, November 25, 2021.
10. "Sustainability as a Transformation Catalyst: Trailblazers Turn Aspiration into Action," *IBM Institute for Business Value*, 2022, p. 2.
11. Madhu Unnikrishnan, "Air France CEO Stays Upbeat on Summer Amid Global Turmoil," *Skift*, March 24, 2022. https://mopays.com/air-france-ceo-stays-upbeat-on-summer-amid-global-turmoil/.
12. Thomas Pallini, "American Airlines Could Pay $1 Billion for up to 250 eVTOLs to Fly Travelers over Congested Cities and Highway Traffic," businessinsider.com, June 11, 2012. https://www.businessinsider.com/american-airlines-order-for-vertical-aerospace-evtols-2021-6.
13. Marcia Gallucci, "Hydrogen-Powered Planes Could Handle a Third of Passenger Air Travel," *Canary Media*, January 26, 2022. https://www.canarymedia.com/articles/

air-travel/hydrogen-powered-planes-could-handle-a-third-of-passenger-air-travel-study-finds.
14 https://www.bts.gov/content/annual-us-domestic-average-itinerary-fare-current-and-constant-dollars.
15 Graham Dunn, "Delta and Virgin Strike Positive Note over Demand Despite Cost Pressures," flightglobal.com, March 15, 2022.
16 Madhu Unnikrishnan, "Air France CEO Stays Upbeat on Summer Amid Global Turmoil," *Skift*, March 24, 2022. https://mopays.com/air-france-ceo-stays-upbeat-on-summer-amid-global-turmoil/.

6 What if airlines could do more with less?

To do more with less calls for airlines to look for new ways to plan and new ways to introduce innovation. The object is, presumably, to use existing resources more intensively (fleet, workforces, airport facilities, maintenance facilities, and so forth) to minimize costs while developing a competitive positioning. Also, the objective is to develop capabilities for an airline to become much more agile to adapt to the marketplace that has become much more turbulent. Think about the impact on airlines of not only the pandemic, that began to spread rapidly at the beginning of 2020, but also the political upheaval in Eastern Europe that started in late February 2022. Both events led to a dramatic fluctuation in passenger and freight demand, making it a challenge for airlines to adapt to these two situations. These two events simply added to the multiple forces of change that airlines had been dealing with since the beginning of this century. Now relating to the pandemic, think about the changes required in networks and schedules due to space closures. Think also about the increase in the price of fuel because of the recent political situation in Eastern Europe. Therefore, the question faced by many airlines is not whether to transform but how to transform so as to do more with less and to do so on a continuing basis.

As stated before, and it is worth repeating, consumers' lifestyles have been changing for many years. COVID-19 has simply accelerated the rate of change. Think about an increase in online shopping, virtual communications, hybrid ways of working, and a much greater focus on having a better life. These changes, in consumer behavior and expectations, are calling for fundamental changes in the marketing and planning functions to reduce costs, develop and provide much more meaningful customer experience, and become much more agile. Relating to the last point, as discussed in the previous book, the airline industry could easily face some other crisis of equal, or even higher magnitude—climate change, cybersecurity, and political conflicts at a regional level but with global implications.[1] The current situation in Eastern Europe is just one example of the third potential change identified. Consequently, risk, and its management, are becoming much more important elements in the planning process. In the previous book, there was a significant discussion, for example, on the need for senior management to develop a relevant purpose. This aspect is now critical to focus on the value

DOI: 10.4324/9781003332824-6

provided to customers, relating not just to price and product features, as well as authenticity and trust, but also to sustainability. This chapter outlines some examples of best practices from leading businesses to help airlines think through some effective ways to navigate through the ongoing turbulence to be able to do more with less.

Let us start with some thoughts on an effective planning framework going forward. Countless books have been written on corporate strategy and planning. Here are just three existing frameworks that might provide value for airline planners to do more with less.

Collaborating by design

How can an airline identify future disruptions to figure out the dynamics of the upcoming marketplace? According to some business researchers, while big data and algorithms have important roles to play, it is the small data that can help identify signals to anticipate major disruptions and develop effective strategies. Again, according to Martin Schwirn, it is small data that can provide clues to big disruptions, and a business should "filter" small data to "identify the small signals of change." The researcher lays out clearly, in his book, the need to filter vital information, identify what matters, prioritize the critical change, and initiate relevant strategies.[2] One point made by the author is very compelling, namely, that change starts with small data and that it is the process of *scanning* that lets planners anticipate the future.

Within the airline industry, what small data could be filtered to "see" the future, for example, of low-cost carriers in the Asia-Pacific region and consolidation worldwide? Low-cost carriers had achieved about a 30% capacity share in the Asia-Pacific market prior to the start of the pandemic. The share varied by country, of course. In India, low-cost carriers had the highest share, approaching almost 70%. Would this share continue to increase in India? Think about the plans of a new carrier in India, Akasa Air. With respect to consolidation, what small data could provide some clues? El Al is moving forward with acquiring Arkia, another airline based in Israel, and making it a wholly owned subsidiary. Would it develop and maintain two brands, as in the case of Air France and KLM? Would a small airline acquiring a large airline be an important signal of change? How about Azul, in Brazil, acquiring LATAM?

Once they identify small signals of change, leading businesses design strategies through collaboration, involving not only customers and employees but also other stakeholders, such as suppliers and partners. Should airlines consider developing a "process" on small data signals to identify and prepare alternative network and schedule scenarios? This framework, beginning to be known as "open strategy," suggests that a business open its strategic initiatives to multiple stakeholders, both internal (e.g., employees) and external (e.g., customers and suppliers). According to Stadler et al., this process provides benefits in three areas—idea generation, analysis and formulation, and implementation. These researchers provide many real-world examples of the use of open strategies. For example, capitalizing on the input from employees,

Barclays Bank used an open strategy framework to transition from the traditional branch networks to mobile banking. In a second example, the researchers discuss how Adidas used this framework to develop and execute a strategy to introduce 100% recyclable performance running shoes. In their third example, IBM used a strategy jam that connected thousands of people across IBM's organization to identify multiple businesses to develop its "smarter planet" initiative.[3] Think about how a global airline could design a well-crafted strategy jam to capitalize on its thousands of employees based around the world.

To do more with less, collaboration across boundaries, previously referred to as integration across functions, is vital. It is not a new business concept for airlines. Except now there is a greater urgency for an airline to get the concept implemented to become, for example, a digital airline by capitalizing on diverse viewpoints, skills, and resources to identify solutions. Keep in mind that the complexity of the airline business has been increasing, not decreasing, leading to a need for effective collaboration to find solutions. New techniques are now available to get cross-functional integration done quickly and effectively. If the concept is not new and new techniques are available, what is a major barrier in the airline industry to collaborate across boundaries? In one word, culture. With the lack of a facilitating culture, it has not been possible to achieve collaboration internally within an airline, across different functions, let alone externally, with other organizations within the ecosystem, for example, between airlines and airports. How would an airline overcome the major barrier of culture and design effective ways to not only collaborate internally but also collaborate within the ecosystem? According to some business researchers, one way to change culture is to use networks. According to these researchers of organizational culture, there are two common ways of determining where an organization stands. One is to use surveys to evaluate employees' values and behaviors and then average their responses to measure where the organization stands. A second approach is to conduct interviews and then develop personas to identify how the behavior of "typical" employees is guided by their values. Both techniques have some value. However, more value can be obtained from knowing who is interacting with whom to determine inner workings.[4]

Think about a parallel situation in the healthcare industry during the COVID-19 crisis.[5] During this pandemic, things that seemed impossible to do in the healthcare system were made possible within weeks or days by changing organizations, taking new approaches, and creating new processes. In the pharmaceutical sector, it used to take several years to develop a vaccine, have it approved, and then launch it through mass production (with all the necessary logistics aspects). During the pandemic, pharmaceutical giants, partnering with start-ups (e.g., Pfizer and BioNTech) to bring to market a vaccine leveraging groundbreaking technology, in a record time. It was reported that China even built a full hospital in one week.[6] Many other companies, outside of the healthcare industry, also came up with disruptive ideas during the pandemic. For example, Dyson went from making vacuums to ventilators in just 10 days.[7] Such companies must have fully rethought their way of working to do more with less.

The next insight from leading businesses to plan effectively is (1) to use a captivating scoreboard with leading and lagging measures of an airline's progress toward meeting customers' changing behaviors and expectations and (2) to use clear but simple key performance indicators (KPIs). A scorecard, particularly if it works within a visual framework, shows in near real time how a strategy is working. It would also be helpful if an airline were to have access to leading and lagging indicators relating to the use of a smart scoreboard. Leading measures would show what the strategy group is doing and lagging indicators would show what the group is getting.[8] The use of a smart scoreboard would help manage innovation effectively. As for KPIs, one of the best practices is to keep KPIs simple, but clear, as stated above. Three practitioners with experience from Agoda, the Asia-based subsidiary of the Booking Holdings travel group, provide an insightful example.[9] These practitioners suggest the use of "a KPI, plus a constraint" concept. They describe the process in detail when they were trying to improve the effectiveness of Agoda's website and a mobile app through which customers searched, selected, and purchased travel products. The object was to increase the conversion rate, or the ratio of website visits to sales. A simple but clear KPI was developed using a comprehensive experimentation process. For an airline scheduler, one example of "a KPI, plus a constraint" could be to maximize profitability without reducing reliability.

Next, there are three organizational changes that could add much value for large legacy airlines: (1) the development of an internal team with the purpose of destroying the airline, and another internal team to recreate a modern airline from the airline destroyed; (2) the development of partnerships with innovative start-ups; and (3) the development of an organizational design practice to solve for "stagility." As discussed later, a previous book in this series already discussed the value of challenging the status quo. Woodward et al. provide a three-step process—creating a "different mindset, habits, and behaviors"; anticipating changes and opportunities; and being willing to "engage with diverse viewpoints."[10] Creating internal destructive teams is also not a new concept in the business world. Jack Welch used it when he was leading General Electric. However, it is easier now, given the availability of new technologies that a team can use to destroy an airline in many more ways and for another team to recreate it, again, in many ways. The application of this concept opens new ways for an airline, or an airport for that matter, to transform itself to do more with less.

Large legacy airlines can benefit by developing meaningful and effective partnerships with innovative start-ups. Although some airlines have developed partnerships, they have not changed their organizational structures to capitalize on the true values of partnerships. There are inherent challenges of having a very large airline partnering with a start-up. The large airline has heavy and complex processes to follow, for example, long decision-making processes. The start-up would be a lightweight, fast, and an agile group. There needs to be a "clutch" between these two structures to work efficiently. The idea is not just to partner, but also to collaborate with an innovative start-up to (a) find solutions for pain points and (b) develop a digital capability (discussed in the next section).[11] Shameen Prashantham provides an excellent case study of how Microsoft developed value-adding partnerships by three basic steps: getting start-up partnering off the ground, extending a deepening start-up engagement, and mainstreaming start-up partnering into the core strategy. The author provides further insights from the work of Microsoft with start-ups: co-aligning with strategy, co-innovating with start-ups, and co-evolving with ecosystems.[12]

In discussions with CEOs worldwide, three partners at McKinsey & Company (Carolyn Dewar, Scott Keller, and Vikram Malhotra) identified an important organizational design practice, coined as "stagility," a practice in which an organization develops both stable and agile disciplines to achieve high performance. According to the CEOs interviewed, stability and agility are not trade-offs. Both need to be present. The authors, Carolyn Dewar, et al, provide an example of the value of "stagility" that dates to 1943. Lockheed Martin created its Skunk Works team to develop a completely new aircraft. Think about one of its achievements. With a clear purpose and empowerment to get things done, the group developed the first jet fighter for the armed forces, the XP-80, in 143 days, from start to finish. According to these business researchers, the best CEOs "*stop the pendulum swing; emphasize accountability; think helix, not matrix; make 'smart' choices.*"[13]

While airlines are aware of the need for transformation of their planning processes, and some are even aware that substantial transformation cannot take place without a change in corporate culture, the latter is not taking place. Effective collaboration is not taking place, for example. The key is the fact that not only are customers' beliefs, behaviors, priorities, and values changing, but so are employees'. Therefore, the change in culture needs to be on a proactive basis as opposed to a reactive basis to achieve effective transformation of the business. Some examples of the need to change corporate culture are the need to have much greater collaboration both inside and outside the organization, the willingness to take greater risks, and the willingness to create learning organizations. Regarding the last point, examples of a learning mindset are the willingness to do more experiments from which greater learning can take place and the willingness for decisions to be driven by data. Some executives may ask if data-driven decisions make any sense in a time of accelerating change and increasing complexity. The answer would appear to be yes, given the ability to collect data in near real time and from multiple sources, not to mention the ability to use artificial intelligence (AI)/machine learning to see patterns. The COVID-19 pandemic has clearly made travel more complex for airlines and travelers. For travelers, for example, the search is not just based on price and schedules, but also on restrictions, charges, in-flight connectivity, and the impact of the itinerary on climate change. And for airlines, complexity has increased, relating not only to the uncertainty of the demand but also to supply, given the uncertainty, in recent times, relating to the availability of crews.

At many airlines, the business still lacks true focus on customers, employees, and innovation. All three require a change in culture. The CEO, the

C-suite, and the middle managers are still not on the same page, a situation that leads to confusion at the frontline staff level. To start with, there are insufficient incentives to change. For example, it is difficult to understand, let alone explain why digital transformation is needed. Employees need to know that they are respected. They need more satisfaction, and they now have a greater need to balance their work and life.[14] A better work–life balance, relative to pay, has been on peoples' minds for many years prior to the pandemic. The pandemic simply got many people to change their careers to improve this balance. Just as experience and value are in the eyes of customers, culture is in the eyes of employees. It is important not only to get timely feedback from employees but also to understand it and take visible actions.

The airline industry is complex and one way to deal with complexity is to increase collaboration within the ecosystems. Think of the process to turn around an aircraft that can take up to two hours for large transoceanic flights. There are many people involved and many third parties. Effective collaboration, using data, mobile applications, and biometrics, will not only save costs but also improve customer service or experience, or both, not to mention achieve operational excellence. The key lies in the improvement of collaboration, both within the airline and within the ecosystem. For example, the flow of information within different parts of the airline and between different organizations outside of the airline may have been reasonable relating to past standards, but they are not adequate to handle the new situation in which the marketplace is much more dynamic and certain actions that are needed are much more time-critical. The information needs to get to the right person at the right time through the right communication channel and with greater speed. This requires the use of integrated platforms.

Think about the flow of information between a pilot of an incoming flight and the ATC, the airport, the operations control center, gate managers, ground controllers, the ramp supervisor, ground services providers, and dispatchers. Of course, the flow of this information exists now. But think about the additional value that can be generated if the information was available in real time, and among all partners—the assignment of a new gate in a different terminal, the need for five passengers to deplane quickly and be escorted to their gates due to the lateness of the arriving flight, the sudden increase in the number of passengers to be boarded due to another flight being canceled, the additional fuel to be loaded due to strong winds, the additional baggage to be loaded from another flight coming from a different gate, the failure of an in-flight system, and the sudden drop in temperature combined with the start of rain to require the airplane to be de-iced.

Finally, it is important to point out that it is not just the need for collaboration, but that the process for collaboration must be designed. The design aspects of the collaboration process need to be facilitated as, according to experts, design and facilitation are part science and part art.[15]

Building digital resiliency capabilities

Technologies are clearly enabling some companies to become digital companies. Consider how Amazon has used digital technologies to extend the scope of its business (from books to consumer electronics to groceries) and to do it with scale.[16] Scale was a desirable feature as it added value for customers in terms of lower costs and better customer experience. In the case of an airline, its businesses became more complex as the airline expanded in size or the breadth of its operations or both. What insights could an airline gain from Amazon that seems to have managed its complexity by digitalizing its operating systems that relate to customers' orders, the breadth of products offered, recommendations based on customers' preferences, and fast delivery times? Scale, scope, and learning can be achieved using digital technologies, vast amounts of data and analytics, and changes in the processes themselves. Of course, airlines are good at forecasting demand and matching capacity, having taken into consideration all aspects of flight and ground operations—crews, maintenance, airport facilities, and so forth. See the discussion in Chapters 2 and 3. However, Amazon seems to have raised the bar for the demand–supply–delivery optimization. From Amazon's experience, it is the combination of AI/machine learning, data, algorithms, and analytics that is the engine that drives the demand–capacity–service optimization. Think about the functionalities of the Alexa system, built, presumably, with input from third parties. Think about the possibilities of similar systems for airlines that could be built with input from third parties.

Just to see how AI is transforming everything, from "society, economics, politics, and foreign policy," readers are referred to a new book by Kissinger, Schmidt, and Huttenlocher, in which they describe how advances in printing in the 15th century changed people's lives by making knowledge accessible to the public and how now AI will also change the way people live through the availability of new information.[17] Similarly, Martin Ford suggests that AI is "altering every dimension of human life, often for the better." However, he also warns that artificial intelligence has the capacity to do harm, through the creation, for example, of "AI-generated audio and video events that never happened."[18] Nevertheless, AI, along with other technologies and the availability of huge amounts of data and analytics, will help airline marketers push the boundaries of their marketing strategies. Raja Rajamannar, chief marketing officer of Mastercard, suggests, for example, "Just like Quantum Physics came in where classical physics failed to tackle, Quantum Marketing will step in where classical marketing fails."[19] The author first discusses the existing four paradigms of marketing—product, emotional, data-driven, and digital and social—and then adds a fifth paradigm, quantum. In his concluding chapter, he provides 21 key attributes of quantum chief marketing officers and concludes that "[m]arketing cannot be run by pure common sense. It takes a fine blend of the art and science of marketing."[20] In a similar way, Simon Mulcahy, chief innovation officer at Salesforce, and Karen Semone, senior director of innovation at Salesforce, go further and suggest that there is a need to focus on the "art, science, and magic" of selling.[21] Leading airlines have already begun to use AI, not just to improve revenue, operations, and customer experience (e.g., AI-powered chatbots and virtual assistants), but they can now go much further to learn about the changing customer behavior, with the use of smart digital customer-engagement platforms.

Think also of the blockchain technology that has been transforming business sectors from the financial sector to supply chains, affecting many businesses. Applications in the airline industry range from increasing efficiencies in the maintenance, repair, and operations sector, to adding more value to distribution systems and loyalty programs. For example, could blockchain technology help an airline to reduce its distribution costs and provide more personalized products and services? See two thought leadership pieces in Chapter 8, one by Christopher Gibbs (relating to maintenance) and the other by Evert de Boer (relating to loyalty programs).

Going forward, the changing needs of customers and employees can best be explored by using digital platforms. Some business researchers are concluding, for example, that the creation of a superior end-to-end personalized customer experience, at scale, requires the effective use of algorithms and data. Coincidently, state-of-the-art platforms are now available that not only can accommodate multiple buyers and suppliers, but being digital, they also have embedded algorithms that can analyze data and patterns and have the language processing capability to solve consumers' problems.[22] Additionally, while big data is generally described in terms of three attributes, volume, velocity, and variety, some business researchers are pointing to a fourth attribute, value, that can be derived from the use of analytics and machine learning to achieve differentiation.[23] Kane et al. point out the importance of developing a mindset for value and how value can be derived from data. They call this mindset "data as a strategic asset."[24]

As for employees, it is now imperative to invest in employees and their work experiences. One competitive advantage, according to a business researcher, Jack Altman, is to focus on people strategy.[25] While the concept of the value of a people strategy is hardly new in the airline industry (think about the achievements of Southwest Airlines), the challenge has been to implement an effective people strategy through the remaking of culture and building a truly operative engagement system. And just as the concept of empathy is critical for improving customer experience, it is just as critical for improving employee experience. The challenge, however, is to identify tactics relating to people, culture, and performance. Altman discusses in detail what people want out of work—purpose, community, and growth. Businesses can solve problems of customers and employees if they develop a different mindset to empower people to drive change to create value.[26] To improve employee experience, it is important to know what now motivates employees as they evaluate their place of employment. Is it pay, insurance benefits, training benefits, and so forth, relating to material offerings? In recent years, according to human resources experts, it appears to be more on how employees feel about the company they work for, more than the material benefits.

For some insights on digital transformation, airlines may want to investigate the experience of the financial community that has been going through a digital transformation. Banks, for example, are engaging with their customers to offer personalized products and services, at the right times, to become relevant. They are thinking about how to provide end-to-end services, facilitated by technologies, such as open platforms, public cloud, digital identities, and ONE Order. In the case of airlines, open platforms can help customers get access to a variety of services, relating to end-to-end travel, for example, other modes of transportation, hotels, and different retailers of products and services at destinations. The point is that these products and services can be marketed at scale with the flow of intelligent data, supported by the cloud, and integrated into the cloud. Going forward, digital identities can facilitate the recognition of customers for the development and provision of personalized services. The availability of a ONE Order feature simply makes it easy for a customer to order multiple products and services coming from multiple selling partners.

Strategizing for positional superiority

The capability to do more with less, also requires innovation that is related to the brand. What if an airline were to move effectively from insights to actions to drive brand growth? In a highly competitive and low-margin business, as in the case of airlines, shouldn't the object be to grow the value of the brand? This strategy requires a different type of thinking and planning than the thinking for effective scheduling and revenue management. The object would now be to develop and position the airline for a competitive advantage. Airlines clearly do substantial amounts of consumer research relating to problems experienced by customers and potential solutions for these problems. The challenge seems to have been not in the stage of identifying the problems faced by different segments of consumers but at the stage of identifying the effectiveness of solutions from the perspective of customers, not airlines.

Compare the value proposition of an airline in the form of a pyramid shown in Figure 6.1. The bottom layer might be the value of an itinerary and the price. The next layer might relate to on-time performance and the loyalty program. The layer above might relate to the purchase of the itinerary and the experience relating to the trip (on the ground and in the cabin). The next layer might be related to the peace of mind, relating, in turn, to such aspects as the passenger being taken care of during a disruption. The final layer might be the capability to make an end-to-end reservation at one place either at the initial time or at any time during the entire journey. How would an airline display an image of these attributes on a perceptual map?

Think of the automotive industry with a perceptual map with two dimensions. As demonstrated by Kimberly Whitler in her book, the vertical axis could, for example, be practical and affordable at the bottom, and classy and distinctive, at the top. The horizontal axis could be conservative on the left-hand side and sporty on the right-hand side. Different cars could then be displayed in

Figure 6.1 Value propositions of an airline

different locations in the four quadrants.[27] How would such a perceptual map be developed for the airline industry? One could start with a simple display of basic and full service along the *x*-axis and regional versus global networks along the *y*-axis. See Figure 6.2. How could different airlines display themselves even on this very basic perceptual map? Think about the possibility of American (AA), Etihad (EY), and Singapore (SQ) on the bottom right quadrant. Think about Ryanair (FR) and Wizz Air (W6) on the left-hand side, and Bangkok Airways (PG) on the top right-hand quadrant. The point is not the exact location of these airlines, but how much space is open for airlines to display themselves even on this very basic map. Who would be the "Mercedes" or the "Toyota" or the "Ford" of the airline industry? While some airline brands are better than others, it is a relative statement. Is there an airline that is the "Apple" or the "Disney" or the "Amazon" or the "Nike" of the airline industry?

An airline, measuring its brand relative to other airlines may not make much sense any way since consumers compare airline brands to other well-known brands to which they relate. The point is not for an airline to just position itself for competitive advantage relative to other airlines, but also to position itself for competitive advantage relative to other global brands. While the strategy is clear, the tactics on how to do it are less clear. The tactics require more than promoting on-time performance and competitive prices. See the discussion by Glenn Hollister in his thought leadership piece in Chapter 8. There is also a need for developing a purpose from the perspective of consumers. There is a need to show authenticity and very clear value propositions. While the need to develop a purpose has become a high priority for leading businesses, the process to do so is a challenge. Some business

What if airlines could do more with less? 103

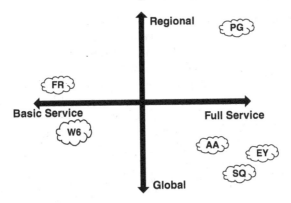

Figure 6.2 A simple conceptual map of airlines

researchers are even raising the question: "What Is the Purpose of Your Purpose?"[28] If the purpose is cause-based, then there needs to be clarity. For example, Patagonia says it is in business "to save our home planet."[29]

What if an airline hired a chief marketing officer (CMO) who had served as a CMO of Procter & Gamble (P&G) but had no experience in the airline industry? True, one cannot compare products like Tide and Pampers with products like flights in the New York–Los Angeles market and flights in the New York–London market. However, are not the processes to gain insights into customers and competitors similar? Also, are the processes to evaluate the capabilities of an organization and the competencies of the business, similar? How about the process to create a compelling brand and the communication of its value? Are they not the same across industries?

What if a global airline decided, even with a significant marketing cost, to own the "air travel space" and become a clear choice for consumers? How would it brand itself? True, it would face challenges, such as the lack of route authority to serve markets worldwide, but it could develop creative ways to work with partners in the ecosystem. True, it would mean that part of its brand will now be under the control of its partners in the ecosystem. However, the key challenge and the opportunity would be to identify consumer problems and see what solutions the airline can provide to solve the problem and then how to brand itself accordingly. The challenge is not how to develop a new route or a new bundle but how the product would solve a customer's problem. The challenge is to identify a customer's problem and to see if the solution provided helps the customer. And, of course, the problem may not be the product, but rather the experience, as discussed in Chapter 4. Most important, the object is to solve a customer's problem, not an airline's problem, for example, if the flight needs to leave at a specific time, due to the availability of a gate or a crew or maintenance or air traffic control.

What are the sources of data to identify consumers' problems—surveys, social media, third parties, purchase behavior, or employees? What are the effective ways of listening to and then observing consumers? The challenge can also be not just to identify problems but to know if consumers are willing to pay for their solutions as well. A customer may want an airline to get her to her destination on time. But if the cancelation of the last flight requires the customer to be placed on a competitor's flight, would the customer be willing to pay the higher price charged by the competitor? Some airlines tried offering concierge services at airports, but the demand for such services was minuscule. There are options for security clearance that offer a better customer experience, for example, precheck (fast-track) and the organization Clear. However, many consumers do not subscribe to these services, presumably, due to their costs, and therefore, they end up standing in long lines.

How does an airline decide what promise to make? Should it be the lowest price or the best on-time performance? What can an airline do to develop brand value in terms of built-in benefits, both tangible and emotional? What KPIs can an airline use to evaluate its brand promise and its brand image? What is the brand today and what should be the desired positioning? And how can an airline get there? The point is to understand how consumers make decisions, how they made them in the past, and how they will make them in the future. How do consumers compare brands, for example, American, Delta, and United in the US and Air France, British Airways, and Lufthansa in Europe? Of course, in some cases, the decision may be made by the corporate travel policy. The brand evaluation decision becomes more complex in international travel. For example, in the New York–London market, the evaluation is not just among American, Delta, and United but also with British Airways and Virgin Atlantic. It becomes even murkier when a consumer is faced with two airlines in a partnership, involving a marketing carrier, and an operating carrier. What would be the axes of comparison? Think about the auto industry where the axes could be practical versus luxury and conservative versus sporty. From another perspective, should an airline use marketing influencers to shape consumer behavior using social media, Twitter, and WeChat, for example? For some examples of non-airline businesses (for instance, Volkswagen and P&G) using key influencers, see the book by Kimberly Whitler.[30]

What is the image that consumers have of an airline's brand? On what knowledge is this image based? How does the behavior change relative to the image? How familiar are consumers with the brand, and in any case, who are the consumers (all segments of the population or just the targeted consumers)? How is the image developed from this knowledge? For example, is the image related to such attributes as innovation, reliability, and trustworthiness, or specific attributes, such as the boarding process, in-flight services, and on-time performance? And let us not overlook the gap between what is stated and promised in a brand (reliability and customer care) and what is actually delivered. What if an airline says, you missed the connecting flight, and you are on your own not only to find a hotel but also to pay for the hotel accommodations, given the fare category of your travel? Think about Walmart's brand promise: "Save Money, Live Better" or "Super Value, Lowest Prices."

Empathy, another dimension of the brand relates not only to engaging with customers to understand their needs but also to accessing information to develop insights to find solutions to their problems. What if an airline really began to understand how customers become aware of an airline's products and how their products can fulfill customers' needs? How do customers develop trust that an airline will deliver on the value promised? How do airlines truly find out if customers are really satisfied to a degree that they will become promoters? Consider how much effort an airline devotes to the development, pricing, and distribution of its products. How much effort is devoted by, even a large airline, to the positioning of not just these product features but to the brand of the airline as well?

The previous five chapters discussed a new era in airline planning because of fundamental changes in the dynamics of the marketplace, not to mention important changes in consumers' lifestyles and, in turn, their shifting behaviors and expectations. This new era calls for airlines not only to plan in near real time but also to do more with less, the subject of this chapter. What if a new airline was formed from the combination of two existing airlines, not just to gain scale at the starting point but also to deploy the concepts discussed in the previous five chapters and in this chapter? What if this airline were to undertake dynamic scheduling and dynamic pricing with total cross-functional integration between all subfunctions in the commercial and all subfunctions in the operational areas? What if this airline also strategized to achieve positional superiority? The next chapter discusses the conceptual framework for such an airline, Agility Airlines.

Highlights

- Risk, and its management, have become major elements of the planning process within the airline industry.
- Airlines need to strategize to develop superior positions to develop and grow the value of their brands. Therefore, airlines should build digital resiliency capabilities.
- Technologies can enable airlines to become digital companies.
- Airlines now need to collaborate, internally and externally, by design.
- This strategy requires a different type of thinking and planning than the thinking and planning of schedule and price management.

Notes

1 Nawal K. Taneja, *Airlines in a Post-Pandemic World: Preparing for Constant Turbulence Ahead* (London, UK: Routledge, 2021), p. 2.
2 Martin Schwirn, *Small Data, Big Disruptions: How to Spot Signals of Change and Manage Uncertainty* (Newburyport, MA: Career Press, 2021), p. 11.
3 Christian Stadler, Julia Hautz, Kurt Matzler, and Stephan Friedrich von den Eichen, *Open Strategy: Mastering Disruption from Outside the C-Suite* (Cambridge, MA: MIT Press, 2021), pp. 52, 159, 190–191, and 205.
4 Peter Gray, Rob Cross, and Michael Arena, "Use Networks to Drive Culture Change," *MIT Sloan Management Review*, Winter 2022.
5 Gerald C. Kane, Rich Nanda, Anh Nguyen Phillips, and Jonathan R. Copulsky, *The Transformation Myth: Leading Your Organization through Uncertain Times* (Cambridge, MA: MIT Press, 2021), ch. 10.

6 https://www.bbc.com/news/world-asia-china-51245156.
7 https://www.popularmechanics.com/science/health/a31943465/dyson-ventilators/.
8 Chris McChesney, Sean Covey, and Jim Huling, *The 4 Disciplines of Execution: Achieving Wildly Important Goals*, 2nd ed. (New York: Simon & Schuster, 2021), p. 81.
9 Omri Morgenshtern, Robert Rosenstein, and Peter L. Allen, "The Quest for a Killer KPI," *MIT Sloan Management Review*, Spring 2022, March 8, 2022.
10 Ian C. Woodward, V. "Paddy" Padmanabhan, Sameer Hasija, and Ram Charan, *The Phoenix Encounter Method: Lead Like Your Business Is on Fire* (New York: McGraw-Hill, 2021).
11 Shameen Prashantham, *Gorillas Can Dance: Lessons from Microsoft and Other Corporations on Partnering with Startups* (Hoboken, NJ: Wiley, 2022).
12 Shameen Prashantham, *Gorillas Can Dance: Lessons from Microsoft and Other Corporations on Partnering with Startups* (Hoboken, NJ: Wiley, 2022), pp. xxxiii and lix.
13 Carolyn Dewar, Scott Keller, and Vikram Malhotra, *CEO Excellence: The Six Mindsets That Distinguish the Best Leaders from the Rest* (New York: Simon & Schuster, 2022), pp. 86–87.
14 Donald Sull and Charles Sull, "10 Things Your Corporate Culture Needs to Get Right," *MIT Sloan Management Review*, September 16, 2021. https://sloanreview.mit.edu/article/10-things-your-corporate-culture-needs-to-get-right/.
15 Philippe Coullomb and Charles Collingwood-Boots, *Collaboration by Design: Your Field Guide for Creating More Value When Bringing People Together* (Sydney, Australia: wheretofromhere?, 2017).
16 Marco Iansiti and Karim R. Lakhani, *Competing in the Age of AI: Strategy and Leadership when Algorithms and Network Run the World* (Boston, MA: Harvard Business Review Press, 2020), pp. 9–12.
17 Henry A. Kissinger, Eric Schmidt, and Daniel Huttenlocher, *The Age of AI: And Our Human Future* (New York: Little, Brown and Co., 2021), ch. 7.
18 Martin Ford, *Rule of the Robots: How Artificial Intelligence Will Transform Everything* (New York: Basic Books, 2021), front flap.
19 Raja Rajamannar, *Quantum Marketing: Mastering the New Marketing Mindset for Tomorrow's Consumers* (New York: HarperCollins, 2021), front jacket.
20 Raja Rajamannar, *Quantum Marketing: Mastering the New Marketing Mindset for Tomorrow's Consumers* (New York: HarperCollins, 2021), ch. 18 and p. 197.
21 https://jbarrows.com/blog/simon-mulcahy-karen-semone-art-science-magic-of-selling/.
22 Ram Charan and Geri Willigan, *Rethinking Competitive Advantage: New Rules for the Digital Age* (New York: Currency, 2021), ch. 4.
23 Gerald C. Kane, Rich Nanda, Anh Nguyen Phillips, and Jonathan R. Copulsky, *The Transformation Myth: Leading Your Organization through Uncertain Times* (Cambridge, MA: MIT Press, 2021), ch. 7.
24 Gerald C. Kane, Rich Nanda, Anh Nguyen Phillips, and Jonathan R. Copulsky, *The Transformation Myth: Leading Your Organization through Uncertain Times* (Cambridge, MA: MIT Press, 2021), p. 106.
25 Jack Altman, *People Strategy: How to Invest in People and Make Culture Your Competitive Advantage* (New York: Wiley, 2021).
26 Brant Cooper, *Disruption Proof: Empower People, Create Value, Drive Change* (New York: Grand Central, 2021).
27 Kimberly A. Whitler, *Positioning for Advantage: Techniques and Strategies to Grow Brand Value* (New York: Columbia University Press, 2021), p. 78.
28 Jonathan Knowles, B. Tom Hunsaker, Hannah Grove, and Alison James, "What Is the Purpose of Your Purpose?," *Harvard Business Review*, March–April 2022.

29 https://www.google.com/search?q=patagonia+purpose+statement&rlz=1C1GCEA_enUS950US950&oq=patagonia%27s+purpsoe&aqs=y2.69i57j0i10i13j0i13i3012j0i8i13i3012j0i39014.13381j0j7&sourceid=chrome&ie=UTF-8.
30 Kimberly A. Whitler, *Positioning for Advantage: Techniques and Strategies to Grow Brand Value* (New York: Columbia University Press, 2021), pp. 169–171.

7 What if airlines could truly differentiate themselves?

What if an airline, existing or new, applied all the principles discussed in the previous six chapters? That is, could an airline, in answering all the big, transformational questions posed in this book, truly differentiate itself from its competitors? Could it gain a significant and maintainable competitive advantage?

To answer this question, let us discuss the characteristics of an airline that applied all the principles in this book. To make the example more interesting, let us discuss a hypothetical airline in the context of a merger between two existing airlines. Why choose two existing airlines? The major thesis of this book is that airlines need to ask themselves major transformational questions and that answering these questions requires a practical mindset. Discussing the application of the principles deliberated in this book is much easier when dealing with a real-life example—say, a merger between JetBlue Airways and Alaska Airlines.

Applying the principles in practice

JetBlue Airways

JetBlue, the seventh-largest airline in North America (based on the number of passengers transported), operates more than 1,000 flights a day to destinations in the US, Latin America, and, recently, Europe. JetBlue has about 20,000 employees and operates out of six focus cities. The three larger ones are New York, Boston, and Fort Lauderdale. The three smaller ones are Orlando, San Juan, and Los Angeles. The airline operates a fleet of about 280 aircraft, mostly Airbus (220s, 320-200s, 321-200s, 321LRs, and 321neos), and Embraer 190s. Although JetBlue is not a member of any of the three major alliances, it does have codeshare agreements with about 20 airlines, including some in the three global alliances.

Since its beginning, JetBlue has already focused on differentiating its products and services. To start with, the carrier developed a vision to "bring humanity back to air travel." Although a low-cost carrier, JetBlue started operations with all-new aircraft with operations from New York's Kennedy (JFK) Airport. The airline started with a differentiated onboard service (seat-back entertainment), live television, and satellite radio. The airline also offered

DOI: 10.4324/9781003332824-7

more legroom, no cost for checking bags, and little to no fees for changing reservations. The key element of using the JFK Airport was the ability to capture many airport slots. The carrier also acquired the smaller Embraer 190s to open new, smaller markets. These marketing strategies paid off as JetBlue was able to compete much more effectively with the low-cost divisions of the larger established airlines—Delta's Song and, United's Ted. In 2014, JetBlue introduced its Mint service in transcontinental markets in the US, a bold strategy that produced effective competition. Then in 2021, JetBlue started to offer transatlantic service, between New York and London, a market in which not only is the demand very high, but the fares are also very high.

Alaska Airlines

Alaska Airlines, based in Seattle, is the sixth-largest airline in North America (based on the number of passengers transported), and has about 15,000 employees. Alaska Airlines, along with its two regional partners, Horizon Air and SkyWest Airlines, operates a large domestic route network, focused on connecting passengers from the Pacific Northwest, West Coast, and Alaska to more than 100 destinations within the US, Canada, Costa Rica, and Mexico. Alaska Airlines has four focus cities (Seattle, Portland, Anchorage, Los Angeles), with a primary hub in Seattle. It is now a member of the oneworld alliance. The airline operates a fleet of about 250 aircraft, mostly different versions of the 737, and about 40 aircraft that are in the 320 and 321 families. There are about another 100 operated by the subsidiaries—Embraer 175s and the Bombardier Q400s. Alaska Airlines does not fly to Asia but partners with other airlines to fly from five West Coast gateways (Vancouver, Seattle, San Francisco, Los Angeles, San Diego) to destinations in Asia, such as Beijing, Hong Kong, Osaka, Seoul, Shanghai, Singapore, and Tokyo.

Alaska Airlines has been ranked, by J. D. Power and Associates, as having a very high level of customer satisfaction for many years. In 2016, Alaska Airlines acquired Virgin America, creating a premier airline in the West Coast. Three examples of good service are reported to be (1) that the airline understands the difference between multichannel and omnichannel, (2) that the airline finds creative ways to provide perks to flyers, and (3) that the airline empowers its employees to find solutions to customers' problems before they intensify. Alaska Airlines has also shown innovation in introducing subscription plans.

Characteristics of Agility Airlines

For convenience, let us refer to the new combined JetBlue–Alaska entity as "Agility Airlines" to represent an airline that is extremely agile in its planning practices.

Some airlines, including Agility, are recognizing the emerging social changes and starting to transform their processes to extend the boundaries of their businesses, to go beyond their traditional domains. Think about the brand vision "to enrich the lives of our customers." But how can an airline adapt its products and services to improve the lives of its customers? While the concept is not new, how to do it effectively remains a challenge. Traditional ways of doing market research and the use of big data (and data science) can help. But people's lives are changing at a faster rate, not just by the expanded use of social media but also the influence of the digital revolution and hyper-connectivity. And as mentioned in this book, in addition to the use of big data, there could also be much value in the use of small data to "see" signals of change, to "see" emerging patterns, and to "see" the emerging needs of customers. Agility will focus on understanding customer behavior, customer expectations, and customer needs to identify the important, unsatisfied needs of its customers. Recall the discussion in the book on how the developers of mobile phones began to develop product features to meet the changing lifestyle of consumers—text messaging and emailing capabilities, taking pictures, and making videos with their phones, and having access to a broad spectrum of apps and the internet. Agility can focus not only on strategies to address the unmet needs of customers but also on the skills needed to acquire new customers.

Using some of the points discussed in this book, Agility can redesign its products and services well beyond renovation and iteration stages to totally transform its products and services through the generation of new ideas and with new ways to scale them, particularly with the extensive engagement with its customers and its employees. It can introduce intrapreneurship within the company by partnering much more effectively with start-up groups. It can develop a broader ecosystem of partners to deliver value to customers during their end-to-end traveler journeys by removing friction at each and every touch point. JetBlue has already been trying to evolve from being an airline to being a travel company, transforming, for example, not only its services in the ultra-short-haul segments but also to become a lifestyle brand.

Network and schedule planning

The starting point for Agility Airlines can be the development of its network in a different way, with agility, and schedules that are economically much more viable and operationally much more robust in the near term. Solutions can be based on the use of new data (e.g., shopping data), new techniques (e.g., dynamic scheduling), and new technologies (e.g., machine learning). The midterm goal can be to develop new products, such as viable nonstop services in low-density markets, door-to-door services, new forms of cost-effective urban air mobility, and intermodal transportation. Agility will already be starting with a large network, using all the assets of the two existing airlines—JetBlue and Alaska. The realigned network will enable it to compete effectively with the incumbent large US carriers. And it can develop the capability to achieve marketing and scheduling innovation by implementing dynamic scheduling and dynamic pricing to create many more point-to-point services (even in long-haul international markets) by operating single-aisle aircraft only, even across the Atlantic (and the Pacific!).

What if airlines could truly differentiate themselves? 111

Agility can capitalize on three key points. First is the value of the quality and the timeliness of data, as well as the value of using smart technology, such as artificial intelligence (AI)/machine learning, and their impact on the quality of the schedule. Second, Agility can think simultaneously of the steps in the scheduling process while making sure that all operational constraints are met and the profitability of the schedule is not diminished. In other words, suboptimizations, resulting from the separation of key decisions in a sequence, are avoided. Third, Agility can address not only all known weaknesses of the traditional scheduling approach but also a capability to undertake clean-sheet scheduling and use the dynamic scheduling features to produce schedules that are both profitable and reliable.

To illustrate these points, let us consider a route map of the major hubs and focus cities of JetBlue and Alaska Airlines as they exist today (Figure 7.1).

Let us further illustrate the possibilities when applying clean-sheet scheduling to the combined network of Agility Airlines. One important use of clean-sheet scheduling is to identify new route opportunities. In the particular case of Agility, one obvious opportunity to explore was new transatlantic and transpacific routes that would complement the domestic network of the combined airline.

In examining the opportunities for new intercontinental routes, decisions must be made around existing equipment. Both JetBlue and Alaska Airlines currently fly single-aisle aircraft, particularly the A320 and B737 families (as discussed earlier), so it would be logical to consider acquiring long-haul,

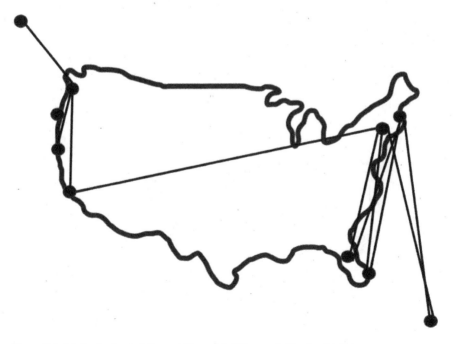

Figure 7.1 Major hubs and focus cities of JetBlue and Alaska Airlines

112 *What if airlines could truly differentiate themselves?*

single-aisle aircraft for these intercontinental missions. The A321-XLR aircraft has a range of 4,700 nautical miles, so it was chosen for this analysis.

Several Asian and European destinations were chosen as candidates for new international routes. Of course, given the length of routes over the Pacific compared to the range of the A321-XLR, the Asian destinations were limited to Tokyo Narita, Osaka, and Seoul. A variety of European destinations were considered including London Heathrow (LHR), Manchester, Paris CDG, Frankfurt, Madrid, Marseilles, and Barcelona.

These possibilities were analyzed using one of the leading scheduling forecasting solutions available in the industry.[1] Results indicate that several of these routes were economically viable[2] as shown in Figure 7.2.

Interestingly, the commercially viable new routes in Europe were the result of flying to secondary cities in Europe, specifically Manchester, UK, and Barcelona, Spain. The large airports considered—London Heathrow (LHR), Paris (CDG), and Frankfurt (FRA)—were already well served from JFK and BOS and competing with existing service affecting the commercial viability of new service from Agility Airlines. It is likely that other services to secondary European cities from Agility Airlines hubs and focus cities would also be commercially viable.

In addition to the possibilities found by examining new intercontinental routes, the results from the clean-sheet scheduling exercise also indicated that further improvements in profitability could be possible by deploying Agility's assets within its domestic network. These improvements could come from improving connectivity between the former two separate airlines and considering fleet assignments across the entire Agility Airlines network (e.g., using a former JetBlue aircraft on a former Alaska route), if that assignment resulted in a better match of capacity to demand.

It is also imagined that Agility Airlines would take advantage of much of its fleet being crew-compatible and apply the principles of dynamic scheduling. With that opportunity, it could identify and execute profitable and feasible schedule changes closer to departures thus generating more revenue. In

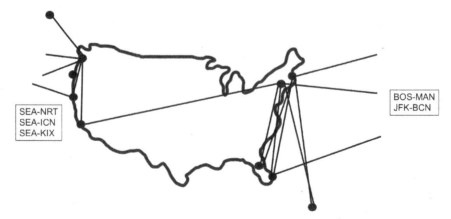

Figure 7.2 Potential transatlantic and transpacific opportunities for Agility Airlines

fact, it was found that the combined fleet size of Agility Airlines could allow opportunities for fleet swaps to be built into the schedule itself.

Finally, another important scheduling practice that Agility Airlines would likely use is building both schedule profitability and reliability into its flight schedule. JetBlue and Alaska Airlines are both premium brands and it is likely that a combination like Agility Airlines would strive to retain a positive brand image amongst its customers. Given the importance of a good record of on-time performance, it is likely that an important part of schedule development at Agility Airlines would be to simulate the reliability of a proposed schedule before it is published and then identify and act on any trade-offs between profitability and reliability.

The net effect of Agility Airlines applying new network planning techniques along with new kinds of data should be better scheduling decisions along with a quicker schedule development cycle. Taking advantage of more time for analysis in the schedule development process should allow schedulers more time for scenario analysis thus further improving their productivity.

Beyond scheduling improvements in the short term, it is expected that Agility would be pioneers in introducing new kinds of products. As discussed in Chapter 2, new disruptive aircraft technologies like electric or hydrogen-powered aircraft will soon become widely available and should bring opportunities to airlines and passengers alike. In addition, the option of traveling via driverless cars could change customer preferences for the mode of travel on short-haul routes thus further disrupting the sorts of products offered to the customer. A modern, forward-thinking airline like Agility would likely be at the forefront of these kinds of innovations.

Revenue and offer management

Agility Airlines can start thinking about different ways to enhance revenue, for example, by customizing and managing offers in real-time and by using new pricing and revenue management techniques, such as dynamic pricing and new ways to optimize revenue from the sale of ancillary products and services. The point is to optimize selling not just core products dynamically but also ancillaries dynamically. In both cases, revenue can be managed in almost real time, while integrating far more effectively network planning and pricing.

Agility Airlines can use an effective offer management system with the ability to personalize offers in real time. Using machine learning, it is now possible to make much more personalized offers that are contextualized using this technology to get a better understanding of what a customer is willing to pay, based on the customer's changing priorities and preferences. Agility can use not only new types of data, for example, comprehensive shopping data but also data on price elasticities of demand by segment, market, and product attribute (such as an itinerary) to implement effective dynamic pricing. In addition, Agility can also sell much more effectively a wider set of ancillary products and services offered by third parties, through partners, and by using platforms.

Agility can integrate its network planning and revenue management practices in real time using cross-functional teams and by focusing on the commonality of assumptions. As such, it can practice both dynamic scheduling and dynamic pricing to balance its supply and demand aspects in almost real time and on a more effective personalized basis. Personalization can relate not only to the product features in an offer but also to loyalty. Some customers may want rewards, and some may want offers. Some may want points, and some cash back, as in the case of some credit cards. With respect to payments, some may want to buy now and pay later, and some may want to use "digital wallets."

And Agility can make loyalty an integral component of its revenue management program. What if Agility transformed its loyalty program for travelers at both ends, less frequent leisure passengers and high frequent business travelers to meet their evolving needs and to add more value for both segments? One change relates to the value of points earned from flying and points earned from the use of credit cards. It is in the best interest of airlines to pay more attention to nonbusiness travelers, as this is the segment that is increasing. At the other end are the travelers paying very high fares for first-class travel in intercontinental markets—the travelers buying $8,000 tickets. Then there is a segment that takes very frequent flights, say, once a week, in short-haul markets. How can the loyalty program be renovated and innovated to meet the needs of all segments?

As a result of applying these practices, Agility Airlines could be expected to generate premium revenue per available seat mile. And further improvements could be possible if it fully embraced the potential of offer management. Think about the use of the choice model discussed in Chapters 2 and 3. For the new intercontinental routes to be flown by the A321-XLR with an all-premium economy product, there is an opportunity to intelligently price this product at a premium. It is likely that this product would interest customers traveling in other premium economy or even business class on other itineraries in these markets. Using the choice model discussed in detail in Jim Barlow's thought leadership piece in Chapter 8, it is possible to identify the price point for the A321-XLR product that maximizes the revenue from customers previously traveling in other cabins. The effect of optimizing pricing in this manner is like the principle of dynamic pricing discussed in Chapter 3, except that it occurs between different cabins of service flown by different airlines. Understanding the choice process for customers selecting different cabins provides an excellent opportunity to identify price premiums. Agility Airlines will develop a much better understanding of profitability by journey and customer, not just flight.

What would these kinds of changes look like in practice? To be sure, airlines analyze data, decide fares, and determine inventory controls today. In the future, with Agility Airlines, today's existing offer management processes would be enhanced in the following ways:

- New sources of data, for example, shopping data revealing true customer attitudes toward price (i.e., underlying price elasticities)

- Better integration between product definition (network planning) and pricing/revenue management, with the goal being no revenue lost because of different assumptions between pricing the product and building it in the first place
- Quicker response to changes in market conditions, for example, competitor price/schedule changes, changes in market demand, and government regulations
- More thought and science behind constructing and pricing the entire offer rather than focus on pricing seats and selling ancillaries
- More personalization in constructing and pricing the offer
- A blending of pricing and revenue management to the point that the selling fare will be determined in real time according to pricing and revenue management principles

It is expected that an airline such as Agility would be a leader in establishing these modern practices.

Designing customer experience through a holistic approach

Customers evaluate not only the products themselves but also their experiences with the purchase and use of products and services. Agility can redesign its customer experience processes, moving from an incremental to a transformative level, to strategize for positional superiority that will convert customers into promoters. It can develop much more effective strategies to win digital customers based on the experience of other businesses. It can provide digital (e.g., mobile-first) solutions that are user-friendly (less complex) to enable customers to manage their travel experiences.

Customer service is part of customer experience, as discussed in Chapter 4, but it is just the experience at one touch point. Customer experience, on the other hand, includes experience during all interactions during the entire journey, from the general awareness of an airline's brand to the purchase of a ticket to the services provided at the airport and during the flight. Travel experience needs to be designed through extensive collaboration and cross-functional teams, using a holistic approach, keeping in mind that customer experience is proactive in the sense that an airline needs to anticipate a customer's needs and then respond to such needs without being provoked. Compare that to customer service that is reactive in that a customer initiates an interaction, for example, to resolve an issue to which an airline responds.

Agility can make sure that its interactions with its customers are not only instantaneous but also continuous to build a deep relationship. During an operational recovery, for example, Agility can respond with urgency and empowered staff to resolve a customer's problems, from a customer's perspective, at any location, at any time, and through any device. All customers' problems can be resolved, not just customers in top-tier status and every customer can be treated with empathy. Glenn Hollister points out, in his thought leadership piece in Chapter 8, that many airlines are "stuck in the undifferentiated middle plot" of the concept described by Michael Porter in his Competitive Scope versus Competitive Advantage plot. Agility Airlines will select a clearly differentiated strategy.

As an overarching strategic goal, it is expected Agility would consistently deliver a customer experience sufficient to justify a revenue premium. It will measure the extent to which it has been able to do this by calibrating a Choice Model described in Jim Barlow's thought leadership piece in Chapter 8. Leading choice models, once calibrated on modern data such as shopping data, are able to detect customer preferences for different airlines. Since revenue premiums are only possible when customers observe and value differences in customer experiences between different airlines, it is important to measure and track preferences for different airlines. Agility will become a leader in measuring and tracking airline preferences and using this information to make further, cost-effective improvements in its experience to drive even more preference.

Sustainability as a competitive advantage

Agility Airlines can not only do its part in making skies cleaner cost-effectively, but it can make sustainability its major competitive advantage, by deploying advanced technologies and collaborating within the ecosystem, for example, with technology businesses and with partners, such as airports. In fact, Agility, in the spirit of a public–private partnership, can strategize to balance its business goals and its goals to reduce carbon emissions. The approach can be holistic and practical. The approach can be holistic in the sense that there can be a dual goal (a goal that is both market-based and cause-based). And the plan can be practical, meaning that it starts with a clean-sheet approach for scheduling and reduces the complexity of measuring, monitoring, and reporting the information on its environmental footprint.

Agility can change its organizational structure and culture in all departments in operations (flight operations, ground operations, maintenance, repair, and overhaul, as well as maintenance and engineering) not just to save costs but also to focus on sustainability. It is important to recognize that this focus on sustainability becomes a shared corporate value, not a task delegated to one individual department. Moving forward, a commitment to sustainability will become at Agility something built into its corporate DNA.

Agility can make communities a part of its strategy because air travel directly impacts communities, not only destinations, infrastructure, and local workers, but, in some cases, also the local economies. Agility can find ways to make these ideas scalable.

Specifically, Agility Airlines can work with the four pillars identified by IATA to create a sustainable aviation industry—technology, operations, infrastructure, and economic instruments. Technology can, in fact, provide benefits in both operations and infrastructure. As such, Agility can partner with technology companies to develop its strategies for sustainability, by gaining, for example, insights from the use of AI and advanced analytics as well as to measure and benchmark its environmental footprint, relating to flight operations, ground operations, and maintenance. Think about another technology, blockchain, that is a trusted, distributed, transparent, and shared-ledger platform. Given the importance of traceability in the real-time management of inventory and maintenance, blockchain technology can make traceability much more effective (from records going back to the date and the place of when and where a part was manufactured).

Regarding operations, fuel efficiency can be increased significantly by optimizing routes, flight paths, and altitudes and reducing aircraft waiting times. While each generation of aircraft is more fuel efficient anyway, sophisticated revenue management techniques can also be used to fly the aircraft with even slightly higher load factors, leading to a significant improvement in the CO_2 emissions per passenger transported. Agility can also explore to identify ways for passengers to travel with less baggage.

Agility Airlines can assume that when travelers make reservations, they would look for information on the amount of carbon emissions relating to particular flights, with the information displayed at the point of sale. Travelers will look for relevant information to choose different modes of transportation, for example, rail versus air, depending on destinations. As such, Agility can work with different organizations within the ecosystem to develop this information and make it available at the point of sale to potential buyers of travel. Agility could even provide travelers CO_2 calculators that can enable travelers to compare easily travel options. A traveler would be able to, for example, "see" the value of a specific trip, in terms of carbon emissions, not just relating to different modes of transportation but also to the type of aircraft being used (by its age and by its fuel efficiency) and the itinerary (nonstop versus connecting flights). A traveler would even be able to "see" the impact of their luggage weight on CO_2 emissions. Agility can not only provide the capability to book intermodal travel, but it can also design the availability of integrated travel, involving both trains and aircraft. And it can start developing end-to-end services and door-to-door travel for customers. To design such planning systems and processes, Agility can involve all stakeholders in the design process, particularly customers, employees, and providers of infrastructure (e.g., airports and technology partners).

Doing more with less

Finally, Agility Airlines can find new ways to do more with less by (1) building digital resiliency capabilities, (2) collaborating in value-adding ecosystems, (3) deploying digital platforms to create superior end-to-end customer experience at scale, (4) deploying "datagraphs" to capture information how travelers use the travel products and services, and (5) developing effective partnerships with innovative start-ups. In each of these five areas, Agility can focus on not just concepts, but on their execution.

The starting point is to identify future disruptions to figure out the dynamics of the upcoming marketplace. While big data and algorithms have important roles to play, and as mentioned earlier, it is also the small data that can help identify signals to anticipate major disruptions and develop effective strategies. In both cases, Agility can work with a framework, beginning to be known as "open strategy," that suggests that a business open its strategic initiatives to multiple stakeholders, both internal (e.g., employees) and external (e.g., customers, airports, and technology partners). The goal could be to become a digital airline, by capitalizing on diverse viewpoints, skills, and resources to identify solutions.

As to the use of "datagraphs," they can help an airline reshape its advantage. Based on the thought leadership of Vijay Govindarajan and N. Venkat Venkatraman, an airline can visualize, using "datagraphics," how its customers interact with its products and services to reshape its competitive advantage.[3]

Although both JetBlue and Alaska had developed partnerships with start-ups, Agility can now change its organizational structures to capitalize on the true value of partnerships. In the past, there have been inherent challenges in having very large airlines partner with start-ups. The large airlines have had heavy and complex processes to follow, for example, long decision-making processes. The start-ups have been lightweights, fast, and agile groups. Large airlines have tended to look for answers. Start-ups have tended to ask questions and have managers challenge each other.

As KLM's Jordie Knoppers, explains in his thought leadership piece in Chapter 8, think about how children ask hundreds of questions. As such, one of his suggestions is to "think like a five-year-old." And Agility can develop new techniques not just to partner but also to think like a five-year-old in terms of asking questions and collaborating to (1) find solutions for customers' pain points and (2) develop a digital capability to do more with less. Technologies are clearly enabling some companies to become digital companies. Just as Amazon used digital technologies to extend the scope and scale of its businesses, Agility can do the same. Agility can use AI, not just to improve revenue, operations, and customer experience (e.g., AI-powered chatbots and virtual assistants) but can go much further to learn about the changing customer behavior, with the use of smart digital customer-engagement platforms. Furthermore, Agility will facilitate the development of digital mindsets of its employees. According to business writers, Tsedal Neeley and Paul Leonardi, a digital mindset encompasses attitudes and behaviors that enable employees and businesses to see how data, algorithms, and AI explore new possibilities to develop compelling strategies in a world dominated by data-intensive and smart technologies.[4]

The capability to do more with less also requires innovation that is related to the brand. In a highly competitive and low-margin business, as in the case of airlines, Agility Airlines' objective can be to grow the value of its two previous brands, JetBlue and Alaska Airlines. This strategy will require a different type of thinking and planning than the thinking for conventional scheduling and revenue management processes. The object would now be to develop and position Agility for a competitive advantage. What is the image that consumers will be seeing from Agility's brand? On what knowledge will this image be based? How will the behavior of consumers change relative to the image?

Agility can work toward developing an image related to such attributes as innovation, reliability, and trustworthiness, as well as specific attributes, such as the boarding process, in-flight services, and on-time performance. And Agility will not overlook the gap between what is stated and promised in its brand (reliability and customer care) and what is actually delivered.

Hopefully, the conceptual example, Agility, deliberated in this chapter illustrates the desirability and feasibility of applying the principles discussed in this book. To conclude, here is a quote taken from the foreword, by Le Hong Ha, president and CEO of Vietnam Airlines: "The book gives a precious blueprint to think about the business model that an airline can pursue. However, you should also be prepared that the book may make you think of totally changing your company's business philosophy."

Notes

1 The solution in question was the Amadeus SkyCAST schedule forecasting solution. Schedules used in the analysis were based on 2019 data. Parameters reflecting customer behavior (QSI coefficients) were calibrated on 2019 data. Industry market sizes were based on 2019 data in Amadeus's Traffic Analytics database. Solution and data were used with the support and consent of Amadeus.
2 Economically viable is defined as expected load factor above 70%.
3 Vijay Govindarajan and N. Venkat Venkatraman, "The Next Great Digital Advantage: Smart businesses are using datagraphs to reveal unique solutions to customer problems," *Harvard Business Review*, May–June 2022, pp. 56–63.
4 Tsedal Neeley and Paul Leonardi, "Developing a Digital Mindset: How to lead your organization into the age of data, algorithms, and AI," *Harvard Business Review*, May–June 2022, pp. 50–55.

8 Thought leadership pieces

Chapter 8 offers several thought leadership pieces that provide international perspectives relating to the theme of the book. These pieces are written by a very diverse group of practitioners with extensive experience, both in the aviation domain and in other business sectors. The contents of some of the thought leadership pieces suggest that managers now need to consider new ways to develop and offer value by thinking non-conventionally on what will be important to existing and new travelers, as they change their lifestyles.

The unifying nature of customer choice

Jim Barlow
Senior Vice President, Network Planning Solutions, Amadeus IT Group

Overview

What does it mean to be truly "customer-centric"? Many companies in many different industries claim to put the customer at the center of what they do. But what exactly does that mean in practice?

This piece argues that the ultimate expression of the voice of the customer is made through their purchase decision. That is, when deciding how best to service their customers, what matters most is understanding what drives actual customer choices. For example, customers may claim they wish to receive premium food and drinks while onboard their aircraft, but if they are not generally willing to pay for them, then any investment in this area will not deliver good returns.

Understanding what customers actually want, as measured via their actual purchase decisions, is also an excellent way to bring alignment between different airline departments. If key airline decisions—for example, deciding the flight schedule, determining which prices to offer, designing a customer service program, and so on—could be made on a common basis of what customers are looking for, then that would bring consistency in airline decision-making. And, arguably, this approach would truly deliver on the promise of putting customers at the center of what airlines do.

However, interpreting customer preferences via analyzing actual customer choices is a complex task. And applying the learnings to actual airline problems is also not easy. In this piece, we intend to show how airline customer preferences can be measured and how these measurements can be used throughout an airline to drive better decision-making and a sense of consistency.

How do airline customers choose flights?

The process by which airline customers generally research and ultimately choose their preferred flight is well-known and can be depicted according to Figure 8.1.

At first, the customer clearly has some purpose for this travel, such as a business trip, leisure activities, or visiting friends and relatives. It is often the case that the specific destination for this travel is immediately apparent, although when researching different leisure options the customer may be interested in examining alternatives. Regardless, at the completion of the first step the customer has a clear idea of origin and destination of their proposed trip.

Next, the customer embarks on a process of searching for different travel options. They could work with a travel agent connected to a global distribution system and review possible options in one step or they could interrogate

122 *Thought leadership pieces*

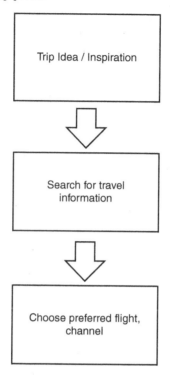

Figure 8.1 Process of choosing preferred flights

different airline direct sites. Or perhaps they are such loyal customers of one airline that they only visit one airline direct site. Or they could look at other channels, online travel agencies, airport sales agents, and so on. In whatever form, at the completion of this step, the customer has identified a number of specific flight options from which they will make a selection.

In the final step, customers will choose their preferred option based on what is available to them and their own preferences. The expression of choice will be made in the form of a booking taking place via a specific distribution channel.

As discussed in Chapters 2 and 3, this choice of available flight options is typically made on the basis of three key variables:

1 Quality of the schedule. As discussed in Chapter 2, examples of schedule effects include nonstop versus connect service, departing at preferable times of day, total elapsed time of the itinerary (including any connecting time), aircraft type, and airport preferences, among others
2 Price
3 Airline preference

Measuring the relative importance of these three effects is the key to understanding airline customer choice. These measurements can then be expressed mathematically into a customer choice model which allows airlines to simulate customer choices under different conditions and identify profitable changes to their product and price.

What does a customer choice model look like?

A customer choice model is a model that represents customer preferences. One simple example is shown in Chapter 3 of this book and is reprinted here as Figure 8.2.

These measurements indicate, for example, that nonstops are preferred by equivalent online connections by an approximate 10:1 effect (note—other interpretations are made in Chapters 2 and 3). These figures are derived from analyzing historical data, especially shopping and booking data which give great insight into actual choices of airline flights. Note that these figures may change by market, passenger type, region, days before departure, or other types of customer segments.

Why are customer choice models important? These models are very useful in simulating the effect of changing choices available to customers. So, one could use these models to analyze, for example, the change in market share from introducing a nonstop into a pure connecting market. Or changing the departure time from an unattractive 5:00 a.m. departure to a more attractive 7:00 a.m. departure. Or evaluating different price levels in a specific market and identifying a new price level consistent with maximum revenue.

In general, customer choice models can be used to simulate the impact on market share and thus revenue from many different kinds of product/price combinations. With that, decisions can be made to improve the schedule, offer a different fare structure, and/or change fare inventory levels.

For those familiar with schedule planning, notice that a Quality of Service Index (QSI) model is, in effect, a choice model. These types of models are not

Effect	QSI Points
Nonstop	1.00
1-Stop Direct	0.17
Single Connect	0.09
Double Connect	0.01
Interline penalty	17%
Codeshare penalty	54%
Elapsed time (vs. fastest connect)	EXP(−0.65*hrs)
Price	EXP(−1.83*$100s)

Effect	QSI Points
Widebody	1.22
Narrowbody	1.00
Regional Jet	0.84
Turboprop	0.74
Legacy airline	1.00
LCC airline	0.90
ULCC airline	0.80

Figure 8.2 Customer preferences for schedule, price, and airline

new to airlines. What might be new to some airlines, and is the primary topic of this piece, is that the scope of these models could be expanded throughout the airline. One interesting example is in the area of understanding customer preferences for different airlines.

Measuring airline preferences and applying those preferences

Notice, in Figure 8.2, customer preferences for US legacy airlines (i.e., AA, UA, and DL) were measured to be roughly 11% more than for LCC airlines (e.g., B6, AS, and HA), other effects being equal. That is, at an equivalent schedule and price, US legacy airlines are slightly more preferred than LCC airlines.

What accounts for this preference? What could airlines do to improve the preference for their brand? Are these preferences stronger in certain markets? Are these preferences stable over time?

The act of measuring these preferences, important in the context of customer choices and separating out schedule and price effects, offers the promise of answering these kinds of questions. Notice that when funding a program to improve customer service, airlines today implicitly ascribe some value to reflecting improved service in affecting future purchase decisions. Implementing a corporate-wide customer choice model would allow this value to be more explicitly measured.

What sorts of customer service programs could be analyzed in this manner? The following list of customer service programs assumes, in part, that some of the corresponding benefits come from strengthening the airline brand, which would ultimately be manifested in affecting future choices.

1. Loyalty program. The logic is that improved rewards should lead to more airline loyalty. In this sense, loyalty should be ultimately expressed in market share above some expectations based on the airline's schedule and price.
2. On-time performance initiatives. Of course, much of the benefit in improved on-time performance comes from reduced disruption costs. However, in addition, many airlines assume that if customers believe that if one airline is more reliable than the others, it will receive preferential market share. How large is this premium? Is it worth the incurred cost?
3. "Hard" and "soft" product attributes. Do customers really perceive a difference between airlines in the nature of their products, either with regard to the seat itself or various aspects of service? If so, can this difference be measured in the context of actual choices? If not, is there really a difference in the first place?
4. Advertising. Are airlines able to significantly differentiate themselves from their competitors in their advertising? Can this differentiation be actually reflected in terms of choices made by real customers? What sort of preference can be generated through advertising?
5. Channel strategy. Airlines invest large amounts in designing their airline. com channel to appeal to customers. In this sense, airlines compete with

one another to convert shopping requests into actual bookings. Are some airlines better at this effect than others? Can this difference be measured in terms of premium share?

To summarize this point, airline preferences can be accurately measured, in the context of scheduling and pricing effects, by implementing a customer choice model. In turn, these preferences can be further analyzed to understand the factors that drive customer attitudes toward different airlines. With this knowledge, airlines can evaluate cost-effective ways to improve their brand.

Embedding customer choice throughout the airline

Referring to the original statement of a truly "customer-centric" airline, what would it look like in practice if an airline understood how its customers chose its products and embedded this knowledge throughout the airline? This principle is illustrated in Figure 8.3.

The principle being illustrated is that a common customer choice model could be developed and maintained centrally. This common model could then be used throughout the company to support any decisions that rely on an understanding of customer choices. This common model would bring consistency amongst many decisions made across the company as well as ensuring that the decisions themselves will be based on the best possible understanding on their effect on customer choices.

Implementing a customer choice program

What does it take to implement a program of analyzing customer choices and applying the learnings throughout the company, as described earlier? The following list suggests some important steps in this process.

1. Gain access to a data source that represents actual customer choices. An ideal source would be shopping and booking data since these data provide the most insight of what customers were looking for, what was available to them, and what they chose.

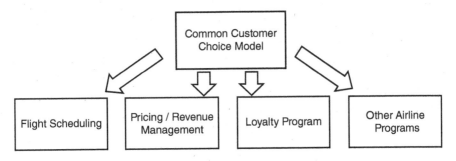

Figure 8.3 Customer choice at the center

2 Assign a centralized, cross-functional team to analyze customer choice data and develop a corporate-wide customer choice model. This team should consider different market segmentations and continuously keep the model up to date.
3 Apply the corporate-wide customer choice model to existing applications in network planning and pricing/revenue management. It is highly likely that both departments already have some version of a customer choice model which could be enhanced by integrating results from a corporate-wide initiative. In particular, using the model in this manner should allow greater integration between network planning and pricing/revenue management, for example, adapting revenue management forecasts for recent schedule changes.
4 Analyze and test measures of airline preference for accuracy. Note that, in the previous example, airline preferences were expressed in terms of groups of airlines (e.g., legacy airlines, LCC, ULCC). With sufficient data, it is quite possible to measure customer preferences for individual airlines.
5 Analyze airline preferences and determine key factors which account for differences in preferences between different airlines.
6 Use knowledge gained in Step 5 to evaluate new customer programs in the context of how these programs could ultimately move market share (or not).

Summary

Analyzing newly available shopping and booking data holds the promise of better understanding actual customer choices. With this knowledge, airlines can improve not only their scheduling, pricing, and revenue management decisions but gain a better appreciation of airline preferences in the context of actual choices. More important, this knowledge can be used to integrate and align decisions throughout the airline around what ultimately drives airline customer choices.

Turning air into magic

Evert de Boer
Managing Partner, On Point Loyalty

Frustrated by a missed promotion, Charles Revson went on to cofound a company specialized in cosmetics in 1932. Revlon, as the company was called, would grow to become a multinational cosmetics, skin care, fragrance, and personal care company. When asked about the success of Revlon, Revson said: "*We don't sell lipstick, we sell dreams.*" With that, Revson captured the essence of the offering—and looked far beyond just the functional features of makeup products. An interesting parallel with airline loyalty programs can be drawn by encapsulating the promise of future travel in a loyalty currency, the program operators have gone beyond the mundane realities of running an airline. Where airlines are bogged down in dog-eat-dog competition, in a very challenging operating environment, the loyalty programs have been able to bottle the magic appeal of travel in one-mile increments. By doing so, they have successfully pushed the boundaries of the traditional model—and opened new avenues of growth and value. Against that backdrop, and with their proven track record, no exploration of "what if" for airline business models can be complete without considering what has become arguably one of the most successful (and profitable) business models within the industry. For the programs themselves, new and different strategies can be explored. But to ensure an equitable and sustainable relationship between the program and the airline, certain strategies work better than others. We will demonstrate that programs that can deliver high degrees of *preferentiality* (a measure of customer value offered) and *equivalency* (a measure of avoiding opportunity costs for its key principle the airline) will prosper—both now and in the future.

Loyalty programs as the beacon of airline innovation

Airline loyalty programs are masters at pushing boundaries. Over the last two decades, the programs have successfully transformed their scale and scope—culminating as the lifeline for many airlines as evidenced during the pandemic of the last years.

From their humble beginnings as gimmicky marketing tools (invented to deal with the arrival of increased competition), the programs have transformed into broad-based customer loyalty programs. In many cases, the loyalty program represents the single largest customer repository for an airline, offering unrivalled data and access to consumers. As an example, according to the International Airlines Group (IAG) in 2019, 33% of passenger journeys were made by program members; 38% of passenger journeys on top routes were made by program members and 44% of flight revenue came from program members. For some airlines, more than 50% of the flight revenues are generated by members of the loyalty program, typically showing a distinct pareto principle with a relatively small number of customers generating the lion share of revenues. On the rewards side as well, the programs have grown into very large distribution channels. For IAG, more than 8 million flight rewards are delivered in a single year. Although the numbers vary from airline to airline, awards can make up for between 5% and 10% of total revenue passenger miles, making it into effectively the single largest distribution channel for airlines. And for those who think that award travel (redeeming loyalty currency for a ticket) is, by definition, yield-dilutive—think again. More redemption products (including combinations of cash and miles or points) and more sophisticated revenue management approaches, in combination with huge external revenues from the sale of miles or points to partners are delivering yield-accretive results for the airlines. The numbers from IAG illustrate how airline loyalty programs have evolved from a niche product targeting premium business customers to currency exchange powerhouses, offering access to the most attractive redemption category—travel.

Today's success of airline loyalty programs is the product of ongoing innovation in the core model. The loyalty programs were able to expand beyond the core airline business by successfully pursuing external partners. Instead of merely offering miles for tickets flown, the programs were able to monetize the allure of travel by selling miles as a travel currency to partners. Loyalty programs also pushed the boundaries of their own organizational model, with new and innovative models being progressively introduced over time.

Loyalty programs have proven themselves adept at change over time. Admittedly, some of the change was driven by the shortcomings of the original model. One eye-catching example is the original logic used to award miles or points in the programs. Historically, distance was used but awarding miles based on distance flown proved to be a poor proxy of customer value. Over time, the programs evolved and introduced sharper economics, including the move to spend-based programs. Under a spend-based program, members are awarded miles or points based on the fare paid, effectively aligning revenue generated with the amount of loyalty currency earned. This rectified the situation whereby a customer would pay significantly more for a short-haul flight (e.g., $1,000 to fly between Chicago and Minneapolis using a same-day return) but would receive less miles than a low-yielding long-haul customer (e.g., Chicago to Shanghai which covers more than 7,000 miles but can retail for less than $1,000). Similarly, new and enhanced elite qualification structures do a better job at recognizing high-value customers—and providing the right incentive for members (essentially spending up instead of buying more). Likewise, more programs are offering elite qualification structures that recognize the value of non-air partner spend, specifically co-branded credit cards, which generate lucrative external revenue streams for the programs.

Despite their intrinsic ties to the airlines, the programs are also a bit of an odd one in the family. It is well known that the airline industry offers many challenges, both on an operational level and on a business strategy level. It requires the purchase and management of expensive capital assets, flying in unpredictable economic circumstances where a few factors (e.g., fuel) largely outside the control of the airlines, determine the financial performance. Airlines compete for passengers with essentially a commoditized product (think of the handful of vendors that provide inflight entertainment systems, onboard catering, third-party lounges, etc.), overall leading to a financial performance where the return on invested capital (ROIC) hardly exceeds the weighted average cost of capital (WACC). Loyalty programs on the other hand, offer very different characteristics. In many ways they are, when considered on their own merits, a different business altogether. Arguably, loyalty programs are more akin to digital innovators like Uber and Airbnb rather than their core airline counterparts. In simple terms, the main operational benefits of airline loyalty programs result in the cash generated by the spread on points, interest on negative working capital and the breakage revenue. In addition, this activity does not require substantial investments so there are low cash outflows related to capital expenditures. These attractive characteristics came to light especially during the coronavirus pandemic as we will see in the next section.

Pulling the curtains on the true value of loyalty programs

Airlines have historically used their loyalty programs to raise capital in tough times, with the preselling of miles to partners being a tried-and-tested approach. As early as 2004, Delta Air Lines, scrambling to avoid an imminent filing for bankruptcy protection, secured $600 million in cash and financing from American Express, most of it as an advance payment for miles that card users would rack up on their American Express co-branded SkyMiles credit card. Similarly, equity carve outs of the loyalty segment started around the same time with Air Canada Enterprises (ACE) selling its Aeroplan division progressively on the Toronto Stock Exchange.

But during the onslaught of the COVID-19 pandemic, airlines found a new and innovative way of raising financing by collateralizing the future cash flows from their loyalty programs (in recognition of some of the shortfalls of the alternative models of raising capital). As part of this process, documents sent to creditors contained a trove of information on the size, margins, and valuations of the programs.

Before the airlines tapped the programs as a vehicle for more attractive capital raising structures, the programs proved their resiliency which undoubtedly enhanced their appeal in the eyes of the creditors. In the first half of 2020, for example, Delta's passenger revenues fell 60%, but the cash the airline got from American Express's purchases of miles for its customers fell less than 5%. A similar pattern can be observed with other programs, where the ongoing attraction of future travel maintained the momentum specifically with non-air partners.

As part of the process, according to United, different options were weighed to raise capital, including preselling of miles and a potential equity carve-out of the loyalty segment. In the end, United, however, chose to maintain full ownership in MileagePlus at that point and invented another structure to deliver the hard-needed cash. For the first time, the financing was based on program related receivables, including MileagePlus program data, agreements, and intellectual property (IP), as well as revenues from the program. United used a combination of secured bond technology and receivable securitization to provide investors with a clear claim against the program. As part of the agreement, an exclusivity agreement was entered between the loyalty unit and United, preventing the airline from participating in any program for the duration of the financing. To safeguard the future, a bankruptcy remote entity was formed to reroute the miles sales revenues. The loyalty program brand assets and IP rights were pledged to investors via the issuer entity. The issue was upsized to $6.8 billion following greater than expected investor demand.

A few months after the United announcement, Spirit and Delta followed suit and announced their own respective transactions to help see them through the crisis. The resulting transactions produced not only some of the largest-ever financial market transactions for airlines ($9 billion in Delta's case), but it also pulled the curtain on the remarkable value attached to the airline loyalty programs as displayed in the increased financial disclosures. AAdvantage and MileagePlus, according to their projected enterprise values, are significantly more valuable than the respective airline as measured by their market capitalization at the time.

Perhaps as the strongest illustration of how loyalty programs are perceived as a less risky business compared to airlines, these financing structures realized a risk discount of between 2% and 3.5%. Loyalty programs, in other words, proved not only to be more profitable than the core airline business, but they are also considered materially different businesses from the airlines by the lenders.

The revelation of the value and its seeming inconceivability sent observers in a tailspin, arguing for and against the notion. At the same time, questions were raised on the sustainability and viability of the new structures. Observers both inside and outside the industry were captivated by the value of the programs. The dramatic growth and changes happening in the loyalty program landscape, the collateralization of airline loyalty programs under crisis, and the high valuation of the programs demonstrate how loyalty programs have evolved well beyond their original marketing efforts into an increasingly complex entity that interacts with (and significantly impacts) other firm functions.

Innovation implies risk

Innovation is in many ways driven by unconventional thoughts. Doing things in a different way requires challenging the status quo. Loyalty programs are no different in that respect—and lessons can be drawn from historical performance.

One of the most material innovations was the redesign of the organizational structure of loyalty programs. Originally, programs were deeply embedded in the marketing and sales organization, reflecting the background of their original custodians. But as the scale and scope of the programs evolved, airlines sought to design more appropriate structures that would provide a better fit to unleash the true potential of the programs. Programs progressively adopted profit centre structures, interacting with other segments of the company using transfer pricing agreements, replacing the old informal agreements governing the sale of loyalty currency and access to reward seats. Early examples include the Qualiflyer Group, composed of Swissair, Austrian, Crossair and others, which had used a separate entity to run the shared Qualiflyer loyalty program until the demise of Swissair in 2002. In the same year, United moved all its loyalty marketing services into a wholly owned subsidiary called United Loyalty Services (ULS).

Taking it one step further, a number of airlines not only carved out their loyalty segment but also sold some or all of the equity of the new loyalty company to outsiders, either through an initial public offering (IPO) or a strategic investment by an external party (mostly private equity firms). In 2005, Air Canada Enterprises was the first mover and divested its ownership of the Aeroplan program through an IPO on the Toronto Stock Exchange. But when the end of the agreement between Air Canada and the owners of Aeroplan came in sight, Air Canada decided it would not renew the agreement and instead would launch its own program. It stated that by operating its own loyalty program, it would be better able to strengthen its customer relationships and deliver a more consistent end-to-end customer experience. Ultimately, after prolonged negotiations, Air Canada did buy back the Aeroplan program. Other airlines that had followed similar structures (selling a part of the loyalty program) pursued a similar strategy and purchased back the equity in the program held by an external investor. Avianca repurchased Advent's stake in the LifeMiles program, stating it would improve Avianca's future profitability by further aligning the program with Avianca and eliminating future dividend payments to the minority shareholder. Multiplus was delisted from the B3 Novo Mercado (Sao Paulo stock exchange) when LATAM Airlines Brazil acquired 23.49% of Multiplus's common shares. These moves raise the question on how to best structure the relationship between the loyalty program and the airline, in a way that is sustainable, equitable and provides sufficient levels of versatility to deal with major changes coming to the market.

Change is the only constant

Four key trends can be observed in the environment which may have a profound impact on the loyalty programs, offering both opportunities as well as challenges.

Significant changes in payments. It is hard to overestimate the importance of financial services companies in the loyalty ecosystem. Delta Air Lines and American Express have a long-standing partnership with a long-term projection of generating more than $7 billion in the sales of SkyMiles to American Express. In 2019, Delta Air Lines and American Express extended the partnership to 2029. The Delta co-branded credit card portfolio represents approximately 8% of Amex customer card spending and 22% of card loans in

2019. Although the Delta–American Express volume certainly is exceptional in size, similar dynamics are present for other programs too. Generally speaking, loyalty programs are fuelled by financial services companies. Changes in the financial services environment therefore will have a ripple effect on loyalty programs. One particular example is the regulation of interchange (interchange fees are paid by the merchant's bank when a credit card is used when a customer makes a purchase from that particular merchant). In a number of markets around the world, regulators have successfully argued to cap the interchange resulting in a material change in the underlying economics (a significant part of the interchange is used to fund the miles purchased from the loyalty programs). But potentially even more impactful changes are on the horizon, with new payment systems starting to make their entry onto the global marketplace. Examples include fintech and direct debit. China, in this regard, is an interesting market, where traditional payment networks never gained a significant foothold. Revenues could also be at risk because interchange is more likely to fall then to rise. In addition, competition with bank-issued proprietary cards has increased in a number of markets.

The rise of the super currency. The fungibility of loyalty currencies has increased drastically over time, but until now, no single currency surfaced as a clear winner. Over time, individual loyalty currencies have become more fungible as the result of more partnerships, allowing members to trade or convert their points and miles. Historically, this involved a form of value leakage, with members losing part of the value as part of the exchange. At the same time, there was a realization that if any participant could crack the code and come up with a mechanism to deliver a universal currency without value leakage, the prize could be material. Having a single currency would provide tremendous economies of scope and provide significant leverage with partners. The industry has started to move to dominant currencies. In March 2022, Qatar Airways announced it would adopt Avios (the loyalty currency operated by the IAG Group) as the principal currency for its Privilege Club program, which it will continue to operate as part of the airline.

Aviation under scrutiny. Aviation is attracting a significant share of scrutiny as part of the increasing debate about the environmental footprints of various industries. Loyalty programs have been identified by some as particular culprits, with some calling for the introduction of an "escalating Air Miles levy to discourage excessive flying" to total abolishment of loyalty programs. Although this would appear as a more extreme viewpoint, what is clear, however, is that loyalty programs will need to be more aware of their role in the eco-debate. A range of initiatives show how programs are addressing the consumer demands, ranging from CO_2 offsets to green tiers introduced by for example Etihad Airways and Qantas.

Consumer desires for integrated mobility systems. Loyalty programs serve fragmented parts of the travel journey. Think about a typical trip, involving mass transit or shared ride to the airport, services at the airport, the actual flight, transfer to the hotel at the destination, and the hotel accommodation. A single trip could involve easily five or more separate loyalty programs.

Customers want seamless and frictionless travel experience. With the changing consumer expectations around an integrated travel experience, loyalty programs will have to take into account this change in expectations—and possibly offer a more aligned product.

With the increased focus on the potential enhanced role that loyalty programs can play for the airlines, managers should explore an enhanced role for loyalty programs—both now as well as after the crisis. The loyalty program can play a pivotal role for airlines in pushing the boundaries of the traditional business model. They offer a number of attractive characteristics that position them well as the lynchpin for future expansion—and exploration of new business avenues. At the same time, the historical lessons teach us that this can only be done if all stakeholders involved are rewarded equitably. Therefore, goal convergence is critical between the loyalty program and the airline.

Making the loyalty program go the extra mile

With the changes on the horizon, the role that loyalty programs can play will be more important than ever. With that also comes the question on how to design and structure loyalty programs in a way that provides a sustainable competitive advantage and is value accretive for all stakeholders. As a starting point, it is clear that loyalty programs can go beyond their original mandate of engendering customer loyalty by acting as an extension of revenue management. Putting the loyalty currency into the revenue management mix offers exponential opportunities to market more efficiently to consumers. Examples include the partial use of currency mixed with cash as well as the integration of tier programs can add an additional lens in the revenue management toolkit. But some programs and setups are more successful than others. Considering the historical performance of airline loyalty programs, it becomes clear that in order for a loyalty program to successfully exploit its enhanced potential in a sustainable and viable long-term way, it must deliver on two fronts. The first dimension is the customer value proposition. The most successful programs offer very compelling value propositions, for example, by giving unique access to seats, like international redemptions in premium cabins. This dimension can be defined as **preferentiality**. A loyalty program with a high degree of preferentiality offers access to products and services in the form of rewards and tier benefits that no other channel can match. Think, for example, of the first-class redemption seat or a complimentary upgrade for elite-tier members. A low-preferentiality loyalty program offers little or no differentiation in the pricing to members, with a good case in point being cashback programs (a dollar earned is worth a dollar without further discounts or benefits). High preferentiality ensures utility in the currency, which ultimately pays dividends in terms of members engagement and partner accruals.

The second dimension that is critical for the long-term viability of the model is the economic exchange between the loyalty program and its

134 *Thought leadership pieces*

principal. The economic exchange between the loyalty program and its principal involves the provision of the principal's products and services to the loyalty program in the form of rewards, as well as the purchase of loyalty currency from the loyalty program. In order for this partnership to be viable in the long-term, this exchange must be done in an equitable way. This dimension can be defined as *equivalency*. In the case of Qantas for example, no margin is derived on the sale of points to the airline. At the same time, integrated revenue management techniques are deployed to ensure the right award ends up with the right member. Like many other airlines, Qantas manages the level of preferentiality, with higher value members receiving better access. According to Qantas, they use a very sophisticated approach to allocate seats, including the long-term value, or the lifetime value of a member.

Figure 8.4 shows the four potential strategies afforded by different combinations of equivalency and preferentiality. Loyalty programs that offer a high degree of both preferentiality and equivalency are well positioned to generate value—this type of program is categorized as value accretive programs. What makes these programs stand out is that they offer products or services that are unique in their offering (e.g., a very attractive price, or enhanced availability)—but do so without causing an opportunity cost for the principal. For an airline loyalty program, the best example would be offering access to attractive travel rewards—that otherwise would have gone unsold.

Loyalty program strategies

Loyalty programs that combine a high level of preferentiality (a stronger value proposition) with high levels of equivalency (a more equitable principal releationship) are best places to go beyond their original mandate – and create accretive value.

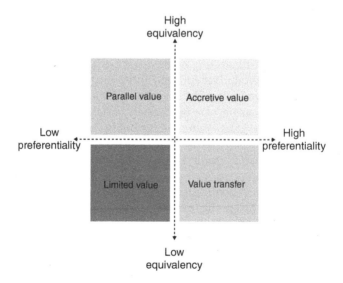

Figure 8.4 Loyalty program strategies

The loyalty program markets the seats in a way that delivers incremental value to all stakeholders involved, including the airline, the program partners, and the members. Programs that offer great value (high preferentiality) but do so at the detriment of the program principal (low equivalency) are categorized as value transfer programs (they shift value from the service provider to the program). Recent examples in which airlines repatriate their previously separated program may offer an indication of the limited shelf life of this model, for example, Aeroplan, Avianca, and Velocity. Parallel value programs not only offer great equivalency (principals incur no opportunity cost), but also offer little preferentiality (no favourable or unique access to products and services). A clear example of parallel-value programs is cashback-style loyalty programs. Finally, limited-value programs are characterized by low preferentiality and low equivalency, marking them as a strategic no-go area.

Final thoughts

Airline loyalty programs have turned out to be a crown in the jewel for airlines. In many ways, the programs resemble successful digital disruptors with their scalable, asset-light business models that match consumers with products and services, delivering superior financial returns. Given their track record of innovation, others in the airline value chain would do well to consider the reasons for their ongoing success. For the programs themselves, the historical performance has taught us that in order for them to thrive in the long run, programs must deliver on two dimensions as previously discussed. For the loyalty program to deliver on all aspects, it must deliver both high preferentiality as well as equivalency. It is hard to overstate the importance of appropriate revenue management techniques to deliver on both dimensions, given its crucial role in pricing and inventory management.

The operation's support for a new airline customer proposition

Christopher Gibbs

Senior Advisor Navier Consulting, Former Engineering Director at Cathay Pacific Airways, and Group Director at HAECO

Maintenance and engineering (M&E), flight operations, and ramp services should be service functions to the rest of the airline and should treat the airline as their customer. As the airline adapts its proposition to evolving customer needs, to changes in technology, to changing staff needs, the airline operational departments need to adapt also. They need not to be islands with different priorities, culture, and values. Safety, reliability, and technical quality will take a higher focus than in other functions, but there is an opportunity to excel, or disappoint, the airline, the end customer, and staff in a number of other areas.

The operational functions need to be truly customer-focused. This requires the senior-level leadership driving top to bottom really good listening to the airline customer and then a high-quality response. M&E and ramp services are fundamental to meeting flight-by-flight customer needs not just by providing an on-time flight but by providing a cabin, galleys, and a cockpit, which are fully functional. Flight ops' cockpit crew are fundamental to safety but can also add value elsewhere, in their announcements to passengers, for example, in liaising smartly with ground staff.

M&E can respond to developing customer needs by integrating between the original equipment manufacturers (OEMs), regulators, and internal product departments to develop new customer propositions. They can add value to new innovative product introductions by pointing out what is viable by ensuring what is fitted is reliable. Finnair's innovative AirLounge business-class seat without actuators, Qatar's Qsuite, and the pioneering narrowbody lie-flat seats flown by such as JetBlue are all testament examples of operational departments and the directly customer-facing product departments working excellently together.

As the airline develops its brand and proposition, the operation needs to become more flexible and responsive. The traditional lead time in opening new destinations, for example, needs to be dramatically reduced. The speed of enabling the airline to, on the day of flight, up- or down-gauge to meet passenger loads on a service must be much faster. Adjustment of cabins to meet changed demand profiles needs to be less slow. The need for nimbleness has been demonstrated in particular during the pandemic with a new range of requirements from cleaning protocols to touch free controls to customer information on aircraft cabin air ventilation. We've seen the recent urgency drive faster responses, but this speed and agility need to be maintained in non-pandemic times.

The airline may be broadening its proposition to be more meaningful to the customer in areas where engineering and flight ops can help. Supporting, for example, customer simulator or hangar visits, enabling customers to join otherwise underused delivery flights, repurposing old seats or aircraft parts. Ramp services would be key for a new end-to-end luggage transfer product.

As well as being a good listener, the operational functions need to be effective modern communicators. In today's environment the customer wants a clear honest explanation of a delay, not a cover-up. The already on-board first-class customer with a mechanic fixing their seat wants a clear explanation of what has failed and what the fix is. Passengers want to see the ramp staff properly handling their luggage as they look out of the plane window waiting to go. The pilot or cabin crew, often international, require the technical staff to be confidently communicating in English and to be treated as customers. Delivering all these skills requires training and development in softer areas often not currently well covered with frontline technical staff and even with pilots.

The culture is usually more conservative in the operational functions but needs to be aligned with the rest of the airline and anyhow staff are, rightly, demanding a more modern, less traditional working environment. A requirement from the workforce for hybrid working can be met in the overhead departments of the operational functions, less so on the front line, but here there is an opportunity to increase the flexibility of working patterns to the benefit of both the staff and the company. Modern information technology (IT) systems, such as those from Jeppesen, Sabre, and AIMS, enable pilots to express their roster preferences while meeting operational needs. Maintenance staff in the hangars should be deployed more intensively off the commercial peaks, which again should appeal to the staff as well as the airline by, for example, enabling more holidays in a northern hemisphere summer.

Driving diversity and inclusion in a currently overly male-dominated operation is essential. This requires working with schools and universities to ensure a diverse workforce entering and pursuing a career in engineering schools, pilot training, and vocational training institutes and then following up with providing great development and careers for all meriting, with some clearly visible role models.

Operational departments, to meet customer and staff needs, must also move away from the current emphasis on staff's time served to one where innovation is more valued, ideas are sought from all staff, and staff are continuously provided with opportunities to develop and learn. Ideally even pilot progression should be less on seniority than currently, more on merit where the definition of merit includes not only command and flying skills, but also attributes meaningful to the airline, such as customer focus and empathy.

The new business environment requires a top-to-bottom digitally savvy team. Again the traditional nature of the operational departments can hold them back. In many airline M&E, flight ops, and maintenance, repair, and overhaul (MRO) departments, still, senior management never uses modern digital tools such as social media. So how can they be expected to lead their teams into an environment with very different ways or working and of interacting with internal and external customers? How can they encourage their pilots or engineers who are already posting to Twitter or Instagram in a way which can be really supportive to the airline? Often these more social media-savvy staff will have thousands or tens of thousands of followers, a tremendous opportunity for the airline if well captured. A good opportunity for upwards mentoring.

Digital transformation will be the key means by which the operational functions deliver more for less cost, as required by the airline customer. Cost reductions can be achieved through ready access to data on the front line; predictive maintenance; aiding lean process improvement, for instance of the supply chain; and automation of back office or even frontline processes. The gains achievable are in double-digit percentages. In transit-line maintenance, just picking one of many examples, staff utilization is rarely above 50%, usually lower. Digital technology, presenting more up-to-date information on the schedule, on the location of the aircraft, on its status, and of the documentation and parts needed to fix, easily holds the prospect of a 20% gain in productivity.

Looking further ahead, emerging technologies such as digital twins and 3D printing, already used in manufacturing but little in maintenance, will need to be evaluated. The parts supply chain with its heavy emphasis on traceability and back-to-birth records is an obvious candidate for blockchain with very little development so far. And the Internet of Things offers the opportunity to join together different currently quite fragmented processes and assets in the maintenance of aircraft and engines.

In the cockpit, we have belatedly finally moved to digital paperless cockpits, a significant productivity leap. The last big leap in staffing was dropping the flight engineer to move to a two-pilot cockpit, much resisted at the time. Thanks to digital and automation technology, the era of single-pilot operation is within sight, first for freighters and first with a second ground-based pilot only for critical flight phases, so able to handle multiple aircraft.

The operation currently almost takes pride in the messiness of their processes, for instance, advertising the number of different steps or parties required to turn a plane around at the gate. Digital technology offers a massive prospect of simplifying and streamlining with all ramp processes on a single platform so that all parties have real-time access to all data and, more important, enabling the airline customer to be presented with a single consolidated view of the status of the aircraft. FedEx and Amazon are achieving on-time customer fulfilment in the high 99.9s. The airline operation owes this to the airline customer. With innovative digital implementation this can be achieved.

All airline functions need to be delivering their product sustainability and supporting the airline-level sustainability imperative. Of course, safety is the first sustainability requirement, and after flight ops, engineering plays a key role, providing a safe defect free aircraft to the cockpit crew. Requirements have moved on from the old days when a certain engine shutdown rate or defect level was tolerated, with zero being the new target and often achieved. The new demands are, of course, well beyond safety. The engineering and ramp services functions are significant energy, water, and chemicals consumers, and opportunities to improve supporting overall company targets need to be driven. How many hangar roofs are today covered in solar panels?

Fuel burn is the top airline-level sustainability target, and the flight ops department plays the biggest role in optimization through using the latest digital analysis tools, collecting data, both current and trends, from the aircraft, the weather, and the individual pilot uplift history. And the flight ops function needs to take advantage of the latest technologies available such as constant descent approaches, shorter flight paths. Engineering can support fuel-burn improvement by providing the most efficient aircraft that includes engine washing to the right frequency, control surface seals in good condition, and the latest fuel-saving modifications incorporated into the engine or airframe. Many of these initiatives need a payback-period calculation, but this needs to be tilted toward the airline customer requirements. If the airline's proposition to the customer is a more sustainable product, as is now close to mandatory, then the operational departments need to be more than supporting; they need to be enabling.

In many areas, a traditional mindset in the operational departments needs to be overcome, but in others, they have a view into the future that they can provide to the airline customer. In spotting new technologies which the new airframe, engine and cabin OEMs are introducing for example. Examples, all with a very direct airline and customer benefit, are in moving to super-light seats in Etihad Airways without loss of room and comfort, adopting the latest satellite technology for fast Wi-Fi in the cabin, and working with the OEMs on lower cabin altitudes even on new metal fuselage aircraft.

In the fleet planning context, engineering has a special insight into the development path of different fleet types or of new technologies, such as carbon fibre, or new ideas, such as folding wingtips. Engineering and flight ops in many airlines took the lead, for example, in endorsing the big twins over the four-engine Boeing 747 and A340–600. This was supported by their positive reliability assessment of the new engines, and of course a view of the maintenance cost advantages of two engines over four. An engineering assessment of the A380 in the 2010s would have quickly come to the conclusion that the engines were outdated, that the aircraft was too heavy since built to be stretched, and that four engines were inefficient unless the aircraft stretched. And now we see twin-engine flying entering a new era as narrowbodies fly over eight hours point-to-point, across the Atlantic, between Australia and Asia, and between the Indian sub-continent and Europe.

The operational departments now face some new evaluation challenges. They need to support the airline make as assessment as to whether, where and when electric propulsion will become dominant. We see that in the car industry the engineers or businesspeople of the major car manufacturers missed the move to electric, leaving a massive opportunity to new entrant Tesla. As well as alternative propulsion, new fuels need to be evaluated; sustainable aviation fuel (SAF) is relatively straightforward, but hydrogen is more challenging. In supporting fleet evaluations, engineering and flight ops may need to assess new manufacturers, such as COMAC. The procurement side of the airline would dearly love to have a wider choice to increase negotiating leverage. An evaluation of a new manufacturer needs to not just include the initial product and its predicted quality, efficiency and timeliness but also service and support ten and twenty years out.

Many of the most successful businesses of the 21st century, such as Apple, Google, and Facebook, are engineering-populated and engineering-driven and pride themselves on the quality of their operation and cost of production. But meeting and understanding clear and developing customer needs with bold innovation. Well-led operational functions in an airline are well placed to support and enable airline success in this environment of very different customers, staff, and technologies.

Everything will remain different—a different view on change

Peter Glade
Chief Commercial Officer, SunExpress Airlines

I love you, you're perfect: now change—Why we need to bid farewell to a loved business model to make it survive

Somehow much of what we are reading in the airline industry—regardless of when it was written—starts by stating that the pressure on the industry had never been as high as today, whenever that was. So, take this as a given and add the pressure of the aftermath of the COVID-19 pandemic and the current extremely high fuel prices. These two developments alone are placing the airline industry in the eye of the storm, which is blowing right into the face of the airline industry, and that is very likely to blow away one or more airlines.

When a hurricane hits a forest, there are two sorts of trees that will survive. On one hand are the trees that have very solid, deep roots and a large trunk, with no parasites. For airlines, those with very solid balance sheets, deep pockets filled with cash, and/or other sources of financial means outside of pure airline economics. On the other hand are trees that are fully flexible, that can bend like a bamboo. In the case of airlines, these would be companies with modern, open information technology (IT) architecture, agile processes, and a leadership team that first acts and then asks for permission and leadership that values and uses the potential of their teams and that are well protected by a network of partnerships that work through bad and worse times.

Not having fully overcome the COVID-19 crisis yet, the industry is now challenged by the crisis in Eastern Europe and the resulting increase in the price of fuel.

No matter what the crisis is, airlines are facing the same issues over and over, because everyone is so busy firefighting that there is never time and budget to truly change. Examples?

- Inertia of airline processes (how many 9-nail-printers still exist at airport gates?)
- Those who are not trying to live fully autonomous are left with anything-else-but-seamless interfaces
- Legacy IT systems that seem to somehow have survived the extinction of the dinosaurs fit into modern IT architectures, like a wienerschnitzel with french fries into Copenhagen's Noma restaurant.
- Internalized every-person-for-themselves mentalities make cooperative open-source solutions scarce.

A tree standing all by itself on a plain has a far lower chance of surviving a hurricane. Forests have become the natural habitats of trees because their different species coexist …

The market may recover between the crises that will always hit the airline business, but it has never really been getting easier. Hence, now is the time to show that airlines, even without the pressure of life-threatening crises in their necks, can question existing structures and jointly rethink everything. And let's face it, even if that miracle happened and the industry would, for example, not take a decade to develop and implement a new distribution capability and then truly support it with all consequences, the industry would still be surrounded by government bodies, infrastructure providers, IT suppliers, and other players that have a vested interest in maintaining the status quo.

Governments around the world will be filling their coronavirus-challenged pockets with "sustainability taxes" for air travel in some form or another—a measure gratified by the electorate, as flying is supposedly a dirty "luxury". What about the increasing kerosine prices, increasing cost for recruiting qualified colleagues as the "war for talent globalizes" and all the investments that the industry will need to shoulder to fulfill their share to reach the 1.5-degree target? Where is there room for this, what was it called again, oh yes—profit?

The situation reminds me a bit of the good old cinema business model. In this business model, the ticket price itself is not how they earn money. Solution? So-called concessions, the sales at the food stalls. Popcorn & Co. are not only making up to 35% of total revenue of cinemas[1] but also are contributing dream-margins. It is the blended calculation of cinema tickets and concessions that a cinema owner is making reliable profits.

We know this; we just call it "ancillaries". Equipped with a similar charm as in cinemas—meals on board, seat reservations, and extra baggage are relevant cash cows already today.

In my opinion, 35% of total revenue for airlines is not aggressive enough of a target. In an industry so prone to external influence on its traditional flight revenue streams, this can only be the beginning. The target should not be more earnings before interest and taxes per flight, the target should be the 300-plus days, on which a normal passenger doesn't even think of flying, is not surfing on airline websites, let alone opening an airline app or walking into a travel agency (some might remember what that was—and I promise you good travel agencies will survive us all, but this a different topic). If the industry really wants to rethink retail, this does not mean to give new names to old systems; it means designing internal processes, currently geared toward compliance and cost optimization, to be able to truly leverage the power of start-ups. This means considering collaboration between competitors in innovative fields as a chance and not as "giving up a competitive advantage". I am baffled every time I read that one carrier alone started a "sustainable aviation fuel" initiative.

We will be looking at an aviation world where it is not passenger streams and slots that determine the design of our networks but the propensity to spend and onboard margins. To the extreme, if coffee has a better margin than beer, a flight might be planned in the morning rather than in the evening. There is no department in any airline that will not be affected by this profound cultural change. Or where is the finance department that already has a product profitability control based on personas and point of sale, as a retailer would? Looking at job ads for cabin crew, the industry is still looking for "great hosts" rather than "great salespeople". Of course, safety is always first, but when will maintenance departments find solutions for product presentations more attractive than catering trolleys? Has anyone ever thought through that no passenger really wants to go to the airport; they just want to arrive somewhere? Why does the airline industry always think their job starts when someone thinks of going somewhere? Where is the airline that has gone the "Red Bull way" and converted its brand to be so strong that selling drinks/flying aircraft becomes irrelevant to the business profits? The competitor of business travel focused airlines is MS Teams, Zoom and Skype, the competitor of leisure carriers is the car dealership at the corner or the kitchen studio down the street. Questions around the tangible (more effective meetings) and nontangible (status, coolness) values an airline can create for its customers to convince them to add the time and hassle and fly somewhere, instead of a quick videoconference will be more important than analyzing daily booking numbers.

Will we, as a small, well-connected airline community, find the right answers within ourselves? Or do we need some large entertainment or retail company to come and disrupt our business model?

Let's not be like the small arthouse cinemas, mostly pure hobby with little to no profitability, charming but somehow fallen out of time—instead, let us have the courage to reinvent ourselves and disrupt the market from inside. Ideas include large-scale cooperation, for example, in sustainability matters across brands, balance sheets, and country barriers. This would need to be based on open architecture of core systems that prioritizes the ability to integrate over the ability to ensure that every special case that might come up can always be handled correctly.

Don't get me wrong: New Distribution Capability (NDC) is already a huge step in that direction, it is just taking far too long to spread throughout the industry. Every airline and many IT providers are already developing their own "dialect" of NDC, and those companies trying to use this "standard" are back to developing individual interfaces. With this added complexity and this speed to market, the industry will struggle to truly convince business partners, relevant to the value chain, to adapt this standard. It is odd that the aviation industry assumes that by slightly amending the existing IT landscape its business model could be revolutionized. An airline that wants to be a retailer has to put retailing into the heart of its IT landscape, replacing its PSS systems as the main source of information storage with persona-based marketing machines that generate the right customer interactions at the right customer touch point at the right price at right point in time.

The main asset that an airline can bring into any partnership along the value chain is not retailing capability or the planning capabilities that so many carriers are proud of. The importance of long-term planning will continue to deteriorate, but it is the fact that to travel on a plane people have to sit on seats in a metal tube not able to escape for a few hours and it is still the fascination of flying. It is embarrassing how little airlines have monetized on these simple two facts. While in modern supermarkets artificial intelligence can tell, after a few seconds, how likely it is for a consumer to buy one or the other product, many carriers are overwhelmed to deliver the correct prepaid meal to a customer who decided to sit in a different seat than written on the PIL (passenger information list). Many airlines are love brands in their core markets, but only very few actually expand this through intelligent brand expansions and partnerships. The image of trustworthiness and safety attitude, many airline brands already are recognized for, is something many other companies would long for using if only as a halo effect.

No, we are not diverse in the global airline leadership. And, as a mid-forties, hetero, white male, I might be the wrong advocate for this, but what unites us more than our sex, race, and educational background is the passion for this business. A business model that is unique will only survive if we change. Fast and profound.

Stop playing copycat

Glenn Hollister
Vice President Sales Strategy & Effectiveness, United Airlines

Something that has long bedeviled the airline industry is lack of differentiation, otherwise known as commoditization. Airline executives are wont to bemoan the customer behavior of switching to a competitor over a $5 to $10 price difference. Those same executives will often point to the price- and schedule-focused shopping displays of air travel retailers (online travel agencies, metasearch engines and corporate booking tools) as the source of commoditization.

While those retailers do create a level of commoditization, there is another, more profound source of commoditization. The commoditization of the industry starts with the decisions made by airlines about the design of their product and service. While some airlines will sometimes design a product starting with a blank sheet of paper, the reality is most airlines' products and services are developed over time through a series of small decisions. And many of those decisions are driven by a desire to match what a competitor has done.

This has been happening for decades. When one airline introduced a separate boarding line for its elite customers, other airlines soon followed. When an airline moved to a simplified fare structure, other airlines followed as quickly as they could. When an airline replaced volume-based corporate agreements with share-based agreements, the others followed. Seating products and services are a frequent area of copying. Angle flat business class gave way to lie flat, followed by all aisle access. Currently the decisions and discussions are about having doors on business class seats. In area after area, the copycat game has played out: agency incentive programs, change fees, global distribution system participation, bag allowances and fees, and COVID-era cleanliness programs are some recent examples.

Ultimately, the copycat game comes about because airlines lack a customer strategy. They have not decided which customers they want to serve. Lacking a defined customer, they also lack a clear picture of what they should and should not do to win customers. When a competitor rolls out a new feature or benefit, other airlines are afraid this feature or benefit will be a competitive advantage and therefore blindly copy it.

Part of the difficulty here is that for large network carriers, their planes tend to carry a lot of different customer types. The typical large, network carrier plane will have a mix of different types of business travelers, some leisure travelers who are willing to pay for a better experience, and some cost focused leisure travelers. This stands in contrast to a highly focused carrier, such as Allegiant, which flies a specific type of route and carries a specific type of passenger. But just because an airline carries every type of passenger does not mean that it should design its products and services to appeal to all types of passengers. Pick a core customer set and design for that.

146 Thought leadership pieces

The famous Harvard Business School professor Michael Porter suggests there are four generic (or basic) strategies as shown in Figure 8.5. The generic strategies are defined along two dimensions: competitive scope and competitive advantage. Within the scope question, a firm (an airline in our case) can choose to focus on one customer segment only, or they can decide to compete in multiple segments. In terms of competitive advantage, the generic choice is between being cost focused or have a differentiated product.

The problem with many airlines is they often have not picked a strategy. Many want to serve multiple customer segments and have competitive costs while differentiating their product. Instead of having a distinct strategy, they are stuck in the middle.

But there is no need to be stuck in the middle. Some of the most successful airlines over time have been clear on their strategy. See Figure 8.6.

- A ULCC that operates in a specific market—taking vacationers from secondary cities to the main entertainment destinations, such as Las Vegas and Orlando.
- An LCC that, while not the absolute lowest-cost carrier, is the cost leader among carriers that serve a wide range of segments.
- A full service Asian carrier that has developed a high-touch, distinctly Japanese product that appeals greatly to a wide range of Japanese travelers.

So how does an airline stuck in the undifferentiated middle plot its way to a distinctive strategy? It is well beyond the scope of this writing to lay out the step-by-step process for developing a complete strategy, but an airline's particular fleet, network and geography provide a starting point and some guidance on which direction to head.

An airline's fleet is an important determinant of its ability to execute a low-cost strategy. There is a reason most LCCs around the world fly either the B737 family or the A320 family—they have the lowest costs per available seat

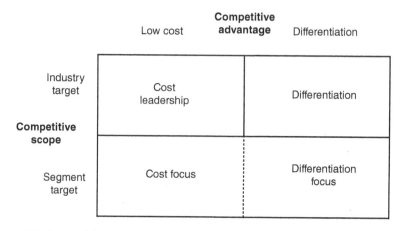

Figure 8.5 Competitive scope versus competitive advantage

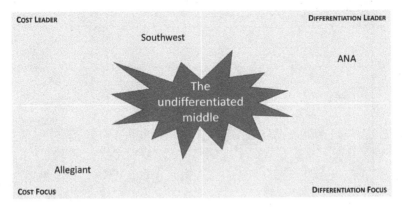

Figure 8.6 The undifferentiated middle

kilometer of any fleet types currently available. Conversely, an airline with multiple fleet types, especially across regional jets, narrowbodies and widebodies is going to struggle to execute on a low-cost strategy, due to the inherent complexity and cost of operating such a fleet.

Fleet size also in a determinant in an airline's ability to execute a segment-focused strategy. If an airline has a large fleet relative to the size of the market it operates in, a single segment strategy is unlikely to work. An airline with a segment strategy that wants to grow without diluting its focus on a single segment will find a difficult path in many cases, due to the limitations on growth across borders imposed by the Chicago convention and foreign ownership rules.

Network itself is a topic as strategy, but one basic way to think about network is whether the primary focus is carrying passengers point to point, or the alternative where there is a high degree of connecting passengers over something that resembles a hub. In general, the nature of a connecting operation tends to push an airline towards a broad strategy, as connecting operations usually need to pull from a wide range of segments in order to fill planes. There can be exceptions, with Icelandair serving as an example of an airline serving a well-defined segment with a high percentage of connecting passengers. But connecting airlines lacking a unique factor, such as Iceland's mid-Atlantic geography, will be hard-pressed to execute a segment-focused strategy.

The key element of geography is not the physical geography, but the market demographics in the geography the airline serves. Understanding the market segments in a particular geography is a deep topic in itself, but a starting point is to look at two key factors: disposable income and the industries that operate in the geography.

Data on disposable income are easily available for most countries and are a good starting point to understand the amount of money available to be spent on airline tickets, as well as the type of product that the segment wants to buy. This area is particularly important for understanding leisure and visiting friends and relatives travel, as those types of tickets are paid for by the traveler themselves. See Figure 8.7.

148 *Thought leadership pieces*

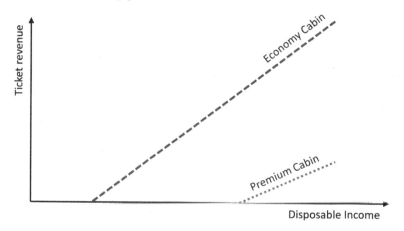

Figure 8.7 Ticket revenue versus disposable income

When it comes to business travel, it is important to understand not just the volume of economic activity but also the nature of industries in the market. Different industries have widely varying travel intensities, with sectors such as professional services (consultants and accountants) and financial services (bankers) traveling extensively and having the ability to pay for premium tickets. On the other hand, sectors such as retail or manufacturing travel much less intensively and are (typically) significantly more cost conscious. See Figure 8.8.

There are many levels of detail beyond the basic strategies. The overall point, however, is not to develop an airline's strategy by looking at what competitors are doing. Instead, look at the unique factors that define your

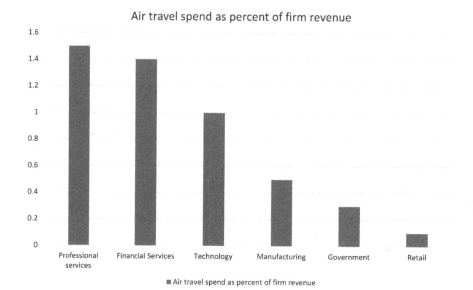

Figure 8.8 Air travel spend as percent of firm revenue

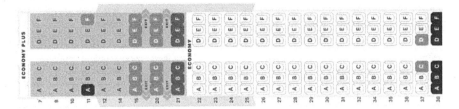

Figure 8.9 Case study: extra legroom seating in the US market

Note: Both airlines have first cabins with 16 seats.

business and develop a strategy to match. Product and service design should flow from your airline's unique strategy, not your competitors' actions. See the case study in Figure 8.9.

Case study: Extra legroom seating in the US market

Sometimes the copycat decisions play out in ways that are clearly not in the airline's best interests.

A famous example is the extra legroom coach seating competition that played out in the early to mid-2000s in the United States. It started with United creating the Economy Plus product by taking out one row of seats and increasing seat pitch in the front of the cabin. United decided on this strategy in order to make their economy cabin more appealing to frequent business travelers who earned elite status in their frequent-flyer program. To offset the loss in revenue from the removed seats, United also developed a strategy to upsell other customers to the extra legroom seats.

American Airlines (AA) saw United's move and did not want to be left out. Clearly not understanding the purpose behind United's move, AA decided to respond by going one better. AA removed *two* rows of seats to create "More Room Throughout Coach". By doing this, AA created a better experience for everyone but at a clear loss of revenue. By giving the better product to everyone they lost the ability to upsell, and so the revenue impact was just the loss of the two rows of seats, without any offsetting upsell revenue.

After a relatively short period, More Room Throughout Coach quietly disappeared from AA's fleet.

Some years later, AA introduced a new extra legroom product called Main Cabin Extra. This time, AA was developing a product based on its own business and designed to fit its market and needs. Not surprisingly the cabin configuration was different than United's.

Neither cabin configuration is inherently better than the other. It is all a matter of how the cabin configuration fits into the overall strategy of who the airline wants to serve, where those people live, the type of network and equipment the airline has and many other related factors.

Enhancing revenue management analyst effectiveness with human–machine symbiosis: learning to work with machines

Jason Kelly
CEO, Kambr, an Amadeus company

Overview

Revenue management (RM) today is at a crossroads. The complexity, velocity, and sheer quantity of decisions that airline decision-makers face is at an all-time high. Decisions that once allowed months of planning and coordination now must be made in days or hours to outpace the rate of environmental change. At the same time, using only batched, inward-looking, and historical data to drive decisions, the technology available to RM decision-makers has not kept pace.

Even when RM teams do have access to excellent low-latency tools for situational awareness, analyzing, synthesizing, and evaluating situations quickly and effectively are challenging tasks. Commercial teams operate in silos. Feedback loops between revenue management, pricing, network planning, scheduling, marketing, and e-commerce teams (if they exist at all) are typically high-latency processes like meetings and email. RM analysts have traditionally been asked to serve the role of bridging the gap between the actual airline business problem and the technological solutions meant to enable them. **What is needed is a reexamination of the way that people and machines work together to solve this problem.**

For example, consider an airline wants to adjust its planned schedule in the future, adjusting the number of flights and times of departure. The RM analyst *may* receive advance notice of this plan through communication with the scheduling team but often will not have a full understanding of how the RM system, pricing, competition, and existing automation will respond until after the flights are loaded and are put on sale. Understanding how customers will react to the new schedule, how existing passengers will be reaccommodated, and how new passengers will flow through the network are crucial to a successful inventory strategy. These effects will not be uniform and can only be modeled in advance to a limited extent. Today it is solely up to the RM analyst to create an integrated picture of this change and respond with strategic adjustments to optimize the new schedule. Compounding this is the time pressure created by the fact that these new flights are already for sale, and that this schedule change is likely only one of 5 to 10 similar situations that the RM analyst needs to handle this week. See Figure 8.10.

The primary constraint on revenue management performance today is the ability of teams to efficiently make decisions in an extraordinarily complex and fast-evolving environment. To best expand the ability for airline decision-makers to achieve (and thus for airlines to achieve), we need to address how to harmoniously leverage people **AND** technology to address this challenge.

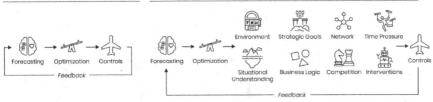

Figure 8.10 The RM analyst bears the burden of translating the airline business problem into the language of the RM system.

Airline decision-makers are **task saturated**—a condition that occurs when there are more tasks than there are resources, tools, and time to address them. Common symptoms of task saturation include a lack of organizational focus, a tendency to reorganize and reshuffle tasks while little is achieved and only the most urgent tasks are executed.

Amplifying the task saturation is the high degree of intrinsic complexity inherent to airline planning problems, which are often multidimensional and require interactions with other parties. While addressing this problem with modern technology seems like a natural next step; we should be cautious: modern technology and communication platforms can easily worsen task saturation issues if they add to the complexity or volume of the tasks needing to be performed.

RM departments have lagged in the integration of machine learning, automation, and statistical reasoning into core processes. Analytic processes that exist are often overwritten or heavily adjusted in favor of simpler heuristic methods. High-quality demand forecasters and optimization techniques that are well understood and carefully crafted have outputs that are overwritten in more than 80% of cases at many airlines. We should not view this as a lack of understanding or of systemic trust but rather as a symptom of our technology not addressing the entire problem and that the human element of strategic problem-solving has been poorly integrated into RM processes to date. **The interface/integration between people and technology is crucial to effectively addressing the task saturation issue and capturing the revenue opportunities that exist in the marketplace.**

The convergence and improvement of human–machine interaction

Before we dive deeper into the issue at hand within revenue management, let's first zoom out and look at the greater macrotrends that can point to the path that lies ahead. Over the last century, we've been experiencing the convergence of human–machine interaction and all technology has been and is being developed around this process of inputs and outputs.

To contextualize this phenomenon, let us look at the specific framework of communications. See Figure 8.11. We as a species relied on ancient means of communication such as the Egyptians' hieroglyphics, wall writing; the Andean

Figure 8.11 The evolution of communications
Image from light the mind.

people's Quechua khipu (also written as quipu), a counting system using knots; and smoke signals, one of the oldest forms of long-distance communication.

The introduction of machine-assisted communication transformed human interaction. In the 19th century, the telegraph, Morse code, the telephone and the radio were all introduced/created, paving a new era of communication. From there on, how quickly and how effectively we communicate with one another has been influenced by the inputs and outputs between ourselves and machines.

Today, all technology is being developed around human–machine interaction and how to improve the process of inputs and outputs of information. We've gone from keyboards and landlines to mobile phones and voice-enabled technology such as Amazon's Alexa and Apple's Siri.

The "magic" of these interactions is how fast information (i.e., data) can be transmitted and received in real time, significantly reducing latency. In the future this symbiotic connection between humans and machines will only integrate deeper with technology such as virtual reality, the metaverse and Elon Musk's Neuralink.

And it's not just communications; every industry has/is undergoing significant change thanks to this human–machine interaction and process of transmitting information in real time. Finance with automated trading, advertising/marketing with programmatic system and entertainment with streaming are just a few of many examples.

However, the aviation industry lags and requires a further fusion with technology (much of the industry was built before the internet era and it shows), but what could this macrotrend tell us about the future of revenue management?

Repetitive tasks and cognition

The revenue management analyst role can be highly repetitive. Analysts are asked to make decisions on relatively similar problems with small variations in the inputs – with feedback being a mix between immediate (i.e., "how did my competitor react?") and long delayed (i.e., "was this decision beneficial to revenue?" that is sometimes not known for many months).

In *Thinking Fast and Slow*, Daniel Kahneman proposes a model for cognition wherein the brain has two systems for processing problems:

System 1:
> High-speed, unconscious decisions that are automatic and effortless. Once prompted with a set of inputs, you "know" the answer immediately or by recall with little additional reasoning. For instance, the answer to 2 + 2, recognizing the face of a relative, or how to drive a car down a road are all examples of things that most people can do with little conscious cognitive effort. System 1 covers more than 98% of the decisions that people make in a day.

System 2:
> Low-speed, conscious decision-making that requires mental effort or reasoning. It is controlled, skeptical, and logical. The role of system 2 is to handle situations that have never been encountered before, for example learning to drive for the first time, answering 2405×3542, or writing a persuasive argument. System 2 accounts for less than 2% of the decisions we make each day.

Why are "system 1" and "system 2" relevant to the revenue management analyst? Most current RM analysts' tasks are firmly in system 1—they can generally assess a situation and map it to a response with little to no time required for effortful reasoning.

Enter machine learning and robotic process automation

With the ubiquity of powerful computing, open-source software, cheap data storage, and the internet—It's now practically possible for the techniques that powered substantial manufacturing productivity gains in the 20th century to deliver similar gains to knowledge workers in the 21st century. Robotic process automation (RPA) and machine learning (ML) open the doors to automating repetitive cognitive tasks. In general, if a decision process can be written down, it's likely that it can be automated.

As of this writing (2022), machine learning can only do "system 1" type reasoning. ML can cleverly understand statistical relationships in data that would not be apparent to humans and can arguably access a substantially larger archive of relevant historical situations. However, ML cannot reason through novel situations or learn to generalize anywhere close to how well people can. ML doesn't form abstract theories and concepts that can be used to generalize in new situations. ML can't set its own goals or understand when pursuing a given objective is no longer relevant.

To escape from task saturation and effectively manage complexity, we need to change the role of the RM analyst from managing the outputs of a technology system, to instead manage the design of the system itself. The RM analyst of the future is a domain-expert and data scientist. The chief roles of this new RM analyst include the following:

- Creating new ideas—What are new approaches to solving the problem?
- Setting goals—What should we be trying to achieve?

- Recognizing broad-spectrum patterns and causality—Where are feedback loops forming? How can we improve the models and processes?
- Complex communication—How can we provide other business units at the airline the contextual story behind the data in a value-added way?

RPA and ML will be able to substantially increase the leverage of each RM decision-maker by extending their process to no longer be bound by execution time. Therefore, it's not about ML (programming an algorithm and letting it go on its own in replace of the analyst) but about "managed machine learning" where human inputs and machines work in lockstep.

It's not a question of human or machine but a matter of human and machine

Seamless integration of ML/RPA decreases cognitive load of the analyst by taking over many of the repetitive unconscious decisions, freeing up the analyst to focus on strategic tasks. To be successful, however, analysts must feel as though process automation and machine learning are faithful agents in executing strategy.

The user experience we need to seek should be something akin to flying a plane on autopilot—underneath it is a highly complex process involving a substantial number of controllers, sensors, feedback loops, physical output, and interaction with an unpredictable external environment, but on the surface most of that is abstracted away to a set of goals controlled by the pilots. Autopilots are a reliable way to reduce workload and allow pilots to focus on planning and higher-level tasks and only achieve this goal because there is a good segmentation of duties and an understanding of limitations built into system design. When inputs disagree or are not consistent with expectations, the automation alerts the pilot and hands over control. Attaining this level of simplicity, the separation of duties and systemic reliability is a core focus of Kambr and a key to successfully integrating RM analysts with ML and RPA.

Value unlocked through automation

One area of recent focus for revenue management is the integration of real-time streaming data, which requires a significant shift from the batch uploads that are standard for airlines today. Additionally, there is substantial value in integrating data-sources beyond traditional passenger service system data to inform better RM optimization—for instance event data, customer relations management, social, or ecommerce integrations. To integrate all this signal is a significant task, and one that is likely limited in value without processes (both human and technological) that are ready to deal with low-latency and non-traditional data. In essence—if we are already task-saturated and bound by the amount of complexity that we can handle as a part of business processes, we can only capture the value offered by adopting additional complexity if we first address the need to better automate our existing tasks.

Kambr is addressing this needed shift in RM with a platform that was built with modularity in mind from its inception. See Figure 8.12. While silos exist in businesses today (especially with data, which often divided between vendors and only readily accessible through silo-specific platforms), centralizing these data into a single platform is critical to getting the most value possible from ML. All information sources and relevant context need to be ingested within a single system so the algorithms powering ML models can best learn about the relationships between all the signals and data flowing through the commercial ecosystem. Building, merchandizing, marketing, and pricing an offer in a coordinated fashion requires that the network of decision makers at an airline all have access to see the entire problem—and the automation and ML that will take actions on their behalf is no different.

Dynamic pricing and dynamic offer initiatives will be similarly unlikely to deliver promised value until some degree of ML symbiosis is achieved by RM teams. In dynamic pricing, offers may be constructed or modified at shop time to improve the expected value of each shop. This requires RM teams to view their interactions with RM systems not as deciding or overwriting system inputs/outputs but rather as setting the goals and logic necessary such that the models act as expected without intervention.

Once properly integrated, ML, RPA, and analysts can substantially increase capacity for making both a higher volume of decisions and better-quality decisions. ML and automation will be reliably trusted to do tasks that don't require critical thinking and continually be optimized by the analyst as systemic and strategic opportunities emerge. If we can best leverage the strengths of each, we should be able to capture substantially more revenue opportunity without a step-change requirement in the costs associated with RM.

- Revenue management platforms have a competitive advantage in efficiently solving an optimization problem and in integrating diverse data sources into a single place.
- ML has a competitive advantage in extracting statistical trends from observed data.
- Analysts have a competitive advantage in strategic thinking and translating business objectives into goals.

It's also critical that human-machine interaction takes place through an efficient medium equally interpretable to all parties. The human must be provided with a frictionless or near-frictionless way of interacting with the machine to carry out a desired action or task that is also easy to understand (i.e., inputting via voice command, heavy use of visualization, and simple, intuitive designs) and the machine must be provided with the necessary information/data to successfully carry out the task with limited ambiguity.

The RM interfaces of the future need to mirror how people interact with each other or with the physical world. Strong design principles promoting intuitive consistency, direct manipulation with immediate feedback, and physical metaphors have been hallmarks of the mobile devices that have

156 *Thought leadership pieces*

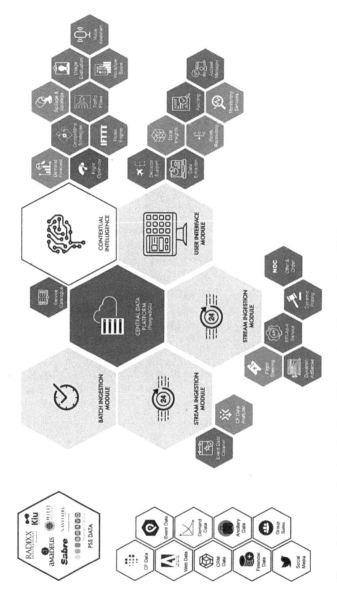

Figure 8.12 An early visualization of Kambr's architecture from 2019

come to define everyday computing. These platforms have successfully become integrated extensions of ourselves, with people able to perform complex and novel tasks with little to no instruction or documentation. **RM platforms must attain this level of simplicity and intuitiveness to allow humans to focus their mental energy on solving higher-order problems** rather than expending effort translating ideas into the arbitrary language of an interface designed for the convenience of machines.

Better together

People will always be a necessary component of revenue management. The analyst role shouldn't be replaced by machines but should evolve to a role where they act as shepherds for multiple models. The analyst of the near-future leverages the mechanical and computational superiority of automation and the statistical power of today's ML technology as instruments of their strategic planning/execution, doing so through a human-centric interface that provides an intuitive experience and business-optimal results.

The biggest and best ideas and companies will be those that best build around the relationship between man and machine. In the case of RM, analysts must free themselves from the trap of high tactical workload of tactical tasks by investing in an "automation mindset"—actively seeking to automate as many easily executed repeated tasks as possible to free up their time for complex problems and strategic functions. Simultaneously, RM system designers must begin to view user experience (and further the experience of integrating ML and RPA) as a critical enabler to system value-add. The best RM results will come from the best human–machine team.

Whatever you do, start with the customer

Jordie Knoppers
Customer Journey Manager Seamless Travel & Biometrics, KLM Royal Dutch Airlines

Creativity as the competitive advantage

Everyone who is working in the airline industry knows it. Aviation is most likely the most difficult and at the same time the least profitable sector in the industry. An industry that is not very adaptive to change operating in a world that is more subject to change than ever. Especially in this enormous turbulent world, it is not easy to survive as an airline. Airlines have to deal with challenges of the pandemic where every country has its own rules and regulations and where harmonization is far ahead of us. We live in a century where sustainability is more important than ever before. Driven by our strong believe in a carbon-neutral airline operation in the future, we feel the responsibility to minimize the environmental footprint year by year. Of course, this is driven by the political and social pressure as well. KLM's purpose of "moving your world by creating memorable experiences" means in this perspective "meaningful" experiences. In addition, the competition is bigger and fiercer than ever. If you cannot compete anymore on price and quality, the next big competitive advantage might be creativity. But it seems to be hard to mobilize creativity and to innovate together as a team, department, and organization, let alone at a country, unity level, or world level.

From the moment aviation arose until today, it is obvious that businesses in the world have made huge transformations. The beginning of the previous century was the era of manufacturing in which everything revolved around creating and optimizing assembly lines. After World War II, the arrival of supply chains made a huge impact and the way the distribution was organized became the distinguishing factor. The next big thing was the era of information and automation, starting three decades ago. Highly disrupting computer technology changed complete business models and the way companies organized themselves. Today, more than ever we are in the era of the customer. Customers are highly demanding, and the level of customer engagement is an important factor for doing business.

Customer experience is a movement, not a department!

Customer experience overtakes price and product as key brand differentiator.[2] That means that the reasons for travel have shifted. Network, fleet, and schedule are, after decades of aviation, still the heart and soul of an airline and are for customers still the first reasons of choice. However, where price used to come in second place, it is now brand and reputation. This means that we need to be keen on designing journeys along the needs and expectations of our customers. After all, our customers are not packages, but inspired persons with feelings. While traveling, they gain experiences with additional emotions such as satisfaction, uncertainty, happiness, or disappointment. Based on these experiences, customers decide whether to travel with you again. In a world where social media is very accessible, sharing experiences, good or bad, is daily business and can make or break your brand image. Wow! That is challenging for airlines whose processes have not changed much over decades.

From the start KLM's founder Albert Plesman wanted his crew to give our customers a warm and personal feeling. Today, after more than a hundred years of operation, this is still a core value of KLM. That does not mean that this is easy to do, but it definitely helps to have this mentality in the DNA of the company. The shift from price to brand and reputation as a reason of choice means that we not only have to design our customer journeys differently; we also have to sell our products differently. In other words, we are going to have to understand how to engage with our customers differently—not in the way airlines want to engage but in the way customers want. And there is not just a one-size-fits-all solution.

Different customers have different expectations on how they want to be engaged. A premium customer paying for a premium ticket has higher expectations than the low budget traveler buying a low-fare ticket. People are traveling for many different reasons. Some are visiting family or friends; others go on holidays. Some go on a business trip; others go for an event. Some have saved money for a ticket for a long time; others fly every month on company's costs. For some, the urgency to fly is extremely high; for others, it is just leisure. Some go alone; others in groups. Some fly with a direct flight; others transfer to another airline or another mode of transport. But regardless of the reason for travel, the sentiment on how people experience the journey is different for every individual. Indeed, the reality of customer experience is complex and designing customer journeys with many internal and external stakeholders involved is hard. That is why customer journey management has to be taken extremely seriously by securing customer experience in the C-suite and by having transversal and cross-functional teams in place to continuously optimize the customer journey. Customer experience should not be considered as a department that takes care of the customer; it is a movement that causes a cultural change within the complete company. And the customer experience movement is in full swing. It is the era of the customer. Great customer experiences do not happen by accident, they happen by design. For 72% of companies worldwide, improving their customer experience is top priority.[3]

Opportunities during emotional connection

Research reveals that 73% of all customer point to experience as an important factor in their purchasing decisions.[4] Every interaction with the company is an interaction with the company's brand. And every interaction counts. Every interaction is an opportunity to emotionally connect with your customer, and every emotional connection is a moment of truth: you can make it or break it. In order to create consistent experiences that fit your brand, integral journey management is crucial. In reality, this is easier said than done. There are many, many dots to connect. Customers face digital and human interactions, on many different channels and at many different touchpoints. That might be directly via KLM employees or indirectly via travel agents, corporate organizations, or partner airlines.

Airlines are silo-driven operational-oriented organizations. That makes it even harder to create customer engagement in every moment in the journey. And we don't just have to manage our own journey. Working with many partner airlines means alignment of customer expectations with each partner, not to mention the hundreds of airports we are flying to. All having their own management, their own infrastructure, their own suppliers, their own governments, and so on.

Outside in

The big question is, Where to start? The answer is whatever you do, start with the customer. Think from the outside in and step into the shoes of the customer. If a sharing economy is the new future that determines the behaviour of the customers, it is quite arrogant to think that as an airline you own the customers and the customers' data when they buy a ticket on your flight. It makes much more sense to think in ecosystems where customers are fully in control and own their own data. As an airline you might orient yourself of being part of an intermodal transport ecosystem, where customers buy the complete journey from door to door in one order, including pre-ordered food and drinks in the train or at the airport. The platform economy is growing, and the technology is available. The question is how we are going to overcome the fear of disruptive change and the mistrust of stakeholders in the ecosystem. Well, think global and act local. To predict the future is hard for everybody, but by continuing to experiment with an end vision in mind you will organically grow in the right direction. In KLM, we use service design methodologies to structure innovation processes. The key point here is that cross-functional project teams are working on customer understanding, ideation, prototyping and testing in order to develop scalable products.

If you ask the right questions and listen really well to the answers, you learn to understand customers' needs, expectations, experiences and ideas. In combination with market trends and corporate guidelines you will be able to create the vision statement and the strategic plan. Once I heard the story of a Western company helping an African village by constructing a drinking water supply system so the women of the village no longer had to walk for hours to get water from a water well miles away. A lot of effort was taken to get the water pipes to the village and get the system running. However, a few weeks later, the system was visually broken intentionally. The Western company fixed it immediately, but soon after the system was broken again. At first it was thought that this was because of the jealousy of a neighbour village, but in the end, the perpetrators turned out to be the women of the village. They did not accept the water supply because their social day trip with other women was taken away from them. This is a typical example of projecting Western theories on an African culture, inside out. In parallel, we cannot determine for our customers what their needs and expectations are. Deep customer research is needed to understand these.

We don't see things as they are, we see them as we are[5]

The biggest challenges in this world are not the huge problems like climate, food industry, environment, cybercrime, diversity, inclusion, or pandemics. It is whether we are able to develop sufficient innovation strength and creativity to be able to solve these major problems.

As Jeff Gaspersz—professor of innovation at Nyenrode Business University in the Netherlands—explains, there are three directions to strengthen innovation power.[6] The first direction is focus. Changing perspectives in order to create focus is very powerful. It is like the photographer who is constantly looking for different angles to capture the essence of his image. Changing perspective also means being able to look at yourself differently, as an individual, a team or a department. Regularly redefining your own value in the organization from different perspectives helps understand what your strengths are and how you can be most valuable for the company. And even more effective, allow others into your network who look differently at what you do.

I have learned from innovation projects that setting your mindset is crucial for creating opportunities, ideas, and insights. This is actually a quick win. Just think of opportunities you have seen elsewhere that leads to an opportunity for yourself. It is similar to how your brain is working when you have the intention to buy a red BMW, suddenly you will develop a strong focus on red BMW cars driving around. In the period I was the program manager for the KLM safety culture program, I did many company visits in other branches with my team to learn and understand what the real game-changers are for behavioural change. Concepts cannot be copied, but building your knowledge in this focused way helps constructively create your mindset. It gave us insights and triggered our creativity to come up with new ideas. Organizing exchange programs is definitely a proven concept that I still use today. From day one, airlines are good at developing networks, developing schedules, and safely running complex operations. Customer engagement is challenging for most airlines. It would be useful to get inspired from exchange programs with Starbucks, Marriott, or Amazon in order to improve customer engagement.

Alone you go fast, together you go further

The second direction to strengthen innovation power is connection. Innovation is not about inventing something new; it is about creating something new by connecting existing solutions. Sharing knowledge through collaboration and cross-fertilization. For example, the collaboration of Sony with Apple's iPhone resulted in video calling with the package deliverer via a security camera at the front door, without being home.

Leadership is crucial. Similar to how military teams are organized, employees should not only be evaluated as an individual but rather the team as a whole. Working with cross-functional teams is the foundation to flood your brain with new impulses, opportunities, possibilities, and insights. For journey management at KLM this is the basic principle. We co-create in teams with stakeholders from every discipline in the customer journey. We co-create with customers across the journey by using customer panels, by designing new concepts together with customers and by testing prototypes in live operation. We co-create with partners in the ecosystem. I strongly believe that co-creation is only successful when putting the customer in the centre of the equation. I was the project lead for KLM in the Aruba Happy Flow project, an end-to-end seamless airport journey based on facial recognition. Facial recognition itself was not new at that time. It was used for border crossing on a large scale. However, by connecting the existing technology to other airport touchpoints and creating a small ecosystem by use of an identity management platform, we were able to create a "hands in the pockets" experience for our customers: the first private-public solution based on biometrics. The idea became a breakthrough innovation. Besides KLM, many stakeholders were involved, from the airport, government, security and suppliers. Every stakeholder had his own interest in the project. The project was doomed to fail because stakeholders were thinking inside out, designing the solution from the point of view of their own processes. The decisive turning point came when we decided to put the customer first and drew up a trust framework with all stakeholders. From that moment, the stakeholders managed to think outside in and the project moved forward fast.

Think like a 5-year-old

The third direction to strengthen innovation power is curiosity. The mindset of organizations should be based on curiosity. Curiosity is characterized by asking questions. A child is able to ask hundreds of questions a day. But at school, children learn to give answers, and they lose the enormous power of asking questions.

It seems to be a no-brainer to keep on asking questions, but in practice, it has proved to be very difficult. In many cases employees are being judged on the achievements of targets, most of the time individual targets. A learning organization needs a safe environment in order to structurally challenge each other and to keep on asking questions. For this setup strong leadership is needed. People are taught to give answers and that is a persistent, hard to change trait.

In the 17th century, the Japanese haiku master Matsuo Basho wrote: "Do not seek to follow in the footsteps of the wise. Seek what they sought." We often learn more from someone's questions than from someone's answers. We use innovation to solve problems or to take advantage of opportunities. But regardless of the issue, the real root cause or potential is most of the time invisible. The "five times why", developed in the early 20th century by Sakichi Toyoda, an inventor and industrialist from Japanese origin as well, is a proven concept. The power is in the repetition of the question. The pitfall is that one starts from assumptions and classical causes of the problem, such as a lack of capacity and a lack of money. Or that one starts from the assumption that innovation will be the new game-changer and will solve it all. Nothing can move our brains faster than a good question. A question gives focus and gives new insights.

Personalization, the next big thing

Airport infrastructures are not sufficient to handle the growth in air travel. The willingness to fly is high and it is expected that air travel is going to continue to grow post pandemic. According to the NEXTT program,[7] three future trends are recognized in the customer journey. The first one is the movement from airport activities to off-airport activities. Second, the advanced processing of data being enabled by digital ID management and automation. The last is interactive decision-making by linking airline systems with real-time, trusted data.

In the end it all comes down to the people. Whether it be the customers, the employees or any stakeholders involved. To become future ready, it is key to collaborate, not only with your own team members, but with every stakeholder in your ecosystem. Trust frameworks and smart contracting help create reliable networks. Seamless journeys from door to door will become reality when ecosystems are adding value for each stakeholder. Real-time information at every moment in the journey is not feasible without connecting airline systems with airport systems, government systems, public transport systems, car traffic systems and so on. Privacy by design methodology is needed to ensure that specific protected data only can be unlocked for a specific stakeholder at a specific touchpoint for the specific process step at the specific moment in the journey.

Personalization is a choice of the customer. It is just a matter of asking your customers on how they want to be served. Notifications should be personalized by selecting from a wide range of options. Algorithms and orchestration in the back end can serve the customer on the personal level of choice. The technology is not new. The challenge is to win trust by adding value for the customer and guarantee data security.

The missing link

Machine learning and artificial intelligence are still in their infancy and so are distributed cryptographically databases like blockchain. I fully believe that in the future we are able to create interoperability solutions between local platforms, cloud platforms and decentralized database networks in order to facilitate 'real' personalization. Having track on the customer's preferences, physical movements and digital behaviour is key to bring customer engagement to the next level. For example, through the right integrations with other platforms and machine learning to continuously filter the data, the inflight entertainment will be customized based on the customers' Netflix, Spotify and eSports behaviour.

The intelligence is in journey management and having the right trusted data from many different sources correctly orchestrated. Besides linking to airline and airport data sources, think of linking with public transport systems, other platforms like Uber and Booking.com and governments' rules and regulations data. For each journey, you need to understand at what moment in the journey and via which channel you will reach out to the customer to serve their needs.

A hands-in-the-pockets experience

The most promising enabler for seamless, touchless and hygienic travel is biometrics. When overbridging trust and privacy legislation, the options are endless. While walking in the airport along several checkpoints, on the move biometric identification and verification are realistic scenarios in the near future. That includes car park, car rental, train stations, hotel entry and so on. Check-in is not needed anymore; we immediately know when customers enter the airport. That gives an important foundation to manage on deviations in the customer journey and to create seamless travel.

Vision without action is a daydream, action without vision is a nightmare. An innovation is worthless if not implemented. To get things done, disciplined execution is necessary. Start fast, fail fast and learn sooner.

I am a huge fan of biomimicry, innovation inspired by nature. Nature proves that species are adaptive to change and that several solutions are feasible for the same problem. There is an enormous diversity in the way birds are flying or catching fish. That is why many aircraft have different wing designs and nose designs, based on birds' wings and beaks. A one size fits all solution is an illusion for Mother Earth.

With new emerging technologies, biometric concepts may differ, as an organic development. Some are driven by an "identity as a service" (IaaS) concept; others by customer experience. Most concepts exist locally; others are cross-airport or even cross-country. Some are based on facial recognition; others on iris, fingerprints or behavioural characteristics. Whatever mix of concepts will arise in the future, the key to success is to have standards developed at the government level in order to create interoperability between the systems.

Brainstorming and "trystorming" are crucial parts of an innovation process. We co-create with customers, employees, and partners in order to discover the optimal solution. As Neil Armstrong in 1969 famously said, "[o]ne small step for man, one giant leap for mankind" is the way we should keep on looking to innovation. Visualize the future, take small steps towards the vision. Just do it, dare to fail and be adaptive for change and advanced understanding. We regret the things we did not do more often than the things we did do. Be open for collaboration with partners inside and outside your industry. Push for industry standards. Last but not least, stay curious and keep on asking questions. Why not?

Creating unexpected compelling experiences to increase bookings and ancillary revenues

Kerstin Lomb
Partner/Leader Customer Transformation Marketing EMEA, IBM Corporation

According to Frost and Sullivan in 2020, digital transformation programs in the airline industry could generate an incremental value of $5 to $10 for every passenger, annually. Such extraordinary value generation would derive mainly from improved productivity, cost savings, compelling experiences—not only inflight—and new ancillary revenue streams.

What's the hold up? The airline industry's obsession on product and price has created a culture of customer experience mediocracy. And airlines are lagging behind other industries, where experience expectations have been set, already prior the pandemic. See Figure 8.13. The role the changing lifestyles are playing forces airlines to rethink rapidly how to leverage digital innovations to not only generate revenues but also create incremental revenues. In the same study, younger audiences with high expectations are demonstrating higher than average frustrations with the industry practices, leaving it ripe for disruption. Furthermore, passengers may become less willing to lower their expectations and accept subpar service under the guise of "safety." A sentiment analysis of TripAdvisor reviews from the United States, Europe, and Asia

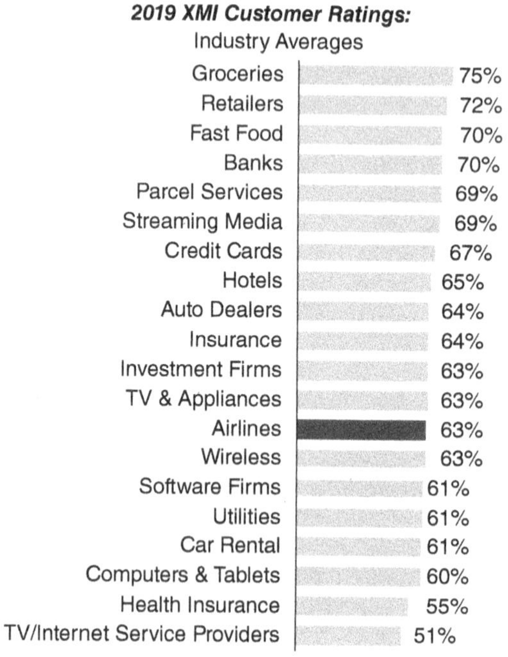

2019 XMI Customer Ratings:
Industry Averages

Groceries	75%
Retailers	72%
Fast Food	70%
Banks	70%
Parcel Services	69%
Streaming Media	69%
Credit Cards	67%
Hotels	65%
Auto Dealers	64%
Insurance	64%
Investment Firms	63%
TV & Appliances	63%
Airlines	63%
Wireless	63%
Software Firms	61%
Utilities	61%
Car Rental	61%
Computers & Tablets	60%
Health Insurance	55%
TV/Internet Service Providers	51%

Figure 8.13 2019 XMI customer ratings

found the emotional intensity of customer reviews increased considerably from 2019 to 2021.

As a result, the question for airlines is how to turn this situation around and reflect on the changes in lifestyles and the impact on customer acquisition and retention, taking advantage of related opportunities to increase revenues and loyalty. Airlines tend to target the end-to-end customer journey. But an engaging and human centered customer experience does not only start on the website. The digital innovations allow already during the customer acquisition phase for meaningful, human centered experiences that then can be carried through the whole customer journey.

Customer acquisition is getting more and more difficult due to emerging new airlines with digital state of the art processes (e.g., Breeze Airways, which offers sign up via Google or Facebook) and third-party cookies being eliminated. Third-party cookies are created by domains that are not the website (or domain) that a user is visiting.

Third-party cookies are mostly used for web analytic purposes. This can happen if a user's web browser loads an advertisement or a so-called targeting pixel that is not hosted on the server of the visited website. The users web browser generates an additional cookie, the third-party cookie, because it is not assigned to the server of the website but to that of the advertiser. Because web analysts are primarily interested in user behavior, the third-party cookie usually documents the page history on a website. However, this cookie often gains really valuable data only when it "recognizes" a user on another website. Since the user's web browser communicates again with the same ad server, it can trace the user's path on the internet and not only that: the behavior on the web reveals a lot about your interests and consumer behavior. This creates a user profile that enables targeted and personalized advertising.

The airline industry since the introduction of New Distribution Capability (NDC), has been heavily relying on performance marketing to drive direct to consumer revenues. Today, marketers have the capability to gather campaign data 24/7 and measure the results as they happen. While in the past, attribution was nearly impossible, data transparency now enables marketers to optimize their campaigns so that they perform better. Performance marketing is the term given for online marketing campaigns where advertising companies pay marketing companies or advertising platforms for results achieved, such as clicks or conversions. Unlike traditional and organic marketing, performance marketing is specifically used to drive actions and track and measure those actions all while attributing the return on investment (ROI) of each asset, campaign or activity.

The third-party cookie elimination is not the only initiative to be concerned regarding ROI and revenue generation through performance marketing campaigns. Mobile device identifiers, privacy protection regulations as well as walled gardens will severely impact marketing campaigns. Already today up to 50% of web traffic is lacking third-party cookies and yet performance marketing is still going strong. Chrome is dominating but Adform developed as early as in 2019 first-party ID solutions for performance marketers, allowing the identification of users in Firefox and Safari. It is expected that more and more so-called new "ID spaces" to retarget and analyze will be developed. The identifiers in the ID spaces are "replacement" identifiers and are expected to provide precise targeting and granular measurement. The key improvement in these solutions is that the user consent is clear and explicit.

These replacement identifiers are built by companies other than the browser vendors. Dedicated ID providers work already jointly on use cases with "data clean room" providers. A data clean room is a software that enables advertisers and brands to match data on a user level without sharing any personally identifiable information/raw data with one another.

Yet marketers need to keep in focus that this is still impacting marketing key performance indicators (KPIs). Furthermore, the intensive advertisement portfolio that airlines have, is creating challenges for media buyers in their efforts to optimize campaigns. Therefore, the opportunity for airlines is to adopt quickly evolving promotional and commerce assets and channels that relate with the new lifestyle driven customer expectations.

For example, weather targeting in advertisement combines weather's ability to impact emotion and action with knowledge in modelling and training artificial intelligence (AI) algorithms to help deliver more effective digital campaigns while minimizing wasted advertisement spend. The approach is designed to recognize the relationships between weather, location, and complex data sets such as health conditions, product sales and consumer activity. This analysis is used to create targeted campaigns without relying on third-party cookie data. Weather targeting is available across the entire digital ecosystem, including programmatic display, social, search, video, email, and digital out-of-home (DOOH). Marketers can anticipate and activate media campaigns based on weather's influence on consumer emotion and behavior in a target area and improve effectiveness by automatically serving ads that are contextually relevant to the user. Further media spending can be reduced by triggering messages only when and where the conditions that contribute to the desired behavior are present. The results achieved underpin the approach: a more than 300% increase in performance versus benchmark for a cold and flu brand, a more than 23% increase sales for a food brand, and a more than 130% increase in ad awareness for a retailer. In the airline industry, it is well known that bad weather periods trigger an increase in vacation flight booking.

The opportunity on hand is to leverage weather impact strategically. Along with the assessment of each media and channel type for their ROI and performance attribution characteristics and by using machine learning to assess the potency of each media type, leading to an optimized media spent through predictive analytics. With machine learning each media and channel type is assessed for their ROI and performance attribution characteristics. Machine learning is used to assess the potency of each media type by cluster in order to update the ROI properties of each media. These should change with the marketing treatments administered and keep the investment decisions always current. This attribution modeling drives real-time analytics for each campaign and enables real-time campaign steering for an optimized ROI and incremental revenues.

Predicting audiences' motivations to purchase tickets can help airline marketers build more effective audience models by identifying which users are most (or least) likely to take a desired action. This is achieved by using advanced AI technology to ingest first-party seed data and augment that information with more than thousands of data attributes. These data signals can include customer demographics, purchase history, online behaviour, lifestyle, interests, media habits and more to help increase the efficiency of media buys across nearly any demand-side platform (DSP) or programmatic partner. The problem, however, is that layering on too many types of targeting variables in the name of personalization impacts the ability to scale.

A leading insurance company leveraged a predictive audience's solution to solve the challenges that layering too many types of targeting variables, combining the latest in AI technology—deep learning with neural networks—to help provide marketers with advanced lookalike models of their target consumer, resulting in greater targeting precision and contextual relevance. They saw an 82% reduction in eCPA (effective cost per action).

In addition to being much more relevant with marketing campaigns, airlines can customize mass communication to a fair degree. One to one, AI-driven creative engagements are nearly anywhere in the digital ecosystem possible. Streamlining the process of talking with customers and providing a more personal experience at the scale of advertising. These innovative advertising solutions help facilitate personalized conversations with consumers virtually anywhere online and are designed to deliver more engaging ads and experiences by using natural language dialog to understand the user's intent and provide answers, recommendations, or next steps. This allows personalization without cookies, showcasing brand empathy and voice. Overall, this advertisement model helps to deepen consumer engagement, confidence, loyalty, and satisfaction. Airlines can uncover consumer needs and trends to inform the future strategy and quantify impact with consumer feedback. The opportunity to promote targeted ancillaries when the likelihood of a purchase is predicted to be high will drive incremental revenues. And it allows airlines to streamline the purchasing process. So why keep the approach to push all ancillaries during booking, leading to lengthy and annoying processes? This is contradicting the expectations of the lifestyle changes.

Addressing the changing consumer expectations and delivering experiences that are known from other industries, airlines can leverage intelligent media management and take advantage of AI-driven creative optimization. Performance-driven dynamic creative optimization technology helps deliver personalized ad experiences at scale for display, video, and over-the-top (OTT) platforms. *OTT* is the term for video content that is delivered via connected television devices (think Roku, Amazon Fire TV, Apple TV, etc.) over a high-speed broadband internet connection. For many years, advertisers have struggled to measure the effectiveness of their television ads. With traditional, linear television, it's impossible to track who is watching what and when so measuring the performance of advertising is difficult. The advent of OTT has finally given marketers line of sight to user-level measurement of ad effectiveness and access to very granular log-level data. Measuring the impact is enabled through log-level data that include attributes from the designated market area and the time of impressions, as well as device characteristics and more.

All these marketing assets use AI to help make sense of real-time consumer engagements and other data signals to dynamically assemble ads that improve campaign performance. Efficient activation reduces resources and time it takes to set up dynamic creative assets. Such an accelerator can be live in a matter of weeks, not months, as it automates the entire creative assembly process. The change in lifestyle leads to consumers expectations of personalized experiences, and data enables airlines to know what helps drive consumer engagement and conversions most efficiently by assembling user- or household-specific ad variations that drive consumer action. Additionally, predictive optimizations through machine learning enables teams to test hundreds of different creative variables and messaging easily, predicting the combination that will deliver on your KPIs, while improving campaign performance. Such a superior performance based on proven technology on average drives approximately 127%-plus lift in performance over time while revealing creative insights by audience and helping to exceed benchmarks.

Another way to catch up with the expectations of customers according to their lifestyle is to take on emerging commerce channels like conversational commerce (APAC is already leveraging messengers as sales channel), T-commerce (addressable TV) and naturally social commerce. Important to note is to reflect customer's behavior and what they are used to from digital experiences in other experiences. Currently most airlines stick with payment and commerce channels that have been introduced way back and are not state of the art or what's possible today. Many airlines feature between 12 and 16 steps/clicks to get a booking done, while we are today all used to one-click online purchases. No surprise when the abandoned cart rate is high. Time to take advantage of the constant growth of social media channels experience and new platforms evolving. Even so the "click 2 buy" discussion in Europe is going strong regarding platform-specific payment solutions, airlines can already adopt and allow for easy payments like PayPal and Amazon Pay. They can dismiss the ambition to try to sell every possible ancillary product right away. Considering predictive analytics, if airlines develop a robust measurement toolkit that is holistic, prioritized, predictive and prescriptive to keep track of customer sentiment and identify the highest-ROI interventions to propose customized and meaningful offerings, it will lead to an increase in ancillary revenues. Through payment methods as outlined earlier, data are transferred and thus for retargeting available. The increasing number of communications between booking and flight can be optimized and reduce the traditional segmentation of offerings.

In conclusion, leveraging the earlier outlined opportunities with AI allow to design a completely new, appealing customer journey that starts truly at the beginning of the customer journey. Airlines have a tremendous opportunity to demonstrate customization already prior to the booking process. Targeted communication and offers that have the highest likelihood that customers will make the purchase. Less is more. But less translates in more revenues and customer loyalty. In line with how today's customers want not just a good experience, but a good "digital" experience. Just how consumers have become accustomed to smart phones, smart TVs, and smart appliances from the value provided, especially smartphones. Creating throughout meaningful and impactful personalized and customized experiences, leading to an uplift in flight booking and ancillary revenues.

What if airports changed into mobility hubs?

Michaela Schultheiß-Münch
Vice President, Market Research and Business Analytics and Fraport AG, Frankfurt Airport Services Worldwide

Dr. Jennifer Berz
Senior Project Manager, Corporate Strategy & Digitalization, Fraport AG, Frankfurt Airport Services Worldwide

The framework for mobility will change substantially due to and after the pandemic. First, the market will change relating to demand, mode of transport and market players. Second, customer needs will change and third, regulation, climate issues and social values will play a decisive role in changing the setting.

Hence, the game-changer for an airport is to develop into a true mobility hub, which relates to an airport as a connecting and transfer point for regional and long-distance mobility and not necessarily from aircraft to aircraft only. It will combine two things: customer preferences for individual, seamless, and flexible travel as well as the demand of policymakers and society for more sustainability, reaching international climate goals and taking into account scarce resources.

Thus, the future mobility hub will be assessed by its quality of connectivity and its quantity of means of transport and a sustainable, environmentally friendly operation.

In line with mobility experts, we believe that there are three key premises for the mobility 2050.

1 *Demand for mobility will further increase after the pandemic.* Human beings are characterized by being mobile. It is their need and craving to socially interact. Even more working from home will probably not reduce demand for mobility in the long run. However, mobility as it is known will considerably change—due to changing concepts of living and paying more attention to the ecological footprint of travel. The collective mindset changes, partly to the disadvantage of air travel. Short haul flights in Europe will strongly decline for the sake of fewer CO_2 emissions. New means of transport will emerge. Sustainability and health aspects will become more important. Where possible, micro-mobility will increase as well as private transport. Technology players will dominate the market. They possess huge cash reserves to invest in innovative technologies like autonomous driving or new modes of transport. They are familiar with big data and will form cooperations and networks. Big ones like Google, Amazon, Meta and Apple could develop super apps for "do everything" or mobility platforms for one-click door-to-door travel.[8,9,10,11,12]

2 *Society will remain consumer-oriented by 2050.* Even during the pandemic you could perceive previous consumer behaviour coming back.[13]

Emerging markets will be the driver as the global economy is said to possibly double by 2050. To discover the world will remain a dream people strive for and will be fostered by still growing wealth.[14,15] At the same time, consciousness for sustainable travel will grow as will health aspects of travel.[16] Mobility will become more situative due to flexible and mobile workplaces instead of the habitualized daily drive from home to work. As the future will bring more hybrid work environments consumers will change from working at home, going to the office by bike or taking the plane for a sales meeting the next day. Thus, choosing their work location and combining it with new concepts of living will change consumers' choice of transport. In addition, consumers want time spent on means of transport to be productive and meaningful. Mobility of the future shall be an experience for which digitalization and connectivity play a key role. Modes of transport could transform into third places besides home and office places, places where consumers feel comfortable and can pursue meaningful activities.[17,18,19,20] And customer experience will become an essential driver for choosing the mode of transport.

3 *The framework for this development will be very much set by political regulations striving for achieving climate neutrality.*[21,22,23] Policymakers will increasingly seek influence in the mobility sector. They will launch policies to promote low-emission transport and foster intermodal travel chains. Politicians want to develop ecological traffic, for example e-mobility, sharing mobility and rail traffic. Within Europe short haul flights shall be climate neutral from 2035 onwards. The availability of sustainable energies will become a decisive factor for a location's attractiveness. Power-to-liquid fuel shall help sustainability already from 2023 onwards, and Airbus announced that to enable emission-free flights by 2035, it would be launching a hydrogen aircraft. Already at present, aircraft fuel consumption has been considerably reduced by about 20%. Corsia (international) and ETS (emission trading system; intra-EU) are two programmes obliging the aviation sector to reduce CO_2 emissions. The EU is pushing hard for its climate protection programme Fitfor55 which contains as core elements the ETS, a kerosene tax as well as the obligation to blend kerosene with an increasing share of SAF from 2025. Finally, there is another driver influencing the market. Business travel will considerably decrease not only due to more home offices and increasing cost consciousness after the pandemic but also due to implementing sustainable corporate travel policies. These promote switching from air to rail and budget the cost of CO_2 emissions of business travel.

The above three main premises hence can be summed up in seven major trend categories for the mobility vision 2050:

Increasing mobility demand: Especially after the pandemic there will be increasing demand for private travel and, in the long run, growing prosperity in the developing countries. More people will be able to afford air travel and new traffic streams may be generated by the so-called VFR (visit friends and relatives) segment. The main trigger will be no travel restrictions anymore due to the pandemic, no global (war) conflicts and the global economy in an upturn. The latter just now—in the light of the war in Ukraine—forms a downside risk the extent of which cannot yet be foreseen.

New technologies: New technologies will influence the mobility market. Alternative infrastructure will be needed for refueling hydrogen or for e-mobility. At airports this applies to aircraft refueling as well as to parking lots and gas stations. Such investment will be triggered by the delivery of such new aircraft in about five years plus.

Change in consumer behaviour: Consumer decision and their choice of means of transport will change with new modes and new ways of intermodality emerging. The change of transport choice will be triggered by a new conscience for sustainable living but also—and probably more—by governmental regulations, for example, reducing short haul flights and diverting traffic to rail connections.

New market/player: The market for public and private travel will change. With new modes of transport available the mix of these will change. With the already existing customer demand for quick search and booking of a journey the different possibilities to travel will need to be displayed in one platform like a showroom and booking as well as ticket purchase to be taken from there. It will therefore be up to big tech players to set up platforms to allow a one-stop shopping for your journey in one shopping basket and create a super app.

Digitalization and interconnection: Digitalization and interconnection will redesign the mobility market. They allow for less business travel as video conferencing becomes more comfortable and speedier. To be connected from almost anywhere also allows a different work–life balance with working places abroad and teaming up with home or leisure.

Regulation: Regulations will come up in favour of intermodality and environmentally *friendly climate policy*. To achieve the climate neutral target, however, incredibly large sums of money are needed to manage the turnaround, scale up new technologies and get to a 100% green standard. It is crystal clear that cost and taxes will raise production and consumer prices, hence ticket prices. All these measures will probably subdue demand in particular on short-haul flights. It will be absolutely essential to implement climate regulations based on a level playing field. Otherwise, there will be harm to European aviation whilst unwillingly promoting outside EU countries and counteracting the target of climate neutrality. It must be assumed that people will find their way through other routes and airports not charged by climate policies (carbon leakage).

Infrastructure: Climate policies as well as available (renewable) energies will influence route choice and infrastructure. New aircraft types can only operate from an airport if the adequate infrastructure has been implemented. Attractiveness of an airport once again will depend on providing a suitable up-to-date infrastructure. Timeline for delivery of first new aircraft types could be somewhat like five years from now. Hence, there is no time to waste.

The added value of a mobility hub regarding these main trend categories

In essence, mobility hubs are supposed to enable a more convenient and easier transfer between means of transport due to local concentration. In addition, they have a promotional effect in favour of multi- and inter-modal mobility. This aims at reducing traffic congestion, while increasing use of public transport. This, in turn, leads to an increase in urban quality of life and makes cities more attractive. In addition, fewer emissions (noise and pollutants) make a positive contribution to environmental protection.

Another added value is the lower hurdle of accessibility. This is aimed both at people who are mobility-impaired due to physical conditions and at people who do not have access to certain forms of mobility, for example because they do not own a car.[24]

Hence, several advantages can be highlighted in favour of a mobility hub:

- Possibility of choosing your means of transport for every journey via the hub, according to your actual situation
- Variety of available transport options offers mobility at any point in time
- Possibility of digital connectivity between different means of transport, for example, through a joint information, distribution and booking platform
- Bundling and network effects leading to higher efficiency of mobility offers
- Higher traffic volume, resulting in more regular frequencies to other hubs or transport stations
- Positive contribution to regional climate goals
- Public relations and marketing effect, thus helping new traffic concepts to get off the ground

What is the impact of these trends on the business model of a hub airport?

The aforementioned trend categories will have a more or less strong impact on the business model of an airport. Figure 8.14 shows the relevance for Frankfurt Airport serving as a best practice example for a hub airport, which should transform into a comprehensive mobility hub. The darker the colour in the table, the more relevant the trend category will be for the listed mode of transport.

Considering the location of Frankfurt and relevant modes of transport we can differentiate three essential mobility scenarios:

- Scenario A: regional transport up to 25 km (rail, car, air taxi, bus)
- Scenario B: supra-regional transport up to 500 km (air travel, rail, car, air taxi and long-distance busses)

176 *Thought leadership pieces*

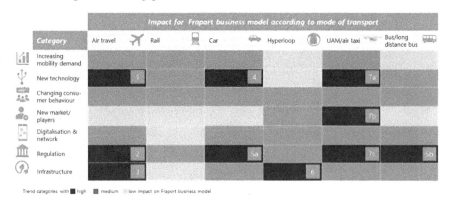

Figure 8.14 Impact of trend categories on the airport business model

- Scenario C: long distance of more than 500 km (air travel, hyperloop)

From these scenarios A, B, C the following fields of action can be derived with numbers below referring to the respective numbers in Figure 8.14:

1 New aircraft reducing CO_2 emissions will require alternative refueling infrastructure for hydrogen and charging infrastructure.
2 Air travel on short haul will become less attractive due to increasing cost and taxes; therefore, alternative routes and modes of transport must be offered. Battery-driven ultra-short-haul aircraft could create a new balance between highways, rail and air travel.
3 New aircraft demand adaptation of existing infrastructure.
4 Considering e-mobility and electric vehicles new charging infrastructure will be necessary in the long run, as well as alternative infrastructure for refilling hydrogen.
5 a/b: Regulating car and bus traffic will mean limitations in the cities which could turn out as an opportunity for Frankfurt Airport to ramp up parking infrastructure as well as its bus station.
6 Hyperloop development needs to be closely monitored. Further development is still uncertain.
7 a/b/c: UAM (urban air mobility) and air taxis are being piloted, however, the adaptation of infrastructure and providing the necessary airspace pose a challenge in densely populated areas.

The combination of new means of transport enabling a high quality of connectivity will be a major success factor for a hub airport in the future. Attracting more and new modes of transport offer the opportunity for additional travel chains, more intermodal chains and, last but not least, becoming more independent from air travel chains. Figure 8.15 shows the impact of an extended intermodal mobility hub for Frankfurt Airport.

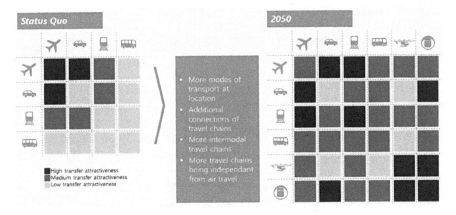

Figure 8.15 Positioning Fraport as an intermodal mobility hub with increased connectivity

First movers already launch new means of transport. Jelbi at Berlin offers an intermodal search and booking platform for public transport and sharing services. Didi Chuxing from Beijing offers ride hailing and is becoming profitable. Mercedes-Benz is testing a "future bus" driving autonomously as public transport at Amsterdam, within a 20-km radius. Virgin Hyperloop One enabled a first proof of concept manned drive. Volocopter is planning the regular air taxi operation at Singapore in 2026. Edmonton International Airport uses cargo drones for commercial transport. Droniq is testing the integration of drones in the air space at Hamburg harbour. Last but not least, Blue Origin already offers touristic commercial space flights.[25,26,27,28,29]

What are customer needs regarding a mobility hub?

Having talked about increasing mobility demand, new modes of transport and corresponding infrastructure let us now have a close look at the customers´ changing needs and desires.

Customer needs

Findings of a largely representative survey conducted at Frankfurt Airport show that facilities of a mobility hub were prioritized according to the importance of means of transport.[30] Parking facilities followed by regional and long-distance train connections were by large the most important elements. This proves that a crucial requirement of a mobility hub is to *provide connectivity between private and public transport.*

When asked *which combinations of means of transport are the most important* at a mobility hub, respondents distinctly favoured the combination between rail and regional public transport, followed by the combinations car/regional public transport and car/rail.

178 *Thought leadership pieces*

When it comes to the requirements a mobility hub needs to fulfil *with regard to route planning*, convenience seems to be the main driver.

The survey also asked for important aspects when booking a trip through a mobility hub (Figure 8.16). *One ticket for all means of transport* was rated particularly important, while route recommendations, combinations of means of transport and a central app to book the trip were also important. Another key feature a mobility hub needs to fulfil is *clear orientation and navigation* through the hub. In this respect digital support as shown in Figure 8.17 is mandatory in particular for finding your way, showing delays and possible disruptions, display routes for transfers and occupancy of means of transport.

Each answer option in the survey got high scorings, which underlines the importance of digital support. This is even more true for passengers who rarely use public transport and consequently have less experience with transfer.

Matching these findings with the current satisfaction index referring to Frankfurt Airport highlights that there is still room for optimization (Figure 8.18). While satisfaction with variety of means of transport and connectivity

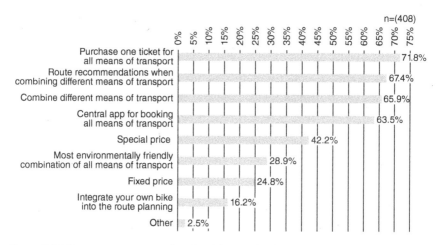

Figure 8.16 Important aspects when booking a trip through a mobility hub

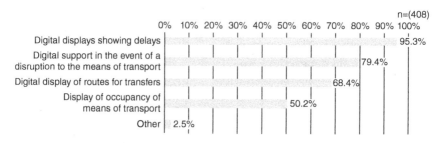

Figure 8.17 Important factors for digital connectivity of means of transport at a mobility hub

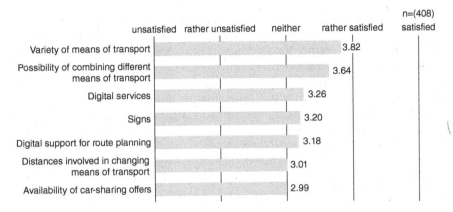

Figure 8.18 Satisfaction levels concerning intermodality at Frankfurt Airport

is ranked high to medium, digital services and support for route planning should be improved.

Quality of connections

Passengers need to have a convincing offer of connectivity between means of transport available at their fingertips. What they do not yet mention but which is certainly in their mind is true door-to-door travel. Being able to book your journey starting at home and ending at your final destination, that is, hotel, apartment, and so on at a specific location. This will need new services for the last mile, possibly to be offered by new modes of mobility as discussed earlier. And it will demand the marketplace that offers the best routing and transport choices combined with one-click reservation and ticketing. This involves procedural and infrastructural fields of action.

First, regarding procedural fields of action, schedules need to be harmonized and/or frequency increased so that seamlessly connecting between means of transport is possible. Second, connectivity needs to be enhanced and route planning facilitated through digital services. The third field of action comprises partnerships and distribution as well as funding as is outlined in the later section "What Else Is Important: Ecosystem and Funding".

When it comes to infrastructural implications, routing and navigation need to support connectivity. This includes navigation between public means of transport, but also intelligent offers for routes that include parking a private car and continuing the trip with public transport. These action items provide rather short- and medium-term improvement and can be acted on right away.[31]

Quantity of means of transport

When it comes to including more means of transport into the mix, decisions will depend on which means of transport will be market ready at which point in time. This interacts with the limited room for development within existing airport infrastructure. In many cases, the existing infrastructure fills the available space so that further development is only possible through deconstruction or expansion of the existing area.

Observing the market and legislation around the admission of new means of transport might be a first step. Therefore, establishing a process to continuously monitor and to define trigger points that set into motion a decision-making process is recommended. As public transport is planned in a long-term Federal Transport Plan, much of which is not very flexible to changing demand, it is also recommended to build relationships with the responsible governmental offices within the country and on a pan-European base to get information first-hand and in a timely manner. Infrastructural changes and/or partnership with providers of new forms of mobility will then be the logical next step.[32]

Infrastructure for multi-and intermodality

In order to develop into an intermodal mobility hub, investments are needed for the physical as well as digital infrastructure.

Physical infrastructure is needed in terms of railways, highway, air and rail terminals, apron space as well as runways and parking lots for private travel. It needs to be enhanced by charging infrastructure for e-mobility, infrastructure for refilling for hydrogen and sustainable fuels and infrastructure to enable smooth transfer of passengers and baggage between the various means of transport.

Digital infrastructure comprises in particular biometric systems for check-in, security and passport control, as well as a joint sales and distribution platform. At the back end, a cross-partner data management system will be necessary to enable door-to-door travel and the cross-functional operations between the modes of transport. Regarding UAM, air traffic control needs to integrate its flight paths into the existing air traffic network control system.

What else is important: Ecosystem and funding

Ecosystem—partnership and coopetition

A mobility hub is more than just physical and digital infrastructure. To make it come alive and viable for customers it demands close cooperation of the mobility partners. An efficient mobility ecosystem will need digital platforms for data sharing and joint product and service offerings, as well as support mobility sharing.

For instance, despite the extensive range of transport services at Frankfurt Airport, there is no truly coordinated partnership regarding sales and marketing and physical transfer support between the individual transport providers. This implies that passengers often must book their journey on different platforms with several tickets. There is no support or easy refund in case of delay or interruption of travel. Even more important, the crucial automated baggage transfer is mostly lacking. Door-to-door travel is still a faraway dream. Harmonization and cooperation of all these aspects in a partner ecosystem could positively impact the quality of connections and incentivize passengers to use a mobility hub.

Responsibility and funding

It is the responsibility of the airport operator to take the strategic decision for the development from airport to mobility. The quality of connections and quantity of means of transport, however, largely depend on the means of transport themselves, that is, the transport system surrounding the potential hub. The airport operator may ensure procedural and infrastructural feasibility. In order to be successful, it will be crucial to involve and cooperate with regional transportation authorities as well as railway, coach and other transportation companies.

Similarly, funding for such an endeavour could be mixed. While it might partly originate from public sponsorships, since a well-functioning mobility ecosystem is in the public's best interest, entrepreneurial decisions to make a business model out of the mobility hub concept should also ensure corporate investments.[33]

How to find the right course and get the feet off the ground?

To evaluate the setting and create a vision of mobility 2050 Fraport liaised with about 170 experts to explore the future trends. Eighteen macro trends were evaluated regarding their impact on aviation (being relevant), the current state of competence of the industry and possibilities for mainstream adaptation. Trends were clustered as shown in this piece and highlighted if high impact trends, because the latter will significantly shape mobility interfaces in the future. In a next step, a working group analysed which innovations will be inherent to these macro trends and derived prioritized fields of action including a time frame. Defined trigger points referring to a certain state of development shall summon for action when becoming necessary. To align the mobility innovation with the current situation of Frankfurt Airport a SWOT analysis was conducted. Thus, the adaptability and current aptitude of the airport hub for changing into an innovative mobility hub was assessed.

Quick progress was made by agile project management and working with flex offices and open space—even though, due to the pandemic, a lot of meetings had to be digital profiting from comprehensive Teams software. Equally essential for such a project is the sponsorship of a board member and direct, close communication and feedback. Alongside with working at the vision of mobility 2050, Fraport already liaises closely with, for example, Deutsche Lufthansa and German Rail to further develop existing intermodality. With Lufthansa, Fraport has formed the

182 *Thought leadership pieces*

FraAlliance, aimed at improving passenger processes and creating added value for its customers.

To give the reader an idea about Frankfurt Airport as an intermodal hub as is at present much value can be taken from the perspectives of Jennifer Berz presented below that relate to the content of this piece.

Digression

To give an overview on the current state of Frankfurt Airport's mobility, the following is a respective part of an article by Dr. Jennifer Berz from the *Journal of Airport Management* (27 January 2022)[34]:

EXISTING MOBILITY OFFER AT FRANKFURT AIRPORT

In general, Frankfurt Airport as a central transfer point already offers all relevant prerequisites for becoming a mobility hub for modern means of transport.

The airport is easily accessible by a wide range of transport modes from the Rhine-Main region and beyond. The German state of Hesse, where the airport is located, is a transit state: half of all long-distance passenger rail services in Germany pass through Hesse; Frankfurt Central Station is the busiest station in Germany. With Germany's busiest Autobahn (German highway system) intersection close by, there are good connections to road traffic frequented by more than 300,000 vehicles daily.[35]

A wide range of transportation options are available: air traffic, long-distance rail traffic, public transport (rail, road), long-distance coach traffic, motorized individual traffic (private car, car sharing, rental car), and bicycle.

AIRPLANE

Frankfurt Airport is primarily—and has been exclusively in the past—a hub for air traffic. In 2018, it was the largest German airport and ranked 4th in European and 14th in international comparison. The airport is used by Lufthansa and other Star Alliance airlines as a hub airport; consequently, 55% of passengers at Frankfurt Airport transfer there. In 2018, 512,115 aircraft movements took place at the airport, and 11% of passengers travelled domestically, while the remaining passengers were on cross-border flights.[36]

TRAIN

Frankfurt Airport is connected to the long-distance rail network and has its own long-distance train station, which is operated by Deutsche Bahn and is structurally connected to Terminal 1. Thanks to the connection to the high-speed network and the operation of high-speed trains, it is possible to achieve travel times competitive to airplanes over shorter distances. As a result, the travel time to Cologne is only 50 minutes and has led to all airlines discontinuing the Cologne–Frankfurt route.[37] The station competes with other long-distance stations in the area, such as Frankfurt Süd and Frankfurt Central Station.

Regional public transport

The airport also has a regional train station, which is served by two S-Bahn lines (German urban-suburban rail system) and several regional trains. The journey between the airport and downtown Frankfurt takes 13 minutes. The S-Bahn trains run every 15 minutes, and an average of 266 regional and local trains call at the airport's regional station daily. In addition, the airport is served by 17 bus lines, which connect it with the surrounding cities and towns. Taxi traffic is also considered part of public transport.[38]

COACH

The airport has a long-distance bus station, which is located between Terminals 1 and 2. The bus station also serves as a dedicated parking lot, which is partially covered by a roof and equipped with several bus shelters. It is served by various German and European long-distance bus companies.

CAR

The airport is connected to two Autobahnen (German highway system) and the regional road network. Adjacent to the airport is the busiest Autobahn interchange in Germany.[39] The airport has 15,460 public parking spaces, which are used for 3.8 million parking operations per year.[40]

MOBILITY SERVICES

Mobility services include ride hailing, ride sharing, ride pooling and rental cars. There is currently no distinct data on the use of ride hailing and ride sharing, but the existence of corresponding services can be verified. Ride pooling is not currently offered at the airport. The 13 rental car companies located at the airport provide a service of 600,000 rentals per year. On peak days, up to 2,000 vehicles are rented.[41]

BIKES AND MICROMOBILITY

The airport is connected to the regional bike path network, which consists of independent bike paths and uses the existing road network. There is currently no offering of shared micromobility transportation at the airport. Since a large proportion of travellers is carrying luggage, bikes and micromobility are rarely used and are arguably primarily an option for airport employees.

To sum up, the paragraphs above show that as of now, Frankfurt Airport enables both multimodality and intermodality. The number of means of transport itself, as listed above, proves that multimodality is already a given. It also seems unlikely that the number of means of transport will decrease. Cars or coaches, which might fall victim to bans in urban centres, could still approach the airport with its location outside of the city.

When thinking about technology and the means of transport of the future as outlined, it is apparent that Frankfurt Airport is suitable for these as well. For instance, urban air mobility providers should find the expertise to cater for their demands already in place, as well as, necessary amendments provided, part of the infrastructure. Another example would be the connection of the airport to a potential hyperloop network. Due to the already existing and well-managed connection to rail services, this should also be a viable and feasible option.

When it comes to intermodality, first steps have also been made. Particularly in long-distance rail transport, there is already a possibility of combining this means of transport with a flight and purchasing it as a holistic product. This means that customers only must make one booking for their entire travel chain, combining the service provided by Deutsche Bahn and the chosen airline. Further expansion is planned for this in the long term.

However, as elaborated with reference to consumer needs and the gaps in customer satisfaction, further measures need to be taken to become a mobility hub with true intermodal functionalities.

A new dynamic approach to network planning

Philippe Puech
Director, Domestic Network Planning, American Airlines

Network planning is the equivalent of solving multidimensional puzzles on a daily basis: where to fly, when to fly and on what equipment in order to maximize profitability. All this needs to be achieved with a plethora of constraints, such as infrastructure and fleet and crew constraints, existing in a dynamic environment that lends itself well to game theory. The outbreak and global spread of COVID-19 resulted in a severe decline in demand for air travel. Almost overnight 97% of air travel demand disappeared. This dramatic decrease, followed by a slow recovery, made network planners' work even more interesting.

How to address the remaining demand during the height of the pandemic was a puzzle that American solved in a creative and collaborative way. With customers in mind, we adapted our network to answer their needs with enhanced integration with other commercial groups, most notably revenue management and operations planning. With their finger on the pulse of the market, the network planning teams could identify pockets of demand, assemble a plan to address them, and use the talent of our Scheduling team to build a schedule that was both operationally and commercially successful. Because change has been the one constant throughout the pandemic, we built flexibility into our processes to adjust our capacity plan to match the shifting demand trends we witnessed more closely. On a regular basis, the team steps back and starts with a clean-sheet schedule to avoid using yesterday's constraints as limitations and instead pushes for an ideal network.

Designing a network and a schedule that is adaptable to what customers want

Our approach throughout the pandemic was to adapt to the constantly changing demand landscape. To cater to this change, we adapted our time-of-day coverage and kept a long tail of markets to keep answering the needs for as many customers as possible.

Adapt time-of-day coverage

Business customers virtually disappeared, leaving only leisure or visiting friends and relatives (VFR) customers wanting to fly, and they valued a different type of schedule. Business customers traditionally have an appetite for early flights to attend a morning meeting or late flights to attend an afternoon meeting before returning home. Meanwhile, leisure passengers prefer mid-morning to early evening flights. The market mix change during the pandemic required a change in the type of schedule we offered.

Address the long tail of markets

Our guiding principle was, and always is, to create the maximum number of options for customers. This means targeting the highest number of nonstop and one-stop itineraries as possible from the spokes American serves. Throughout the pandemic, we leveraged the connecting power of our hubs, most notably our two largest hubs—Dallas–Fort Worth International Airport (DFW) and Charlotte Douglas International Airport (CLT). Pre-pandemic, American operated around 900 daily departures at DFW and nearly 700 at CLT, making them the second and third largest hubs on the planet (see Figure 8.19). These two hubs benefit from advantageous geographic locations and large breadth and deep depth in service, meaning the vast number of destinations they serve and the number of times we serve each of these destinations make them formidable origin and destinations (O&D) creating machines. American's DFW hub is the prime east–west hub and CLT is the north–south hub.

On the network side, connecting two markets either nonstop or one-stop require a spatial and temporal component. When the O&D fulfills both requirements, we consider this a viable O&D, and this is the equivalent of offering a stock-keeping unit, or SKU, for the consumer goods industry.

Let me explain briefly these two components shown in Figure 8.20. The spatial requirement for O&D viability follows the intuition that passengers accept a limited amount of backtrack on their trip when connecting over a hub. In the example above we would consider SBA to TPA over DFW to be viable while SEA to OMA over DFW would not as the circuity would be 64% over the distance of a hypothetical nonstop. The temporal requirement for O&D viability concerns whether the flights connect in the hub. In the preceding example, the DFW–SBA flight leaves at 840 while GSO–DFW arrives at 920. Therefore, a passenger from GSO cannot connect to SBA as the DFW-SBA will have left the hub. On the other hand, TPA–DFW, arriving at 737,

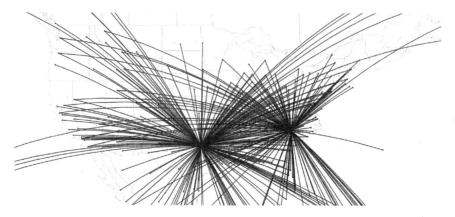

Figure 8.19 Coverage offered by American Airlines' Dallas and Charlotte hubs in July 2021

Network constructors requires two components to consider an O&D as viable

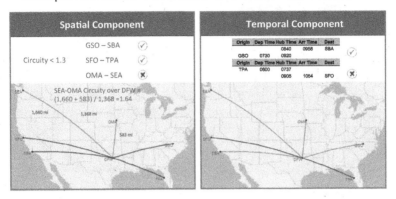

Figure 8.20 Part A and B Spatial and temporal components for O&D viability

connects to the DFW–SFO, leaving the hub at 0905. To illustrate the need to keep the highest connectivity possible, let's take the example of DFW to San Diego International Airport (SAN). This flight shows that 40% of the customers are local; therefore, 60% of the traffic is connecting. The second largest O&D onboard the flight represents around 2% only. In fact, the next 50 onboard O&Ds represent another 40%, meaning 20% of the traffic comes from the 51st to the thinnest O&D, highlighting the importance of the long tail of markets. This coupled with the fact that we saw some migration from large cities to secondary or tertiary ones reinforced our conviction that designing a network our customers want to fly also means offering the largest number of O&Ds possible.

Implication on the schedule side

Our goal was to keep the maximum number of products on the shelf but reduce capacity in response to decreased demand. To do so, we followed a bank cancel approach, which is illustrated on the graph below in Figure 8.21.

This graph represents a 30-minute rolling departure count from DFW before and during the pandemic. Each peak represents a bank in DFW, which typically operates nine banks. In other words, American operates nine waves of arrivals and departures. The largest banks operate around 130 turns, which means planes from 130 airports land in DFW turn within 30 minutes to two hours and then depart to 130 destinations. This leads to thousands of O&D combinations either nonstop or one-stop. You'll notice on the graphs that the peaks are comparable, but the time-of-day coverage changed as we were only operating seven banks instead of nine. Our first wave was around 8:30 a.m. rather than 7 a.m., and the last bank was around 8:30 p.m. instead of 10:30 p.m.

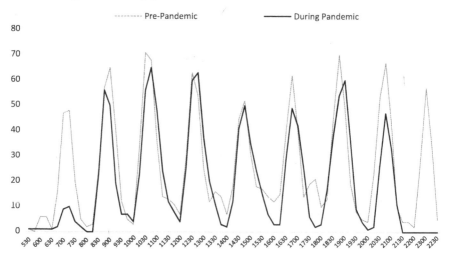

Figure 8.21 DFW 30-minute rolling departure count pre-pandemic and during summer 2020

American, therefore, operated fewer hours during the day but the level of operations during the operating banks were similar to pre-pandemic.

This approach contrasts what comparable airlines were doing. The alternate approach was to reduce lines of flying, or what we colloquially call "plucking." Doing so reduces connectivity in each complex as the number of inbound and outbound markets were drastically reduced. In turn, it leads to less product on the shelf. The results we saw throughout the pandemic reinforced our focus on O&D creation and adapting our network planning practices to what customers want.

Commercial and operational integration leads to dynamic scheduling and reduced lag time in the feedback loops

In normal times, airlines firmed their schedule three to four months before flying and the planning process was typically locked two months prior. In other words, six months before the flight, very little changes were made. Uncertainty both on the demand and supply changed this approach radically.

Multiple times over the last two years we rewrote entire schedules in a matter of days rather than weeks, and within only a few weeks before the first flight date. This was prevalent when new variants of COVID began to spread. Our schedule publication became closer in than pre-pandemic. Additionally, network planning teams used new closer-in data sources to gauge demand and tweak capacity plans accordingly leading to the dynamic scheduling practice.

This closer-in planning environment was also made possible by changes to our network planning processes and deeper integration between planning, scheduling, and operations.

Close-in signal led changes to the schedule

As a system-thinking aficionado, reducing the lag time between an action and its feedback loop has always been a focus of mine. The best-laid plans were, and still are two years into the pandemic, subject to change either because a region implements COVID-19 regulations or because demand is rising somewhere unexpected.

Previously, past performance was the single most important data point in capacity deployment decisions. This disruptive change in demand profile led to a need for early signal identification, which requires recent demand data as input. This led to more widespread forward-looking and real-time performance data to identify green-shoot markets and make planning decisions. For example, our planning team worked with revenue management to examine second derivatives in bookings. We looked at the entire travel ecosystem to create our capacity plans. Restaurant reservation trends allowed to spot places that were open for business and traffic generally followed leisure destinations that were open. We also worked closely with car rental companies. When they were running low on inventories, it was a leading indicator of booking decelerations. This was an outcome of the airlines' desperate quest for leading indicator of demand as we were navigating unchartered territory.

Use of computational horsepower to tweak capacity plans

The pandemic led to an increased use of Demand-Driven Dispatch at American. We can use computational horsepower to evaluate aircraft equipment change opportunities. It could allow us to make adjustments such as increasing from a 128-seat aircraft to a 190-seat aircraft (almost a 50% increase in seat for a single frequency). From a schedule standpoint, American is adding operational flexibility in the base schedule. From a specific hub, it is increasingly common to see pure business and pure leisure markets on the same equipment family. During the week, the larger aircraft flies to the business market while the smaller gauge flies to the leisure market, and this is reversed on weekends to help redeploy capacity to meet demand. This flexibility is exacerbated by the talent of our new day-of-week team who works with the operational constraints to make commercial decisions at a very granular level. This is only possible because their analytical talent can quickly process thousands of data points to refine the schedule in a way that's friendly to the operation.

As close as a few weeks before departures, using booking and operational data we could add, re-time, or change aircraft size on certain flights. This optimization is now part of our permanent processes. As the further-out booking curve returns, so does our planning horizon, but some of the flexibility goodness from the pandemic will be brought into this new normal.

Clean-sheet scheduling

Historically, it was not uncommon throughout the industry to take a past year schedule as a base for the development process. This seed is an anchor that leads to inertia in any process and schedule development processes don't escape that fact. It is especially true for airlines with thousands of daily operations.

We saw earlier that airlines need to adapt their products to the changing needs of their customers. As demand recovers, we see shifts in traffic trends and what was true pre-pandemic no longer applies. Therefore, to capture this quickly changing world, we as practitioners, need to develop processes that build a schedule capturing all the recent learnings. For instance, we can neither use a pre-pandemic base any longer nor can we use a recent schedule as the amount of capacity and demand are growing. It reveals the need for frequent schedule resets.

That involves taking a step back and start with more or less a clean slate, or what Dr. Taneja coins "clean-sheet scheduling." It means to start with no preconceived notions and develop the right network with enough lead time to relax some operational constraints taken for granted. For this to be possible, computational horsepower and extensive forecasting capabilities are a must to optimize all the possible combinations of where and when to fly on which aircraft until the best result is reached.

The past two years have been extremely challenging, but they also allowed network planning teams to work in a more dynamic environment. Experience-wise, these years will count as dog years, but exciting new ways to run the business have been experienced. Deeper integration between commercial, network planning and operational teams has been developed. Now that the genie is out of the bottle, the success airlines achieved by tailoring the schedule to customers' needs, the flexibility to optimize the schedule closer-in to maximize profitability, and the ability to step back and reset the airline on a regular basis is here to stay and this is an exciting new chapter for practitioners and customers.

Making clean-sheet scheduling real

Renzo Vaccari
Senior Vice President, Head of Sky Suite, Amadeus IT Group

Overview

In Chapter 2 of this book, the technique of clean-sheet scheduling is presented to generate more profitable flight schedules. Using this technique, airlines make no assumptions about schedule patterns from previous schedules and instead build a proposed flight schedule according to underlying route economics, geography, and costs. The principle is that historical schedule patterns may not necessarily be valid when generating an optimal flight schedule for the future, and that using just incremental approaches may be suboptimal. Therefore, so the logic goes, when planning a proposed schedule, why not check to see if alternative new schedule patterns generated by a system from scratch indeed might generate more profitability?

Of course, the principle of clean-sheet scheduling is not new. Airlines have discussed the idea of solving the flight scheduling business problem to optimality in one single step for many years. In fact, this prospect has often been referred to in the industry as "the holy grail". However, given the size of the problem, the complexity of representing revenue and profitability, the sheer number of operational constraints, and available technologies, this problem has not been solved in a single step yet.

To gain a sense of the underlying scale of this problem, as further described in Chapter 2, notice that the decision space of the flight scheduling problem is very large. Suppose an airline flies to 100 airports. If so, they have a total of 4,950 possible routes. They could conceivably fly these routes at any day of the week and any time of the day. And if they fly, for example, 10 different aircraft sub-fleet types, then they have 10 different choices to fly these routes at the different day/time combinations.

So, while it is conceptually attractive to solve the clean-sheet scheduling problem, in fact airlines have had to approximate this solution into a series of sequential steps, via a combination of systems and manual interventions, as shown in Chapter 2. As further discussed, this approximation has led to several weaknesses. If indeed an approach to performing clean-sheet scheduling could be found that removed the need for previous approximations, then that approach would represent a real contribution to airlines' ability to optimize their flight schedules.

The purpose of this thought leadership paper is to present an approach to clean-sheet scheduling that is feasible and scalable. Using the approach described in this paper should allow airlines to enjoy the benefits from clean-sheet scheduling in their schedule development process.

Characteristics of clean-sheet scheduling

What does it take to perform clean-sheet scheduling? The following list describes the characteristics of the clean-sheet scheduling problem. Any solution approach that acceptably accounts for these characteristics can be said to perform clean-sheet scheduling:

1   Account for many scheduling possibilities, without having to start from an existing flight schedule
2   Represent passenger market share, connections, revenue, and costs with good accuracy
3   Account for many operational constraints
4   Reduce unnecessary schedule changes
5   Produce a flight schedule in sufficient detail
6   Perform this function with acceptable performance and scale

The first characteristic of clean-sheet scheduling is most important. To perform clean-sheet scheduling well, airlines must "cast a wide net" and consider many different possibilities, often possibilities they would not normally consider. Too often, experience has shown that airlines tend to think incrementally and unintentionally restrict the number of new scheduling ideas they might consider.

Of course, airlines do not need to consider all scheduling ideas which are theoretically possible. For example, an airline might fly to both Portland, Oregon, and Portland, Maine, and thus, it is possible for them to fly directly between these two cities. However, if it is so unlikely that this market could justify nonstop service, it is not necessary when performing clean-sheet scheduling to consider new service in this route.

The state of the art in modeling passenger market share and revenue is with nested QSI (Quality-of-Service Index) models, a file of industry market sizes, connection building rules, and spill/recapture routines. Any approach to solving the clean-sheet scheduling problem will need to be consistent with the data, models, and systems that airlines use in this area.

For any proposed schedule generated via clean-sheet scheduling to be useful, it will need to be operationally feasible. As such it will need to comply with the standard set of operational constraints, such as aircraft count, gates, slots, maintenance, crew, airport staffing, and other constraints. Most airlines model these constraints in their schedule development process; thus, any new clean-sheet scheduling approach will need to access these constraints in the standard formats.

One concern with applying clean-sheet scheduling, or any other schedule optimization techniques, is that they should not generate unnecessary changes to the proposed schedule. That is, they should only propose changes that meet an acceptable number of incremental benefits. It makes no sense to make many large-scale schedule changes to chase $1 of benefits.

The resulting schedule produced by applying clean-sheet scheduling should be able to be easily consumed for manual review. That is, this schedule should be fully timed and routed with sub-fleet equipment assignments and produced in a standard format.

Finally, for any solution approach to clean-sheet scheduling to be truly useful, its results should be available in a reasonable period for any size airline. What is reasonable? When examining how clean-sheet scheduling fits within an airline's standard schedule development processes, a time limit of 12 to 24 hours seems reasonable. Note that there is some natural tension between characteristics 1 and 2 (accounting for many possibilities and representing revenue with sufficient accuracy) versus 6 (system performance). One solution approach could provide acceptable performance and scale but not consider many kinds of scheduling possibilities nor accurately represent the complexity of nested QSI models, for example.

When in their process should airlines perform clean-sheet scheduling?

As described in Chapter 2, airlines typically solve their scheduling business problem—the need to create profitable and operationally feasible schedules—by breaking the problem into separate sub-problems and solving each sequentially. As shown in Figure 8.22, these processes are often performed on a cyclical basis (specifically steps two through six) as further described in Chapter 2.

In this context, clean-sheet scheduling could be performed in the corporate strategy, route development, and schedule planning steps. As part of defining corporate strategy, clean-sheet scheduling could be used to evaluate new alliances and partnerships, as well as new hubs or schedule orientations. It could also be used to adapt the corporate strategy to major new industry disruptions, such as route closures, significantly changed fuel prices, competitors entering and leaving the market, and the like. As part of route development, clean-sheet scheduling could be used to identify profitable new routes, or identify which unprofitable routes to close, in the context of the rest of the

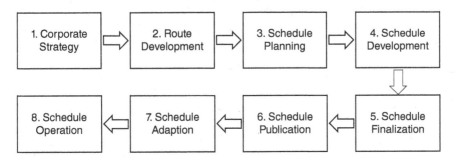

Figure 8.22 Key airline scheduling processes

schedule network. And as part of schedule planning, clean-sheet scheduling could be used to identify a more profitable starting point as part of constructing a new seasonal schedule.

Solution approach

At Amadeus, we solve the clean-sheet scheduling problem by following a two-step process as shown in Figure 8.23.

In the first step, the Amadeus solution "SkyPLAN" is used to determine the routes and frequencies consistent with maximum profitability. As part of this process, it considers the following inputs:

- List of airports served (including new airports to consider)
- Count of aircraft by fleet type (including ranges for optimizing fleet mix)
- Average aircraft utilization
- QSI market share model (either standard Amadeus model or could be adapted to airline's unique model)
- Block times by route
- Industry market sizes (total industry traffic in each origin–destination market)
- Average revenue contribution per passenger for each origin–destination market
- Airline costs
- Aircraft/airport constraints (e.g., slot limits by airport)
- Connection-building rules
- Schedule of competing airlines

SkyPLAN then determines which routes could conceivably be flown and allocates available aircraft to these routes to maximize total airline

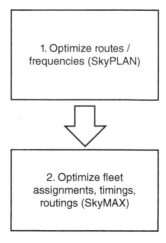

Figure 8.23 Clean-sheet scheduling in two steps

profitability. As part of this process, it estimates revenue in every available origin–destination market via a QSI model and industry market sizes and forms connections according to connection-building rules. It preserves operational feasibility by ensuring a series of operational constraints are always met.

The result is a statement of which routes should be flown with specific frequencies. SkyPLAN explicitly considers different schedule patterns (hub versus point-to-point, hub alignments, hub orientations, etc.) as part of this optimization process. The output provides a sense of the best "skeleton" of the schedule, or basic schedule structure.

At this point, the proposed routes and frequencies are fed into SkyMAX, whereby fleet assignments are made, timings are set, and routings are formed as part of determining a feasible detailed, timed, and routed schedule. It is important to note that fleet assignments, timings, and routings are all solved together in this step, as part of one very large optimization problem, rather than sequentially. SkyMAX also works by maximizing the profitability of a proposed schedule while accounting for the routes and frequencies given to it. Note that the same sets of inputs are used in both solutions (QSI model, industry market sizes, competing schedules, etc.) to ensure consistency.

Of course, one way to govern this optimization is to compare a proposed schedule with a historical schedule and penalize any deviations from the historical schedule to ensure schedule consistency and reduce schedule changes. Setting penalty values to different levels can allow this "consistency effect" to be dialed up or down.

As part of applying clean-sheet scheduling, it is helpful to measure the additional benefits found by adopting this approach. While performing clean-sheet scheduling requires new solutions and takes time during the schedule analysis/development process, the value of new schedules that would otherwise not have been found could be significant. It is therefore important, as is done with SkyPLAN and SkyMAX, to report on the additional profitability found by this approach.

Observations about the solution approach

One first observation about the solution approach is that it would clearly be more conceptually elegant to perform the optimization in one step rather than two steps. However, experience has shown that performing this step with currently available technology is not possible, given the complexity and scale of the problem. In future, new optimization techniques as well as new computing environments, such as quantum computing, hold promise, though. That said, the approximation caused by performing schedule development in two steps, rather than multiple steps as it often is today, is a clear improvement in the right direction.

Another observation is that the results from this process are often not incremental to an existing schedule. That is, SkyPLAN/SkyMAX will intentionally and deliberately use the flexibility available to it to discover new scheduling ideas. In this sense, clean-sheet scheduling can be thought of as a kind of "schedule idea generator" that provides new ideas for manual consideration. At a minimum, clean-sheet scheduling is an efficient way for suggesting profitable opportunities at the beginning of the schedule development process.

An important lesson from performing clean-sheet scheduling is that it is especially good at identifying new schedules when key assumptions about the existing scheduling environment are no longer valid. So, in cases of uncertain demand, changes in competitive schedules, higher route closures, and so on, it will immediately adapt and generate new scheduling possibilities. Presenting airline schedulers, at the beginning of the schedule development cycle, with new ideas of how to adapt their schedule to new conditions should shorten the development cycle and make airline schedulers more productive.

One example of this effect is with modeling higher fuel prices. At substantially higher fuel prices, for example, $100/barrel versus $70/barrel, it may no longer be profitable to serve some routes with existing frequencies. In turn, canceling some routes and/or reducing frequencies may affect connecting services on other routes. Some marginal routes may no longer be profitable if service from key connecting markets has been canceled. Applying clean-sheet scheduling techniques to the problem of constructing new schedules in an environment with higher fuel prices will allow these effects to be accounted for and modeled holistically.

Another key lesson is that, even in highly constrained environments (with limited slots, gates, maintenance, other constraints, etc.), clean-sheet scheduling could suggest changes of up to 50% of the flight schedule. Experience has shown that these changes typically generate significantly more revenue and honor all operational constraints.

Applications of clean-sheet scheduling

Clean-sheet scheduling is clearly an approach best suited for more strategic questions. Experience has shown that clean-sheet scheduling is best suited to the following kinds of scheduling situations:

1 Suggesting new ideas at the starting point of seasonal schedule development
2 Evaluating new schedule structures—new hubs, changes in hub orientation, aligning multiple hubs, changing from point-to-point to hubs (and vice versa), and so on
3 Identifying new routes, especially how these routes will interact with the rest of the schedule network
4 Better matching capacity (frequencies/equipment) on existing networks
5 Identifying connecting market opportunities

6 Proposing changes to the schedule as part of responding to major disruptions, for example, route closures, higher fuel prices, changes in competitive environment, uncertain passenger demand, and the like
7 Evaluating new alliances/partnerships, even mergers and acquisitions; better orienting schedule with that from existing partners
8 Evaluating changes to the fleet mix (new aircraft? retiring old aircraft?) and count
9 Evaluating changes in the airline business model (e.g., transitioning from low-cost to full-service and vice versa)

Summary

Clean-sheet scheduling holds the promise of helping airlines build more profitable flight schedules. In the past, this approach may have seemed somehow speculative and theoretical. However, a solution approach is now available that can solve this problem and generate useful results for airlines.

Notes

1 Source: https://www.statista.com/statistics/185127/revenue-sources-of-us-movie-theaters-since-2005/.
2 Frost & Sullivan. (2016). Customer experience to overtake price and product as differentiator by 2020. *Inform, August 2016.* Retrieved from https://inform.tmforum.org/news/2016/08/customer-experience-overtake-price-product-differentiator-2020/.
3 Forrester Research Inc. (2016). 72% of business name improving customer experience their top priority. *Forrester Media Center*, April 12, 2016. Retrieved from https://www.forrester.com/72+Of+Businesses+Name+Improving+Customer+Experience+Their+Top+Priority/-/E-PRE9109.
4 Puthiyamadam, T. & Reyes, J. (2018). Experience is everything. Get it right. *PwC, 2018.* Retrieved from https://www.pwc.com/us/en/zz-test/assets/pwc-consumer-intelligence-series-customer-experience.pdf.
5 Nin, A. (1961). *Seduction of the Minotaur.* Swallow Press, Ohio University.
6 Gaspersz, J. (2014). Building an Innovation Mindset. *The European Business Review*, September–October 2014, 60–62.
7 NEXTT (2021). *Let's Build the Journey of the Future.* Retrieved from https://www.nextt.aero/en/.
8 PricewaterhouseCoopers (2020). *Wie COVID-19 die Mobilität in Deutschland bewegt.* Available at: https://www.pwc.de/de/im-fokus/mobility-transformation/pwc-mobilitaet-2-abschied-von-urlaubs-und-dienstreisen.pdf (accessed 4 March 2022).
9 Deloitte (2020). *Mobilität nach der Corona-Krise – die Stunde des Individualverkehrs.* Available at: https://www2.deloitte.com/ch/de/pages/public-sector/articles/mobilitaet-nach-der-corona-krise.html (accessed 4 March 2022).
10 McKinsey & Company (2020). *From no mobility to future mobility: Where COVID-19 has accelerated change.* Available at: https://www.mckinsey.com/industries/automotive-and-assembly/our-insights/from-no-mobility-to-future-mobility-where-covid-19-has-accelerated-change (accessed 4 March 2022).
11 Handelsblatt (2021). *Staatskonzerne und Big Tech könnten die großen Gewinner der Coronakrise werden.* Available at: https://www.handelsblatt.com/meinung/homo-oeconomicus/gastkommentar-homo-oeconomicus-staatskonzerne-und-big-tech-

koennten-die-grossen-gewinner-der-coronakrise-werden/26920180.html?ticket=ST-6359390-1o6CtsjNzhmdufw3ynAA-cas01.example.org (accessed 4 March 2022).
12. Deloitte (2020). *COVID-19 Briefing: "Die Route wird neu berechnet"*. Available at: https://www2.deloitte.com/de/de/blog/covid-19-briefings/2020/covid-19-briefing-krise-automobilindustrie.html (accessed 4 March 2022).
13. McKinsey & Company (2021). *The consumer demand recovery and lasting effects of COVID-19*. Available at: https://www.mckinsey.com/industries/consumer-packaged-goods/our-insights/the-consumer-demand-recovery-and-lasting-effects-of-covid-19 (accessed 4 March 2022).
14. McKinsey & Company (2018). *Huānyíng to the new Chinese traveler*. Available at: https://www.mckinsey.com/industries/travel-logistics-and-infrastructure/our-insights/huanying-to-the-new-chinese-traveler (accessed 4 March 2022).
15. European Travel Commission (2020). *Research Snapshot on the Indian Outbound Travel Market*. Available at: https://etc-corporate.org/reports/research-snapshot-on-the-indian-outbound-travel-market/ (accessed 4 March 2022).
16. BMU (2019). *Umweltbewusstseinsstudie 2018: Bevölkerung erwartet mehr Umwelt- und Klimaschutz von allen Akteuren*. Available at: https://www.bmu.de/PM8553 (accessed 4 March 2022).
17. McKinsey & Company (2021). *What executives are saying about the future of hybrid work*. Available at: https://www.mckinsey.com/business-functions/people-and-organizational-performance/our-insights/what-executives-are-saying-about-the-future-of-hybrid-work (accessed 4 March 2022).
18. Microsoft (2020). *The Next Great Disruption Is Hybrid Work – Are We Ready?* Available at: https://www.microsoft.com/en-us/worklab/work-trend-index/hybrid-work (accessed 4 March 2022).
19. ADAC (2017). *Die Evolution der Mobilität*. Available at: https://www.zukunftsinstitut.de/fileadmin/user_upload/Publikationen/Auftragsstudien/ADAC_Mobilitaet2040_Zukunftsinstitut.pdf (accessed 4 March 2022).
20. Capgemini (2019). *The Autonomous Car Report*. Available at: https://www.capgemini.com/news/the-autonomous-car-report/ (accessed 4 March 2022).
21. Arthur D. Little (2020). *The Future of Mobility post-COVID*. Available at: https://www.adlittle.com/en/insights/report/future-mobility-post-covid (accessed 4 March 2022).
22. McKinsey & Company (2020), *From no mobility to future mobility: Where COVID-19 has accelerated change*. Available at: https://www.mckinsey.com/industries/automotive-and-assembly/our-insights/from-no-mobility-to-future-mobility-where-covid-19-has-accelerated-change (accessed 4 March 2022).
23. McKinsey & Company (2020). *The impact of COVID-19 on future mobility solutions*. Available at: https://www.mckinsey.com/industries/automotive-and-assembly/our-insights/the-impact-of-covid-19-on-future-mobility-solutions (accessed 4 March 2022).
24. Randelhoff (2016). *[Mobilitätsstationen] Nutzen verknüpfen, Räume verbinden*. Available at: https://www.zukunft-mobilitaet.net/162772/urbane-mobilitaet/mobilitaetsstationen-nutzen-sinn-zweck-verknuepfung/#fn-162772-1 (accessed 4 March 2022).
25. Verkehrsrundschau (2021). *Italien: Erste Auslieferung schwerer Waren per Drohne*. Available at: https://www.verkehrsrundschau.de/nachrichten/transport-logistik/italien-erste-auslieferung-schwerer-waren-per-drohne-2970604 (accessed 16 March 2022).
26. Business Air News (2020). *Volocopter takes steps to secure UAM in Singapore*. Available at: https://www.businessairnews.com/mag_story.html?ident=19944 (accessed 16 March 2022).
27. Roland Berger (2020). *Können Fahrräder und Scooter unsere Städte verändern?* Available at: https://www.rolandberger.com/de/Insights/Publications/

K%C3%B6nnen-Fahrr%C3%A4der-und-Scooter-unsere-St%C3%A4dte-ver%C3%A4ndern.html (accessed 16 March 2022).
28 Manager Magazin (2021). *Didi zum US-Börsendebüt 80 Milliarden Dollar wert*. Available at: https://www.manager-magazin.de/finanzen/boerse/didi-fahrdienstvermittler-aus-china-zum-boersengang-mit-rund-70-milliarden-us-dollar-bewertet-a-fe514fb5-25a4-442c-b3e5-05080b18691b (accessed 16 March 2022).
29 Virgin Hyperloop (2022). *Global Progress*. Available at: https://virginhyperloop.com/progress (accessed 16 March 2022).
30 Müller (2021). Analyse der Bedürfnisse potentieller Nutzer eines Mobilitäts-Hubs am Frankfurter Flughafen. Unpublished BA thesis, Frankfurt University of Applied Sciences.
31 Berz (2022). *How can airports fully embrace multimodal and interoperable mobility ecosystems to deliver sustainability goals and offer a superior passenger experience?* Journal of Airport Management (Volume 16 Number 3, June 2022).
32 See note 24.
33 See note 24.
34 See note 24.
35 Fraport AG (2021). *Facts & Figures – Transportation to and from the Airport*. Available at: https://www.fraport.com/en/our-group/about-us/facts---figures.html (accessed 4 March 2022).
36 Fraport AG (2021). *Facts & Figures – Traffic figures*. Available at: https://www.fraport.com/en/our-group/about-us/facts---figures.html (accessed 4 March 2022).
37 Focus (2013). *Köln-Frankfurt – Keine Lufthansa-Flüge mehr wegen ICE*. Available at: https://www.focus.de/reisen/flug/keine-lufthansa-fluege-mehr-wegen-ice-koeln-frankfurt_id_1795614.html (accessed 4 March 2022).
38 Fraport AG (2021), ref 29 above.
39 Stadt Frankfurt am Main (2021). *Fernstraßennetz*. Available at: https://frankfurt.de/themen/wirtschaft/standortportrait/infrastruktur/fernstrassennetz (accessed 4 March 2022).
40 Fraport AG (2021). *Services*. Available at: https://www.fraport.com/en/our-group/about-us/facts---figures.html (accessed 4 March 2022).
41 Fraport AG (2021); see note 29.

About the author

Nawal K. Taneja, whose experience in the aviation industry spans five decades, is a well-known airline business strategist. He has worked for and advised major airlines and related aviation businesses worldwide. His experience also includes the presidency of a small airline that provided schedule and charter services with jet aircraft and the presidency of a research organization that provided consulting services to the air transportation community throughout the world. On the government side, he has advised worldwide departments of civil aviation on matters relating to the role of government-owned or government-controlled airlines, and their management. Within the academic community, he has served on the faculties of the Massachusetts Institute of Technology (as an associate professor) and at the Ohio State University (first as a professor, later as the chair of the Department of Aviation, and finally, as the chair of the Department of Aerospace Engineering). Currently, he is an executive-in-residence at the Fisher College of Business at the Ohio State University.

He has served on the advisory boards of both public and private organizations. He continues to be invited to provide presentations at industry conferences worldwide, moderate panel discussions, and develop and discuss "what if" scenarios for individual aviation businesses. He advises senior executives in airlines and related aviation businesses, as well as senior government policymakers, on the impact of powerful forces that are converging and intersecting, such as

- the overwhelmingly changing customer behavior and expectations;
- the profoundly changing perspectives of employees;
- the proliferation of smart technologies;
- the emergence of new forms of transportation systems, air and ground; and
- the rapidly evolving aviation regulatory policies.

He has authored an aviation management series that includes 14 books, written at the encouragement of, and for, practitioners in the global airline industry. This series attempts to move the arc of thinking about the airline business to develop and capture real strategic advantages by pursuing creativity and collaboration to drive change. The ambitious objective throughout the series is to stimulate visionary leaders to explore multiple perspectives and to think laterally to sense and seize opportunities. The series also presents best practices from other business sectors for creating, capturing, and delivering value, given that the rules of customer centricity and competition are changing continuously. Moreover, at the suggestion of some readers, the series has begun to include a portfolio of thought leadership pieces that touch upon a broad spectrum of topics, such as game-changing digital technologies, customer- and employee-engagement platforms, state-of-the-art retailing strategies, and new transportation processes and systems. These pieces, contributed by experienced practitioners with diverse backgrounds, provide real-world examples of challenges and opportunities facing different sectors of the aviation industry.

Nawal K. Taneja holds a bachelor's degree in aeronautical engineering (first class honors) from the University of London, a master's degree in flight transportation from the Massachusetts Institute of Technology (MIT), a master's degree in business administration from MIT's Sloan School of Management, and a doctorate in air transportation from the University of London. He is a fellow of the Royal Aeronautical Society of Great Britain.

Index

Adidas 95
Adner, Ron 6
agility 9, 97, 110
Agility Airlines 10, 90, 105, 109–119; to enrich the lives of our customers 110
Agoda 96
AirAsia Group 8; AirAsia Ride 8; BigPay 61; Superapp 61
Airbnb 1, 60
Airbus 82; 220 108; 320 30, 109, 111; 321 7, 112, 114; 350–1000 16
aircraft: electric 8, 30–31, 33, 35, 81–83, 88, 113; hydrogen-fuel powered 34, 82; supersonic 33–34, 88
Air France 79, 81, 87, 94, 104
Air India 23
airline: basic products 4; complexity 95, 97–98; core product 8, 10, 13–16, 21, 28–36, 39, 45, 57–58, 113; operations control center 18; scheduling considerations 17–28
Airline Tariff Publishing Company 41
Air New Zealand 22
airport slots 16–17, 22–23, 109
air taxis 31–32
air travel space 102
Akasa Air 94
Alaska Airlines 23, 56, 61, 108–109, 111, 113, 118; Baggage Guarantee 61; Horizon Air 109; SkyWest Airlines 109; Virgin America 109
algorithms 18, 20, 24–26, 41, 50, 52, 65, 68, 74, 94, 99–100, 117–118
Alitalia 23
Allbirds 69
Allegiant Air 7
Altman, Jack 100
Amazon 1, 6–7, 10, 16, 39, 55, 60, 62–64, 75, 99, 102, 118; Alexa 62–63, 75, 99; Complexity *see* complexity; Dash Buttons 62; Firefly 62; Go Store 62, 71; 1-Click feature 62–63; Prime 62
American Airlines 10, 14, 61, 66, 82, 102, 104
Apple 6–7, 69, 102; Siri 75
Arkia Airlines 94
ATC 86, 88, 98
automotive sector 2, 13
Avianca Airlines 22
Azul 94

Bandara, Indika 70
Bangkok Airways 102
Barclays Bank 95
Barlow, Jim 18, 45, 114, 116
Berz, Jennifer 28, 69
Bezos, Jeff 63
BioNTech 95
Bloomberg, Jason 63
Boeing 27; 737 109, 111; 737 MAX jets 7; 787 30
Boer, Evert de 14, 67, 100
Bombardier, Q400 109
Booking Holding 96
Boom, Overture 33–34, 88
Bouquet, Cyril 5
brands and branding 2–3, 8, 10, 13, 37, 53, 56, 58, 60, 64, 68–70, 74–75, 87, 89, 94, 101–103,104–105, 109–110, 113, 115, 118–119
Breeze Airways 8
British Airways 66, 104
Bryar, Colin 7
building digital resiliency capabilities 99–101
Burse, Doreen xv–xvi
business jets 79

Cathay Pacific Airways 3, 7, 22
Chanel 69

chapter outlines 9–11
Charan, Ram 64
chatbots 70
China Airlines 7
cloud 49, 85, 101
Cobban, Paul 63
Coca-Cola 77
collaborating by design 94–98
complexity 17, 21, 35, 38, 42, 89, 95, 97–99, 116
Concorde 33–34
connectivity 112; digital 69; hyper 62, 110; in-flight 57–58, 97
COVID-19 2–3, 16, 21–22, 26, 43, 71, 79, 84, 93, 95, 97
culture 1, 18–19, 22, 64, 71, 89, 95, 97–98, 100, 116
customer: beliefs 97; centricity 1; choice model 44–46; desires, behavior, expectations 3–5, 8, 10, 20, 25, 28, 39, 41, 51, 53–54, 57, 59, 61–62, 64–67, 69, 71, 73–75, 79, 83–84, 88, 90, 93, 95–97, 100, 103–105, 110, 118; experience 2–3, 5–8, 10, 14–15, 21, 23–24, 28, 38–40, 42, 44, 57–72, 74, 86, 93, 98–101, 104, 115–118; feedback 24, 61, 67, 70; intelligence 68; journey 4, 13–15, 28–29, 33, 37, 40, 45, 59–60, 68, 70–72, 74, 101, 110, 114–115; listening to 6–7, 103; personalization 10, 37, 39–40, 48, 56–57, 64–70, 75, 114–115; preferences 8, 10, 13–16, 22–23, 25, 35, 38, 41, 45, 64–65, 68, 73–74, 99, 113, 116, 121; problems, concerns 100; profiles 55, 71; relationship management 72; satisfaction 38, 44, 61, 109; segmentation 39, 46–48; service vs. experience 59–62; surveys 87, 103; 360-degree view 65; trust 66, 74, 94, 104–105, 119; types 16
cybersecurity 2, 93

dashboards 87
data: analytics 41, 59, 65, 68, 80–81, 99–100, 116; driven culture 97, 99; location and movement 55, 68, 70, 85, 115; market information data tapes 20; new types 68, 114; patterns 21–22, 27, 46–47, 52, 58, 62, 73–75, 97, 100, 110; privacy 2, 66; processing power 20; quality, reliability 17, 19, 23, 27, 35, 65, 111; sensors 67; sharing 38; shopping 9, 20
datagraphs 117–118

DBS Bank 10, 63–64, 75
Delta Air Lines 3, 9–10, 14, 57, 66, 104; PARALLEL REALITY 61; Song 109
demand-driven dispatch 27
demand, pent-up 84
Dewar, Carolyn 97
digital: experience 71–72; resiliency 10, 99, 105, 117; revolution 2; transformation 56, 63, 98, 101; twins 85; wallet 4, 66
Disney 102
distribution 14, 20, 37, 40, 55, 57, 100, 105
Doerr, John 80
doing more with less 10, 117–119
door-to-door, travel services 6, 8, 28–30, 60–61, 110, 117
Doosan Mobility Innovation (DMI), Korea 32
drones 32; DJI M600 drone 32; 42air 32
Dyson 95

EasyJet 23
ecosystems 3–4, 10, 90, 95; co-evolving with 97; collaboration in 2, 6–7, 9–10, 30, 64, 70, 89, 95, 98, 100, 116–117; control of 64, 103; integration within 40; open 6; partners 110; platforms 68; public and private 87; selling 47
Edelman, David C. 65
El Al 94
Embraer 79; 175 109; 190 108–109
empathy 5, 104
employees 38, 59, 63, 94, 118; behavior of 95; branding 87; empowerment of 5, 66, 109; engagement with 5–6, 117; to evaluate 95; expectations of 66; feedback from 98; investments in 10, 100; involvement 29; needs of 5–6, 8, 66, 98, 100; purpose-focused 87, 91; satisfaction 98; shift in power of 1; as stakeholders 29; as supporters 62; turnover 21; value for 3, 97; work environment 2
end-to-end travel 4, 10, 28–30, 35, 59, 65, 70, 72, 74, 100–101, 110, 117
Etihad Airways 81, 101
EURAIL 3
Euromoney 64
Eurostar 69
eVTOLs 8, 33, 82; Elroy Air's Chaparral 33

Facebook 7, 65, 68, 84
Finnair 46
Fitzpatrick, Stephen xvii-xviii

FlySafair 56
Ford, Martin 70, 99
Ford Motor Company 102
frequent flyer programs *see* loyalty programs
Frontier Airlines 7

general data protection regulations (GDPR) 2
General Electric 96
generation Z 87
Gibbs, Christopher 85, 100
Glade, Peter 44
global distribution systems (GDSs) 39, 51, 57
Google 4, 72, 77, 84; Assistant's Interpreter 61; DeepMind 74; Flights 68; Home 75; Search 68
Govindarajan, Vijay 118
green tickets 8
Gucci 69
Gupta, Piyush 64

Hainan Airlines 7
Hawaii 80
healthcare landscape 2
Heart Aerospace 31, 82
Hertz 3
high-density markets 31, 34
Hillman, Jonathan E. 1
HNA Group 7
Hollister, Glenn 37, 102, 115
Hyperloop 9, 34

IATA 8, 30, 41, 57, 84, 116; Dynamic Offers Maturity Model Matrix 41; electronic miscellaneous document 38; four pillars for a sustainable aviation industry 84, 86; NDC 41, 48, 51, 56–57; ONE Order 56, 101
IBM 78, 80, 95
ICAO 80
IKEA 69
intermodal, multimodal 5, 28–29, 35, 69, 110, 117
International Airlines Group 5
Internet of Things *see* technology
Intrapreneurship 3, 110
ITA Airways 23

Japan Airlines 34
J.D. Power and Associates 81, 109
JetBlue Airways 8, 23, 66, 108–113, 118; bring humanity back to air travel 61,

108; Paisly 8; Technology Ventures 8; Travel Products 8
Joby Aviation 8

Kane, Gerald C. 100
Kelly, Jason 52
Kenya Airways 23
Khanna, Ro 1
Kissinger, Henry A. 99
Klingenberg, Christoph xix–xx
KLM 94
Knoppers, Jordie 69, 118
Kreiken, Boet E. J. xxi–xxiii

LATAM Airlines 94
Le Hong, Ha xxiv, 119
LinkedIn 65
List, John A. 5
Lockheed Martin, Skunk Works 97
Lomb, Kerstin 71–72, 74
loyalty 2, 14, 42, 53, 61, 64–65, 70, 74; programs 5, 13, 37, 60, 66–67, 71, 73, 75, 83, 89, 100–101, 114
Lufthansa German Airlines 104

machine learning *see* technology
McDonald's 59, 66
McKinsey and Company 97
Mercedes 69, 102
Mesa Airlines 81
Microsoft 78, 81, 97
millennials 87
mobility 2–3, 5, 24–25, 31–32, 69, 84, 110
Mulcahy, Simon 99

Neeleman, David 8
Neeley, Tsedal (and Paul Leonardi) 118
Nescafé 69
Netflix 1, 60
Net Promoter Score 60, 64
New Distribution Capability (NDC) *see* IATA
Nike 10, 69–70, 102
Nokia 11

ONE Order *see* IATA
online travel agents (OTAs) 55
open strategy 30, 94, 118

Pampers 103
Patagonia 103
personalization 64–70, 115; *see also* customer; challenges 65; hyper 48, 66; opportunities 65–70

Pfizer 95
Picoult, Jon 66
platforms 1, 6, 10, 30, 34, 41, 65, 68, 72, 75, 98, 100–101, 113, 117–118
Porter, Michael 116
Prashantham, Shameen 97
price elasticities *see* revenue
pricing *see* revenue
Procter & Gamble 103–104
public–private partnership 78, 116
Puech, Philippe 21

Qantas 1
Quality-of-Service Index 15, 18, 20, 24

Rajamannar, Raja 99; Quantum Marketing 99; Quantum Physics 99
Reichheld, Fred 60
revenue management 9, 14; algorithms 52; ancillary 9, 13, 36, 41, 44, 71; better shopping displays 56; complexity 38, 42; cross-functional teams 50; customer choice model 44–46, 51, 53; dynamic pricing 9, 46–49; in-flight shopping 57; MIT/PODS study 47; NDC and distribution 57–58; network planning integration 49–51; new pricing schemes 55–56; new techniques, next generation 42–55; offer management 39–42, 46, 113; passenger mix 50; price elasticities 41, 45–46, 48, 114; real time 51–52; seat buy-back 42–44; selling differently 9, 55–58; strategic pricing 53–54; subscription pricing 55–56; traditional approach 36–39; value pricing 46; willingness to pay 26, 41, 53
Ritz-Carlton 59, 66
Rowland, Becca 80
Royal Bank of Canada 6
Ryanair 7, 23, 102

Salesforce 99
Samsung 69
scale 5, 10, 23, 37, 39, 41, 46–48, 64–65, 70, 75, 81, 99–101, 105, 110, 117
schedule planning: clean-sheet 21–23; complexities 17, 21, 35, 116; dynamic 9, 26, 110; improving forecast accuracy 25–26; operations-friendly 24–25; profitability and reliability 23–24; reliability 21
Schultheiß-Münch, Michaela 28, 69
Schwirn, Martin 8, 94

Semone, Karen 99
Singapore Airlines 61, 102
Smith, Gerald 53–54
SNCF 79
social changes: implication 2–3; trends 1
Song, Chang-Hyeon xxv
South African Airways 22
Southwest Airlines 11, 100
Spirit Airlines 7
Spotify 1, 6–7
Stadler, Christian 30, 94
stagility 96–97
Starbucks 77
strategizing for positional superiority 101–105
Sun Country Airlines 9, 61
sustainability 5, 28, 32, 34; carbon (dioxide), emissions 5, 78, 80, 83, 86–88, 117; Carbon Offsetting and Reduction Scheme for International Aviation 80; complexity 89; core of an airline's business strategy 88–90, 116; Environmental, Social, and Governance 79; greener flight 88; implications on airlines 84–88; net-zero-by-2050 scenario 10, 83–84, 90; Paris Climate Agreement 79, 84; reasons for increasing focus 87; Sustainable Aviation Fuels 80–82; Sustainable Development Goals 79
Sutherland, Rory 69

technology: artificial intelligence, machine learning 9, 20, 25–26, 41, 47, 52, 64, 68, 72–74, 80–81, 85, 97, 99–100, 110–111, 116, 118; biometrics 98; blockchain 61, 64, 85, 100, 117; digital twins 85; Internet of Things 85
telemedicine 67
Tencent 64
Tesla 3
thinking: A.L.I.E.N 5; conventional 4; nonconventional 29–30, 68
thought leadership pieces 120–197
Tide 103
Tiersky, Howard 71
Tinder 1
tourism 83, 90
Toyota 102
train, high speed 28, 79
Twitter 104

Uber 3, 16, 60; Uber of the Air 31
ultra-low-cost carriers 13

United Airlines 10, 14, 34, 66, 81, 88, 104; Ted 109
United Nations 79; Climate Change Conference 80
urban areas, populations 31

Vaccari, Renzo 17, 23
Valmorbida, Decius xxvi–xxvii
Venkatesan, Raj 72
Venkatraman, Venkat N. 118, 119
Vertical Aerospace 31–32; VX4 32
VFR 17, 45, 67, 79
Vietnam Airlines 61, 119
Virgin Atlantic Airways 66, 104
virtual: assistant 63, 100, 118; communications 79, 93; interactions 67
Volaris Airlines 56

Volkswagen 3, 6, 104

Waddell, Dee K. xxviii–xxix
Walmart 104
Washington Post, the 1, 3
Wayfair 6–7
WeChat 68, 104
Welch, Jack 96
Whitler, Kimberly A. 70, 101, 104
Wizz Air 7, 102
Woodward, Ian C. 96
work-life balance 98

YouTube 69

Zakaria, Fareed 1
Zane, Leslie 69
Zara 69